Pâtisserie Made Simple

THE ART OF
PETITS GÂTEAUX

Pâtisserie Made Simple

THE ART OF PETITS GÂTEAUX

Maxine Scheckter

Photography by Amber-Jayne Bain

KITCHEN PRESS

To my mum, for nagging me,
my dad, for believing in me,
Ben for supporting me,
and to everyone else who helped me get this far.

Contents

007   Introduction
009   Equipment and ingredients
014   Techniques

Recipes

037   Spring
077   Summer
113   Autumn
165   Winter
209   Celebrations
237   Base recipes

243   Thank you
244   Index

Introduction

I'm writing this book for a 16-year-old me. When I started out I knew I wanted to temper chocolate, make shiny mirror glazes, and other more advanced pastry techniques, but I couldn't find a book that explained these techniques in a way that I understood. There are plenty of beginner baking books, and plenty that are intimidatingly advanced, but I couldn't find anything that bridged that gap. I wanted to be the person to write it. So here it is! I hope that as you work your way through this book you'll grow not only your understanding of pastry techniques, but also your confidence, so that you can make these recipes your own. Mix and match components from different recipes. Change up the flavours. Use your creativity to create a petit gâteau that encompasses everything you love in a dessert and decorate it however you like. The more you make, the better at it you will become and the more your own style will start to take shape.

I've split the recipes into five main sections: Spring, Summer, Autumn, Winter and Celebrations. (There's also a final section full of base recipes.) Cooking seasonally helps you get the most out of produce when it's at its best. The seasons also tend to match what I feel like eating at that time. Gâteaux in the Spring and Summer sections are lighter and generally more fruit based, whereas the Autumn and Winter desserts embrace warmer flavours and feel a little more comforting. However, as many of the recipes use frozen fruits and other ingredients available all year round, you can really mix and match your gâteaux, making them with whatever's available and whatever you're craving.

As you read the recipes, you'll notice some repetition. Basic elements like mousses, sponges and crémeux feature regularly. This is because pâtisserie is all about technique. The more you practise the better you'll get. That doesn't mean every crémeux is made the same way, or every sponge uses exactly the same recipe, but the skills and techniques are transferable. Think of it like a house. Each house may begin with a similar foundation, but as construction progresses every new component contributes to its overall structure and aesthetic. Just as a well-built house stands the test of time, well-crafted pâtisserie can leave a lasting impression.

Equipment and ingredients

Before you get started

Looking at a full gâteau recipe can be a little overwhelming at first, with all the different elements, ingredients and techniques. But please don't let that put you off! Each gâteau in this book can be broken down into stages and made over multiple days; freezing between each step until you're ready for the next stage (the freezer is a pastry chef's best friend!). Although everything you need is right here in the book, I find that writing myself a prep list is helpful — it will make things feel much less intimidating, too. You could write down each task for the gâteau you're making, and the order you need to do it in. At the same time, make sure you have all the ingredients you need before you get stuck in. There's nothing worse than being mid-mousse and realising you don't have enough cream!

To make your life easier, start out with a clean bench. Clean as you go; I find the less mess I have around me, the clearer my head is for baking. And of course, put some tunes on and relax! Baking shouldn't be stressful.

I admit I never read the beginning of cookbooks (until writing this one!), but I highly recommend you read through the beginning of *this* book before you start cooking. It gives you important information about what ingredients to use, and more in-depth instructions about techniques that will really help you as you bake your way through the book.

Disasters in the kitchen

Talk to any chef and they'll have a laundry list of disasters they've experienced — I've sure had my fair share. As painful as they are at the time (I most definitely have cried over cake more times than I would like to admit), these disasters are how you learn for next time. For me, a mark of a good pastry chef is someone who can fix things when they go wrong — a skill that only comes after many, many failures. Something I always remind my students of is that if you've made something with love and care, no matter how it looks, it'll still taste delicious. If all else fails, spoon it into a bowl and call it a trifle!

A note on recipes, and where they come from

As a pastry chef, I often encounter the misconception among home cooks that I possess an innate natural ability to create recipes and know exactly how much of each ingredient to use. This isn't the case. Recipes are a science, based on precise ratios. Some are simple, like a pound cake, which is composed of equal amounts of flour, butter, sugar and egg; some are more complicated, like a crème pâtissière or a chocolate mousse, which require much more care and attention to detail.

As my abilities have grown throughout my career, I have learned how to look at a recipe and understand the function of each ingredient. With this knowledge, I can take a professional recipe and turn it into one that works for the home cook by adjusting the ratios or removing unnecessary ingredients.

No recipe is truly original, though the final product each creates is. The recipes in this book all come from somewhere, but they have been tested, altered, adapted and modified into something all my own, that I want to share with you.

What is a petit gâteau?

Petit gâteau is French for 'little cake' (gâteaux with an x is the plural, meaning cakes). The English word cake usually means a baked sponge covered in icing, but in France and many parts of Europe, gâteau refers to a multi-layered dessert. There's no exact requirement for a petit gâteau besides the size. A petit gâteau is generally the perfect size for dessert for one person. Any smaller and it becomes a petit four, which are bite-sized. Any larger and it loses the 'petit' and turns into a gâteau. There are normally at least three components in a gâteau, with multiple textures and flavours, to give the perfect bite.

There's a few things you need to consider when designing your petits gâteaux.

Obviously, flavour always comes first. It's a bit more complex, however, than thinking of a nice flavour combination; all the flavours need to work in harmony with each other to create the perfect mouthful. This means you need to think about the quantities of each component. For example, in the PB&J gâteau that you'll find on page 89, the raspberry compote is quite sharp in order to cut through the richness of the mousse. Too much of the raspberry would mean you lose the peanut butter flavour, and not enough would mean the peanut butter overtakes the raspberry.

One thing I pay a lot of attention to is the overall sweetness of the gâteau. I try to add sharp elements to balance out the sweetness, like in the banana, passionfruit and coconut recipe on page 69. The passionfruit crémeux is quite tart, the coconut is more subdued, and the banana is sweet. This creates the perfect bite that's neither too sweet, nor too sour. The only way to really know if a pastry is well balanced is to eat it, and eat the whole thing — it's a tough job, but someone has to do it!

Once you're happy with the flavours, you need to consider texture. A lot of petits gâteaux can be very soft and heavy on mousse. If that's what you'd like, perfect! But sometimes you want other textures in there too, like a crisp biscuit or the crack from a chocolate shell. In my speculoos petit gâteau recipe on page 216, I've used crushed speculoos biscuits in the outside coating to add a crunch to all the soft elements.

Finally, you must think about decoration. Whenever you're adding something for decorative purposes, you want to think about what impact it has on the rest of the gâteau. Is it adding flavour, and is it a flavour you want added? Does it add texture? Your finishing touches don't always need to contribute to these other aspects, but you need to make sure they aren't detracting from them, either. Gold leaf, for example, is flavourless, so its impact is purely visual. Adding a chocolate decoration can add texture if it's a crisp, tempered chocolate, and it also adds sweetness. I particularly like using herbs, such as basil leaves inside as well as on top of the yuzu basil petit gâteau on page 187; it brings freshness as well as a pop of colour.

As you work your way through the book, feel free to mix and match recipes to create your own gâteaux. This is the point of the book; I want you to make these recipes your own. Experiment with flavours, textures and decorations, and don't be discouraged if they don't work out the first time. It can take multiple tries to get the balance of flavours and textures right. As you make each element from the book, give it a taste. The more you taste, the better your palate will become, and the easier it will be to match flavours in your head.

Inspiration for your gâteaux can come from anywhere. You may start with a decoration you want to try and work your gâteau around that, or you can be inspired by flavours you find in other food or drinks. I often start with something simple — maybe an ice cream that I love, or a fruit that I want to showcase — and build from there.

Equipment

I have tried to simplify the equipment needed for the recipes in this book as much as possible. Don't be overwhelmed if you don't have, for instance, a stick blender. For each item, I've included possible substitutes that you will likely already have at home. These substitutes may be harder to use, but will get the job done in the meantime, as you slowly build up your equipment collection.

The tin: The inspiration for this book came after I realised my customers' favourite classes were the ones that involved only one tin. The recipes from these classes were the easiest to recreate at home, and suited all skill levels. Those who wanted perfection could get it, and those who didn't care about being picture perfect still made something delicious and pretty! Best of all, the tin itself is nothing special; it's a brownie pan I got from the supermarket. The dimensions are 16 x 26cm, and 3.5cm deep. If you can't find a tin the exact same size, don't worry. Anything roughly the same size will work. You can even just use a standard cake tin if you want. Just don't go much bigger, or your gâteau will be very thin and difficult to handle.

Scales: All my recipes are in grams. Measuring in grams is more consistent than cups and this will show in your baking. I recommend investing in a good kitchen scale. You don't need to buy the most expensive one but, as someone who has spent far too much on cheap scales that break every few months, I can tell you it's definitely worth buying a solid set. I recommend digital scales that have an accuracy of one gram; the more accurate the scales, the more accurate your baking will be. You'll notice all liquids in the book are measured in grams rather than millilitres, again to improve accuracy. You will put those scales to good use! For ingredients that are very light and are needed in small quantities, such as pectin, baking powder, or baking soda, the quantity is given in teaspoons. Home scales, no matter how good, are not accurate enough to be measuring 1–2 grams of these lighter ingredients (unless you have fancy micro scales but, again, I always break mine).

Piping bag: It's much easier to pipe decorations with a proper piping bag. While a snipped-off zip-lock bag will do the trick, it is worth buying a large roll of disposable piping bags. You can get them easily online and they can be quite affordable. Reusable or cloth piping bags tend to be hard to keep clean and dry, and go mouldy very easily, so I stay away from them. You can find biodegradable piping bags on specialty cake websites if you're wary of using too much plastic.

Piping tips: While there are a lot of cool shapes you can make with a piping bag and some scissors, having a small range of piping tips can really help improve the finish of your gâteaux. The most common shapes I use are a 1cm round tip, a 0.5cm round tip and a grass tip. You can get these from a cake decorating store, and like everything else, you can build up your collection over time. Remember that you don't need to decorate your gâteaux the exact same way I have, so if you don't have the piping tip required for a certain recipe you can improvise with whatever else you have on hand.

Offset palette knife: An offset palette knife is key to making perfect layers, and being able to properly spread each mixture flat makes the whole gâteau building process much more achievable and enjoyable. I like to have two offset palette knives on hand: a 10cm one for spreading layers; then a larger 20cm one for glazing and any finishing work. However, if palette knives are unavailable, you can use a spoon, spatula, or any similar kitchen tool. The layers of your petits gâteaux may not be perfect, but it will work. A smaller offset palette knife is also the perfect tool for moving your delicate petits gâteaux around.

Stick blender: There are a few recipes in this book that require a stick blender, often to emulsify butter with whatever mix you're making. If you don't have a stick blender, you can use a conventional blender. When blending a hot mixture, allow it to cool down before using any kind of sealed blender, to avoid getting burnt. If you don't have a blender, whisk your mixture as much as possible, then pass it through a sieve to remove any lumps.

Freezer: As I've said, the freezer is a pastry chef's best friend, and an essential piece of equipment for all the recipes in this book. If you've ever looked in the window of a pâtisserie, you will have seen perfectly cut cake slices. The trick to getting such clean cuts is the freezer. Nearly every gâteau in this book must be frozen before it is portioned to get a smooth, clean cut — it's much easier to handle a frozen gâteau than a warm, squishy gâteau!

Oven: An oven is a necessary piece of equipment for a pâtisserie chef. However, no oven is perfect. I've lived in my share of rubbish houses with equally rubbish ovens — I've even had an oven door explode while it was preheating. No matter how crappy your oven might be, you can still work with these recipes. The sponges and other baked elements of the recipes will bake very quickly, as they're small by design. This means there's less time for problems in the oven. I recommend purchasing an oven thermometer. You can get a decent one for a reasonable price. My current oven, although only a couple of years old, can be about 30 degrees off the set temperature, sometimes more, depending on what setting I'm using. The baking temperatures in the recipes are for a fan oven. If you don't have a fan oven, keep it at the stated temperature and just bake for a little longer. Trust your cake instincts and it will be fine! Cake instincts are: colour, smell, touch and time. Does it smell delicious and done? That's the first sign your baked good is cooked. Has the cake set to the touch, as directed in the method, and does it have a nice golden-brown colour if it's supposed to according to the recipe? If the answer to these questions is yes, then you're good to go. You shouldn't need more than an extra 5 minutes for any of the small recipes in this book, unless your oven has some serious issues.

Thermometer: In a few recipes you will need a thermometer. Cheap digital thermometers always break on me, so I use inexpensive old-fashioned glass thermometers for cooking and a laser thermometer for tempering chocolate (a note that laser thermometers can be expensive, and struggle to gauge the temperature when you are cooking something that produces steam, like the pâte de fruit in the strawberry shortcake gâteau, as they tend to read the temperature of the steam rather than of the actual product). If you're going to try tempering chocolate and don't want to buy a laser thermometer, I recommend starting with a digital thermometer. If you use it enough, you can then treat yourself to a laser thermometer. A word of warning about my recipes: as much as I love baking, I am also very lazy. I'll never ask you to do an extra step or process unless it's absolutely necessary. So if a recipe requires a thermometer, it's because you really need it. Trying to make that recipe without a thermometer will mean it won't set properly, or may easily overcook and burn.

Stand mixer: This is the most expensive item on this list, and the most useful. Being able to whip egg whites in a stand mixer is a game changer! (If you've ever tried to whip egg whites by hand you'll know this.) However, I have spent many years without the budget or the space for a nice stand mixer. If you're in the same position, then I recommend picking up a small, inexpensive handheld electric mixer. While it won't last you a lifetime, it will save your arms until you're able to purchase a nice stand mixer. In some recipes, where you only need to whip one egg white (which can be a pain in a large stand mixer) a little electric mixer is a life-saver!

Blowtorch: There are a few recipes in this book that are finished with a blowtorch. While it is one of the least important pieces of equipment, it is a whole lot of fun. Blowtorches for home cooks tend to have a tiny flame incapable of brûlée-ing anything, and often come with a hefty price tag. Most Asian supermarkets sell stronger blowtorches and gas canisters at a lower price with a bigger punch. Just take care to use your blowtorch safely. Always use your blowtorch on a heat-proof surface, like a baking tray that isn't lined with baking paper (trust me, no matter how careful you are, the paper will catch fire) and make sure the gas is fully turned off after each use.

Equipment and ingredients

Ingredients

As a general rule, the higher the quality of the ingredients you use, the better the result will be. But how you use your ingredients can be just as important as their quality. Here are a few important tips on how to get the most out of your ingredients, and to help improve the consistency of your baking.

Agar-agar: As a natural setting agent that comes from seaweed, agar-agar is often used as a vegetarian gelatine replacement. Due to its ability to set while still hot, it is not ideal for mousses, as it sets immediately upon contact with whipped cream, and also melts it at the same time. It is, however, an amazing setting agent for making thin drapey veils, like the one used in the mulled wine and pear petit gâteau (page 193). It can be found at specialty supermarkets and Asian food stores.

Butter: This is an unpopular opinion in the baking world: I always use salted butter. It's what my mum used when I was a child, and she wasn't going to buy me any special butter to bake with, so send any complaints to her. I believe it makes a positive difference to my baking. If you don't use salted butter, add a little salt to the recipe to enhance the flavour.

Chocolate: When it comes to chocolate brands, there is a whole world of choices. As always, the better the chocolate, the better the end product. I prefer to use Valrhona, a French brand known for its superb chocolate made with ethically sourced cocoa that's been created with pastry chefs in mind. Callebaut and Lindt also work well, and both are available at specialty food stores. You could also consider trying a local bean-to-bar manufacturer. Such manufacturers often have a large range of cocoa percentages and flavour notes, and it can be a lot of fun choosing a chocolate that pairs well with the recipe you are making. Make sure the chocolate you choose is a couverture chocolate, containing cocoa butter. Compound chocolate, made with other vegetable fats, will not work in many of these recipes. The easiest way to check if your chocolate is couverture or compound chocolate is to read the ingredients list. If cocoa butter is *not* listed, you've got compound chocolate.

Edible flowers: Flowers are a great colourful decoration for your petits gâteaux. If you have a green thumb (I sure don't) you can grow your own, otherwise specialty food stores and occasionally supermarkets will sell fresh or dried edible flowers.

Eggs: For consistency, I always use medium free-range eggs. Each egg weighs approximately 55 grams with the shell, and contains roughly 30 grams of egg white and 20 grams of egg yolk. If smaller eggs are used, adjust the quantity accordingly.

Flour: There are two main types of flour available in New Zealand: low-grade (also known as plain or standard grade) or high-grade flour. High-grade flour is similar to bread flour and contains a higher gluten content, making it ideal for yeasted dough or baking that requires more structure. On the other hand, low-grade flour, or plain flour in the UK (or all-purpose in the US), has a lower gluten content, making it great for cakes and pastries. Unless otherwise specified, the recipes in this book use plain flour. In some countries you can find a wider variety of flours with different levels of refinement. The more refined your flour is, the higher the gluten content. Less refined flour means less gluten and more flavour from the grain. Having these options available means you can experiment with different flours to find what you think works best for a recipe. For those who require gluten-free options, many of the recipes in this book can be adapted by replacing regular flour with gluten-free flour. If this is possible, it will be noted in the ingredients list.

Freeze-dried fruit: An incredible way to preserve fruit, freeze-drying gives you all of the flavour of fresh fruit, concentrated into a tiny bite. Freeze-dried fruit by itself is a great garnish, or you can put it through a spice grinder or push it through a sieve to get a powerful powder that is great for flavouring your gâteaux. The berry pavlova gâteau on page 226 is a perfect example of freeze-dried fruit powder being put to good use. Freeze-dried fruit and powders can be bought online, at specialty grocers and even at supermarkets. They easily absorb moisture, so I keep mine in an airtight container in the freezer, which keeps them fresh and crisp.

Fruit purées: Many recipes will call for a fruit purée or juice. In professional pastry kitchens these come readymade, frozen, pre-puréed and strained. But at home you have to make them yourself. Don't worry though — it's very easy! Start with either fresh or defrosted frozen fruit. (Frozen fruit has a bad reputation — often seen as being lower quality than fresh fruit — but it's a great way to preserve the best of the season's fruits). Blend the fruit with a blender until smooth. Then strain the blended fruit through a sieve to remove any seeds or large chunks. Depending on the fruit you are using, you will end up with purée or juice. Store the purée or juice in the fridge and use within a week. Any leftovers are great for making fancy cocktails, stirring through yoghurt, or purées can be turned into a quick jam for toast. I always weigh my purées after making them, as often a significant amount of weight can be lost when straining out the pulp to create a seedless purée. The amount specified in the recipe is always for the puréed weight, not the weight of the fruit before blending.

Gelatine: Gelatine is used to make things set. In this book I use gelatine to set mousses, gels and glazes. I use leaf gelatine in my recipes, as it is easier to work with than other types of gelatine. Leaf gelatine comes in different strengths — gold, silver and bronze — but I've found the distinction to be unimportant in a home setting. The 'stronger' gold gelatine is lighter in weight than the 'weaker' silver and bronze sheets, meaning leaf for leaf, they're interchangeable. If leaf gelatine is unavailable, for the recipes in this book, one sheet of leaf gelatine can be substituted with half a teaspoon of gelatine powder, soaked in one teaspoon of cold water. An important note: leaf gelatine is typically made from pork and gelatine powder from beef. Keep this in mind when considering the dietary requirements of the people you are baking for. Unfortunately, I have yet to find a vegetarian gelatine replacement that works well for mousses and other pâtisserie techniques.

Gold leaf: I don't think there's anything more fancy than a touch of gold leaf on a gâteau. When buying gold leaf, or gold lustre dust, make sure it's edible. Edible gold is pretty easy to get hold of these days; almost any cake decorating store will sell it in powder, sheets or flakes. Flakes are my go-to — they are normally the offcuts from the square sheets, and are significantly cheaper and easier to work with. A pair of tweezers, a toothpick or a small, soft paint brush are all great tools for handling finicky gold leaf.

Liquid glucose: Sometimes called corn syrup, liquid glucose is readily available at supermarkets and is the key to making shiny, coloured glazes. Don't skip this one!

Microgreens: Microgreens are vegetables and herbs in the early stages of life. They are a small touch that can make your pastries extra special. It's important to pick a microgreen that matches the flavour profile of your gâteau. A tropical flavour pairs well with micro coriander, and a berry-based gâteau works great with micro basil (also called baby basil). These little greens can be expensive, and are not a make or break. Your gâteaux will be stunning with or without them!

Milk and cream: In New Zealand there is typically only one type of cream available, so that's the cream I use! In contrast, many other countries offer a wider variety of cream options with differing fat percentages, which influences the setting, mouthfeel and flavour of a recipe. In the UK and the US you should use whipping cream, which has a fat content of about 35%. Using full-fat milk and cream is essential for achieving the desired outcome in many recipes, as fat plays a significant role in the setting of any pastry recipe.

Pectin: Pectin is a natural setting agent that comes from fruit. It comes in different types; the most common is powdered yellow or citrus pectin. Pectin can be purchased at bulk-food stores, specialty food stores and organic stores. It thickens compotes, jams or gels without dulling the flavour. It can be used without adding too much sugar, giving you a fresh-flavoured product with a gorgeous mouthfeel. Pectin must be mixed with some sugar before adding it into your liquid or purée, otherwise the pectin will form lots of little lumps that won't dissolve. I typically mix one teaspoon of pectin with 20–30 grams of sugar, unless specified differently in a recipe. In some cases, you can replace the pectin with cornflour, but cornflour dulls the overall flavour quite a lot, and it doesn't work in every recipe. So it's definitely worth trying to get your hands on some pectin.

Sugar: Caster sugar is the sugar of choice in any professional pastry kitchen and is used in the recipes in this book. It dissolves faster than other sugars, making it easier to work with. When brown sugar is used, it is always soft brown sugar, unless otherwise specified. Feel free to experiment with different sugars, like muscovado or coconut sugar, for a different taste. Generally you can replace one sugar for another in a 1:1 ratio.

Substitutions

One of the most common questions I get asked is if a recipe can be made vegan. The short answer is no. Pastry recipes are a science. The majority of plant-based alternative ingredients aren't able to be used in a simple 1:1 swap to make a recipe vegan. There are some amazing pastry chefs creating incredible vegan pâtisserie, whose recipes are created specifically to work with plant-based ingredients.

While the recipes in this book have been vigorously tested, they have been tested as they are written, so I cannot say if they will work if you swap or change any ingredients (other than those I have specified).

Techniques

Pâtisserie is all about technique. Understanding what is happening in a recipe, and identifying and learning from mistakes, is crucial to becoming a more confident pâtisserie chef. Here are a few techniques that will be used a lot in this book — reading through this before starting any of the recipes will help you to feel more confident as you bake.

Lining your tin

This one is pretty basic, but every gâteau requires it! You will want to start by cutting a piece of baking paper that is the same length as your tin and about 10cm wider. Spray your tin lightly with spray oil (fig. 1) and then press the baking paper in (fig. 2), so that you have an overhang on each long edge (fig. 3) to help you to pull your gâteau out later.

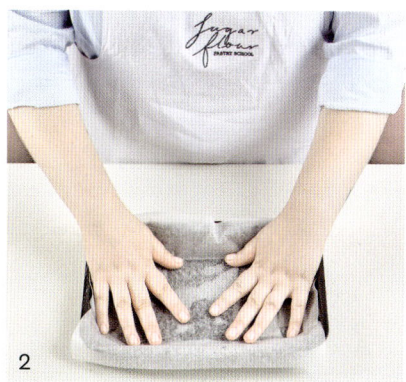

Soaking gelatine

Soaking gelatine is quite straightforward, but it is essential that you do it properly to avoid having bits of crunchy gelatine in your gâteaux. Start with a bowl of cold water (add a few cubes of ice if it's particularly warm in your kitchen). Submerge the gelatine completely in the cold water (figs 4, 5) for a minute or two until it's completely soft and squishy (fig. 6). Gently squeeze out any excess water and use as instructed in your recipe. I tend to soak gelatine as the first step in a recipe, to give it time to hydrate while I get the other ingredients ready.

Layering

Consistent layers are the key to making your petits gâteaux look like a professional product. You will want to check a few things before you get started with a recipe. The shelves in your fridge, freezer and oven should be flat. Otherwise each layer will be on a lean and your finished gâteaux will be thicker on one end. Perfectly flat shelves are a bit of a luxury — I've only had this in two kitchens I've worked in during my career. The solution is to make doorstop-type wedges of tinfoil to lift the lower end of your tray and make it level. Also, when layering your gâteaux make sure the previous layer is in the state asked for by the recipe — don't pour your perfectly whipped mousse all over a hot sponge, or it will melt in front of your eyes. And don't forget: everything takes practice. Your first few gâteaux might be a little wibbly-wobbly here and there. The only way to make them better is to try again. And remember what we discussed earlier: it will taste great, no matter how it looks.

Techniques

Mousse

Mousse is often the main component of a petit gâteau. There are a variety of mousse recipes in this book, and they all share a similar technique. Each consists of a base, with whipped cream folded into it. The base, which holds the flavour, varies between the recipes. There are two main base options, fruit or chocolate. A chocolate base is used for chocolate mousses, and mousses that are flavoured with nuts, caramel or anything else that pairs well with chocolate. Fruit mousses are made with a fruit purée as the base, which gives the mousse a strong fresh fruit flavour. An important note about chocolate mousse: dark, milk and white chocolates all require different mousse recipes. Each type of chocolate will set differently, so don't just swap out one type of chocolate for another. Get familiar with each recipe. Below you'll find a detailed step-by-step guide to make a mousse that works for every recipe in this book, as well as some troubleshooting tips for when you get stuck along the way.

Step one: First, soak the gelatine leaves in cold water until soft. On particularly warm days, you may need to add ice to cool the water and stop the gelatine leaves disintegrating. The ideal temperature for a pastry kitchen is 18°C, so if your kitchen is anything over 20°C, you should add some ice.

Step two: Next, heat the base liquid up to dissolve the gelatine into. For a chocolate mousse this is usually milk, boiled (fig. 7) and poured over the chocolate and gelatine (fig. 8), then mixed until smooth and glossy (fig. 9). For a fruit mousse, a small amount of fruit purée is heated with the gelatine until melted (figs 10, 11, 12), before being added to the remaining purée, which will help keep the base mixture cool (fig. 13).

Step three: The mousse base then needs time to cool. It won't take long for the base to reach the desired temperature (about 30°C). Often I whip my cream by hand in the time it takes for the mousse base to cool. If your mousse base cools too much, gently warm it over a pot of simmering water, stirring constantly, until it's fluid and has reached the desired 30°C.

Step four: Once the mousse base reaches the correct temperature, you can gently fold in the whipped cream. If cream is folded into the mousse base when it's too warm, the mousse base will melt the cream and you will lose all the air you've whipped into it. This results in a dense and sometimes rubbery mousse. Alternatively, if you wait for it to cool down too much, the gelatine will start to set and won't combine with the cream nicely, meaning there will be lumps of gelatine in your mousse. Unless otherwise stated, cream should be whipped to medium peaks, which is a point where the cream is stiff enough to hold a point that slightly folds over when the whisk is lifted out of the cream. Always pour the cream on top of the mousse base, and then fold. If you pour the mousse base on the cream it will push some of the air out, and keeping air within the cream is essential to a wonderfully light mousse. When folding, use a large spatula to gently scrape the base of the bowl, scoop up and bring the mixture over itself (fig. 14). In between each fold I like to rotate the bowl slightly to ensure everything is mixed evenly. Fold the mousse

mixture until it is only *just* combined. It should look like a homogenous mixture, and ever so slightly streaky. The more the mousse is mixed, the more it will deflate. And if you are not gentle, the mousse may split. Once your mousse has split there isn't much that can save it, unfortunately. The fat within the over-whipped cream will have separated from the other liquids. A split mousse will have a grainy mouthfeel when it has set. Be aware: the more fat in a mousse, the more likely it is to split, so mousses made with nuts or caramel require a particularly delicate touch.

A frozen mousse can be kept in a freezer for a month, and will last three days in a fridge once defrosted. Mousse, along with any other food item, should not be frozen again once it has been defrosted, as this poses a food safety risk.

While the majority of the mousse recipes in this book use a fruit- or chocolate-based mousse, there are a couple of variations. Mousses that have a particularly liquid component, like the Pimm's mousse (page 90), have the addition of a Swiss meringue in the base. This is a pasteurised meringue that helps the liquid base and the thick cream combine together. The other variation is bavarois, which is a type of mousse made with an anglaise, or runny custard base, then folded into whipped cream. A bavarois tends to be richer and works well with certain flavours, like the brown butter bavarois in the piece of toast gâteau (page 172). Both of these mousses follow the same principles as explained above.

Whipping cream

Whipped cream is a key component of any mousse; it's what makes a mousse light and airy. It's a pretty straightforward process, but here are a few key tips to get perfect whipped cream. Firstly, make sure your cream is cold. When we whip cream we're incorporating air, which gets trapped by the fat. If your cream is warm, the water and the fat in the cream separate out, rather than trapping those air bubbles. The same thing happens if you try to freeze cream and then whip it. You can whip your cream in a stand mixer with the whisk attachment, with an electric whisk or by hand. If doing it by hand, use a large bowl and a decent-sized whisk; this will make it much quicker to whip up. Any recipe that calls for whipped cream in this book will specify soft (fig. 15), medium (fig. 16) or stiff peaks (fig. 17). This is a guide for how much the cream should be whipped, and following the description is essential to making sure your mousse is delicious and light as well as ensuring that it won't split when you fold your cream into your mousse base. Always whip your cream just before you need it, otherwise the water can separate out as it sits.

15

16

17

Techniques

Meringue

There are three different types of meringue: French, Italian and Swiss. French meringue is unpasteurised meringue, meaning it needs to be cooked to make it safe to eat. Italian and Swiss meringues are both pasteurised. Italian meringue is pasteurised by pouring a hot sugar syrup over egg whites as they're being whipped. Swiss meringue is pasteurised by heating the egg whites and sugar over a pot of simmering water (fig. 18) until the mix reaches 75°C. It is then whipped in a stand mixer or with an electric whisk (fig. 19) until you have a thick meringue (fig. 20). Both of these methods yield a stable meringue that is safe to eat raw. Swiss meringue is what's most commonly used in this book for making mousses and for finishing touches. I find it much easier and more consistent than Italian meringue. French meringue is used in a few recipes, such as the berry pavlova (page 226), where it gets piped out into mini meringues and dehydrated, or cooked in a low oven until dry, for decoration. These meringues will add a great crunch to your gâteaux, whereas Swiss meringue adds a light airy quality. Like cream, meringue can also be whipped to soft, medium or stiff peaks, and this will always be specified in the recipe.

Pâte à bombe

A pâte à bombe is a mixture of egg yolks whipped with a hot sugar syrup to pasteurise them. It is used in a couple of recipes in this book inside mousses where a richer flavour is desired, such as the butternut and maple gâteau (page 129). Although it is traditional to use a hot sugar syrup for your pâte à bombe, I prefer to apply the same method that we use in the Swiss meringue — whisking the egg yolks and sugar together over a pot of simmering water (fig. 21) until they reach 75°C, which pasteurises them fully. It is much easier than working with the hot sugar syrup. Like with your Swiss meringue, once the mixture has reached 75°C, you'll move it to a stand mixer or electric whisk and continue to whisk it. A pâte à bombe will never reach stiff peaks the way a meringue will. Instead we look for the ribbon stage, or figure 8 stage (fig. 22). To check for the ribbon stage, pull your whisk out of the pâte à bombe. Your whisk should bring a ribbon of the pâte à bombe out with it. Use the whisk to draw a figure 8 with the ribbon on the surface of the bombe mix. You should be able to draw a full figure 8 before the ribbons disappear back into the mixture. If the ribbons melt back in before you've finished drawing your figure 8 then you need to continue to whisk your pâte à bombe until you can draw a full figure 8.

Whisking

Many of the techniques in this section call for you to whisk ingredients, which I have full faith you can do without a detailed paragraph on how to do it. There are, however, some times when an electric whisk or stand mixer is best, and times when whisking by hand is ideal. Whenever it's appropriate to use an electric whisk or stand mixer, it will be noted in the instructions. If you don't see a reference to either of those, it means that a hand whisk is required.

Caramel

My goal in life is to stop the spread of caramel misinformation on baking shows. I know a lot of people find caramel very difficult because they think they can't stir it, but that's actually not entirely true!

There are two types of caramel, dry caramel and wet caramel. A dry caramel is made by cooking sugar in a pot without any added liquid, and a wet caramel is made with the addition of water. Dry caramel is much easier, faster and less temperamental than a wet caramel, so it's my go-to whenever possible (like I said, I'm lazy — if I can do something an easier way, I will). But, due to the nature of how dry caramel is made, it's very hard to control the colour of your caramel, with a light-coloured caramel being tricky to achieve. Wet caramel can be more of a pain, but you'll be able to stop the caramel at an earlier stage if required, which can be useful in some scenarios, such as for the glaze on the macadamia and caramel petit gâteau (page 49).

Dry caramel

Dry caramel is much easier to cook. Cook sugar over a high heat, full blast on gas, or 1400–1600 watts on an induction cooktop. Stir as soon as the sugar starts to liquify around the edges (fig. 23). Keep stirring until the sugar melts and becomes a deep amber colour. It will look weird and clumpy for a little bit here (fig. 24), but it will come together very quickly. Occasionally a few lumps of sugar won't dissolve (fig. 25). Don't worry about these, you can always fish or strain these lumps out once you've added liquid to cool the caramel down.

Wet caramel

For wet caramel, put sugar and water in a pot, and stir until just combined. Then cook it on a high heat without stirring — for now (fig. 26). On television shows everyone mucks around with a pastry brush dipped in water, brushing down the sides of the pot so no sugar crystals ruin the caramel. Here's an industry secret: no one has time for that! The fear of a tiny little sugar crystal falling in and ruining your caramel is greater than the likelihood of it happening. When you add water to sugar, all the sugar crystals dissolve and turn to liquid. Occasionally a stray sugar crystal will not dissolve into the water properly, but it won't cause any harm. If you stir the caramel, you risk that stray crystal clinging to another, forming a chain reaction, known as crystallisation. Before you know it, your caramel is a sandy white mess. (This is a good place to note that sometimes we want to make that sandy white mess, like when making the caramelised peanuts for the caramel, chocolate and peanut petit gâteau on page 178). Caramel is most susceptible to crystallising

Techniques

between 110 and 120°C, as that's when the correct ratio of sugar and water is present to crystallise. To avoid crystallisation, I always cook wet caramel on a high heat to skip over this danger zone. This normally means having your gas burner on full force, or your induction cooktop at about 1400–1600 watts. As soon as the caramel starts to become a light gold colour (fig. 27), it has passed the crystallisation 'danger zone' and you can stir it without fear until it reaches your desired colour.

After caramelisation

Now that you've done the caramelisation, you need to stop it cooking further. The finished caramel is incredibly hot. It will most likely be smoking, even if you don't burn it! The sugar will be holding a lot of heat and simply removing the pot from the heat won't be enough to cool it down. As soon as your caramel is at the desired colour, you need to turn off the heat and add something to immediately cool it down and stop the cooking process. When I say immediately, I mean *immediately* — the moment you're happy with the colour, tip your addition in (fig. 28). A few seconds delay is enough to turn a perfect caramel into a smoking burnt mess. The most common additions to caramel are cream, water, butter or a combination of the three.

27

28

Depending on the amount of fat used (cream or butter), you may or may not need to use a stick blender to emulsify your caramel. I tend to blend caramel after making it, as this significantly improves mouthfeel. This is particularly important for caramels containing a lot of butter, such as in the caramel, chocolate and peanut petit gâteau (page 178). In that recipe, if you don't blend the butter in, the caramel will become grainy and likely split. Each recipe will specify if the caramel needs to be blended or not. The ratios of cream and butter vary from recipe to recipe. Cream gives the caramel body and keeps it liquid, whereas butter gives the caramel a smooth mouthfeel. Most recipes use both to achieve the desired texture. Should your caramel split, you can often save it by whisking or blending in one teaspoon of cold cream at a time until it's back to the desired consistency.

From here, you have two options: proceed with the recipe, or put it back on the heat and keep cooking it. The longer you cook the caramel the thicker it will become, as more water will evaporate. From this stage on you have a lot of control over the final consistency, and you could turn your caramel into anything from a nice sauce to a chewy caramel bar.

Anything after the caramelisation stage is the easy part. You can play around with cooking times, temperatures and fat ratios to reach a caramel consistency you like. I don't specify certain temperatures that the caramel should reach in the recipes in this book, as my preference is a liquid, pipeable caramel, which is normally achieved through the ratio of cream and butter in the recipes. Having caramel ooze out when cutting a petit gâteau adds more drama to the experience. However, if you want to make a chewy, candy-bar caramel, aim for at least 120°C at the final cooking stage, however this will change depending on your recipe and ratios.

Glazing

Glazing is another technique that can be quite difficult, but once you understand the process you will be able to do it perfectly every time. The purpose of a glaze is strictly visual. Glazing rarely adds to the flavour or texture, so it's a step you can skip if you're not bothered about your petit gâteau's appearance.

Glazing happens when a gelatine-rich mixture makes contact with a frozen surface. The high concentration of gelatine in the mixture and the low temperature of the surface causes the glaze to set rapidly, resulting in a glossy layer. A good glaze can be difficult to achieve, as the rapid setting time leaves little margin for error. Generally, you will glaze only the top of your gâteau, before it is portioned or trimmed, leaving the edges of your gâteau exposed. Otherwise the glaze is applied after it has been portioned, coating your petits gâteaux completely. For gâteaux made in a tin as we are doing, I prefer to glaze the top only, as glazing the sides makes it harder to move the petits gâteaux around without damaging them. In such small portions, having less glaze also helps to keep the sweetness in balance.

I use a few different glaze recipes in this book. The coloured glaze, made with white chocolate (page 239), is the simplest; not only is it easy to add colour to, but it is also the most forgiving glaze recipe in terms of application.

Once the glaze has been made according to the recipe, let it cool down. Each recipe will state the required temperature that the glaze must reach. Make sure to stir the glaze mixture every five to ten minutes so it cools evenly. Use a spatula to stir your glaze, rather than a whisk, to reduce the air bubbles. I test the consistency with a thermometer, and also by feel. Dip the tip of your finger in the glaze and let it drip off. It should evenly coat your finger without all running off or clumping up on the end. If the glaze is too hot, it will be too runny. Not only will it melt the outside of any mousse, it will be thin and, for lack of a better description, kind of ugly. If the glaze is too cold, it will immediately set on any mousse before you have a chance to spread it with your palette knife. You'll be left with a thick jelly layer that will coat the top of the mousse, which doesn't taste or look good.

Once the glaze is at the correct temperature and consistency (fig. 29), and not a second earlier, you can remove your gâteau from the freezer. Remove your gâteau from the tin, discard the baking paper it's on, and put it on a fresh sheet of baking paper. Pour the glaze over one side of the mousse, moving quickly from the top corner down to the bottom (fig. 30). I do this by pouring from the top left corner to the bottom left, then dragging the glaze to the right side, but your technique may differ depending on your dominant hand (I am right-handed). Use a large palette knife to drag the glaze to the other side of the gâteau (fig. 31). You need to completely cover the top of the gâteau with the glaze in one or two swift movements. After that it will start to set and you'll cause some serious damage trying to move it around. The edges of the gâteau will not be pretty. The main part you want to focus on is the centre of the gâteau, as the edges will be trimmed off before portioning (and snacked on by the chef!) and your

gâteau will transform from a slightly ugly duckling to a beautiful swan right before your eyes.

Allow the glaze to set. At this point you will have a gâteau (not a petit gâteau) ready to be portioned. The key with pouring the glaze is to be confident. Pour more than you need and let the excess run off. Once the glaze has set, don't disturb it, as touching it will make obvious marks and imperfections. There's no way to fix such damage; pouring a second layer to cover up any imperfections will result in a thick glaze that isn't nice to eat. I prefer to cover any mistakes up with a bit of tactical decoration — gold leaf can hide a multitude of sins. Any leftover glaze, or glaze that has dripped off the sides, can be reheated and used again. It will last for one week in the fridge and one month in the freezer.

Mille-feuille glaze

Glazing mille-feuille is very similar to glazing a frozen gâteau, although it presents its own challenges. You'll start in a similar manner by pouring your glaze down one side of your mille-feuille (fig. 32), then quickly dragging the palette knife along to coat the top completely in glaze (fig. 33). You need to do this in no more than two swift motions as otherwise pieces of pastry will break off into your glaze. Use the chocolate piping bag you have set aside (as specified in the recipe) to pipe lines of chocolate widthways across the top of the glaze (fig. 34). They don't need to be perfect lines — the feathering in the next step will make them look beautiful — but you do need to work quickly before a crust forms on the glaze. Drag a toothpick up and down through the chocolate to create a feathered pattern (fig. 35). Chill the mille-feuille until the glaze sets, at least 10 minutes, before portioning as instructed in the recipe.

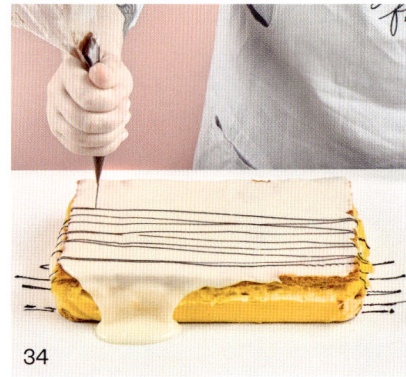

Portioning

Pastry chefs love the freezer. Cutting a frozen gâteau gives a clean, sharp cut that reveals the components and layers you worked so hard on. A large knife with a warm blade also helps. Either go the unnecessary, but very badass, route of warming the blade of your knife with a blowtorch each time you make a cut, or simply dunk the blade of your knife into boiling water. Make sure to dry the blade before making each cut. You always want to wipe the blade with a cloth or paper towel between each slice, as this will help you get the perfect side profile and keep the layers nice and clean. Pastry chefs tend to have rubbish knives. If you're looking for a nice big portioning knife, a supermarket one will do the trick. Please, please, please, do not blowtorch an expensive handmade Japanese knife — it will ruin the blade!

Give your gâteau up to 5 minutes on the bench before starting to portion it, especially if it's been frozen overnight, just to make it slightly easier to cut.

You should start by trimming the edge so you have a nice, clean cut to start with (fig. 36). Then follow the measurements on each recipe to create the desired shape. These measurements are simply a guide, and you can cut your gâteau into any shapes you like. Generally, the measurements provided will result in between 16 and 24 petits gâteaux. (Remember, the majority of the recipes can and should be frozen, meaning you won't have to eat 24 petits gâteaux all at once. But if you want to try, who am I to stop you!)

I like to start by cutting my gâteau into sections that are all the length suggested in the recipe (figs 37, 38), then I cut them into the correlating width to get individual portions (fig. 39).

This section of the recipe will also tell you if your gâteau needs to stay frozen in order to be finished. This is usually when it needs to be glazed or dipped in chablon once portioned, or if you can store it in the fridge until finishing.

I always get asked what happens to offcuts. People tend to assume they get thrown away, but nothing in a kitchen ever goes to waste! In a professional kitchen they'll be put out on a bench for the chefs to nibble on as they walk past, and I do exactly the same thing at home.

36

37

38

39

Melting chocolate

No matter what method you use to melt your chocolate, you should chop it up into smaller pieces to help it melt evenly, especially if you're using a bar of chocolate rather than drops (also known as fèves).

There are a couple of different ways to melt chocolate. When melting chocolate for use in a mixture, like a mousse or ganache, a liquid is heated up and used to melt the chocolate. When melting chocolate to make decorations, or use in a chablon, you need to melt the chocolate directly. I like to melt my chocolate in a bain-marie, mostly because I don't have a microwave (nothing against microwaves, I just don't have space for one). A bain-marie involves filling a pot about one-third full with water and bringing it to the boil, then placing a bowl, preferably metal, over the simmering water. I prefer the bowl to be metal, as it heats up more quickly and can cool down quickly also, helping to control the temperature of whatever you are heating in the bowl (chocolate or otherwise; a bain-marie is also used for Swiss meringue and other pastry techniques). It's important that the base of the bowl isn't touching the water, so as to stop the chocolate from burning.

You can also melt chocolate in a microwave, preferably in 10-second bursts, stirring in between. Chocolate can burn quite easily, particularly in the microwave, so the short bursts are necessary to prevent this. I prefer to use a microwave-safe plastic bowl. Obviously metal and the microwave are a no-go, and glass or ceramic bowls hold a lot of heat, making it hard to cool the chocolate down for tempering. Once you have your chocolate melted, it's ready to colour, if desired, and use as directed in your recipe.

Colouring chocolate

Colouring chocolate is a bit more tricky than it sounds. As chocolate will seize with even a drop of liquid, you can't use the normal food colouring you'd find at the supermarket. Chocolate-specific colouring is fat soluble, and mostly comes in powdered form. You can purchase it at specialty cake shops. Powdered colouring tends to be quite expensive; however, you don't need a lot as it is quite powerful. Natural alternatives include freeze-dried fruit powders and colourful spices, such as turmeric or saffron. When colouring chocolate make sure you pass the powder through a small sieve or tea strainer first, as this will help it dissolve better. I also like to use a stick blender for larger amounts, or a little handheld milk frother for smaller amounts. This helps blend the colouring into the melted chocolate and makes the pigment stronger. The amount of colour you need will vary greatly depending on what brand and type of colouring you use, which is why amounts of colouring are not specified in these recipes. Start with a small drop or pinch, and add more colouring as desired. When colouring chocolate, I like to melt the chocolate, colour it to the desired shade, and then temper it. Recipes for chocolate decorations in this book will assume you start with chocolate that is melted and coloured as described, but not yet tempered.

These colouring guidelines also apply to colouring chablon, the chocolate and oil dip that's used to finish many of the gâteaux in this book. Colouring the coloured glaze (page 239) can be done with any type of colouring as the chocolate has already been emulsified with milk.

Tempering chocolate

Tempering chocolate is a pain in the butt. It took me years to learn to confidently and comfortably temper chocolate. Even now, the thought of it can fill me with dread. It's a skill that will take you time to master.

You'll notice that some recipes in this book require tempered chocolate, and some don't. When coating a frozen gâteau in chocolate, we use what's called a chablon. This is a chocolate that has been thinned by the addition of a fat, normally cocoa butter or oil. The frozen gâteau sets the chocolate instantly and, because it will be stored in a fridge, the chocolate retains the desired snap and shine simply by being cold.

For chocolate decorations or chocolate bars that are handled at room temperature, the chocolate must be tempered. Decorations made with tempered chocolate can be stored in an airtight container in a cool, dry place for up to one month (if they're not going to be used by then, you'll just have to eat them!). Chocolate within a cake, mousse, or crémeux can be used straight from the bag or bar, and does not require tempering.

First, an explanation of tempering: it is the process of heating chocolate, then cooling it to create the correct alignment of crystals inside the cocoa butter, which is the fat inside the chocolate, forming the so-called 'beta crystals'. The beta crystals trap fat and sugar evenly throughout chocolate, giving it a shiny finish, a beautiful snap, and a nice smooth mouthfeel. Chocolate that is not tempered will 'bloom' when it sets — if you've seen a sun-damaged chocolate bar that has become streaky and white, that's what untempered chocolate, or bloom looks like. This is the cocoa butter and the sugar coming to the surface, because they haven't been trapped in the beta crystals.

There are two types of chocolate, couverture chocolate and compound chocolate. Couverture chocolate is made with sugar, cocoa solids and cocoa butter. Cocoa butter is the natural fat from cocoa nibs, and this is the part of couverture chocolate that requires tempering. Compound chocolate is made from sugar, cocoa solids and a solid vegetable fat. It is often used to coat candy bars, and you'll find packets of it labelled 'cooking' or 'baking' chocolate at the supermarket. Due to the inclusion of vegetable fat, compound chocolate can set hard at room temperature without being tempered and without blooming. The vegetable fat also means the chocolate lacks the smooth, creamy mouthfeel of couverture chocolate. It's generally lower quality and cheaper, so while it has its place (I love a good supermarket candy bar!), it's not going to give you the best results. As discussed earlier, the easiest way to tell whether you have couverture or compound chocolate is to look for whether it includes cocoa butter: if cocoa butter *isn't* listed among the ingredients, it will be compound chocolate.

There are two main methods for tempering chocolate: seeding and tabling. Seeding involves cooling down the melted chocolate with non-melted chocolate, and is more suitable for home cooks as it requires less specialised equipment. Tabling involves agitating melted chocolate on a piece of marble to cool it down. Either method will result in tempered chocolate if you execute them properly. You'll see a lot of reference to the melting temperature, crystallisation temperature, and working temperature in all of the tempering methods, which you'll be able to find in the temperatures chart below.

Tempering temperatures

Chocolate type	Melting temperature	Crystallisation temperature	Working temperature
Dark	50°C	29°C	31°C
Milk	45°C	28°C	30°C
White	45°C	27°C	29°C
Caramelised white	45°C	27°C	29°C

Seeding

Seeding is the easier method of tempering chocolate. Using the bain-marie method (melting chocolate, page 23) will help you melt your chocolate without burning it. Begin by placing a metal bowl over a pot of just-boiled or simmering water. Then melt two-thirds of the chocolate, by weight, in the metal bowl. Stir the chocolate constantly until it is all melted and has reached the melting temperature required for the type of chocolate you are using.

Once at melting temperature, remove the metal bowl from the pot and add the remaining third of the (unmelted) chocolate, which is called the 'seed' (fig. 40). The residual heat from the melted chocolate should be enough to melt the seed. Stir constantly until you have a bowl of smooth chocolate (figs 41, 42). Use a thermometer to check the chocolate has cooled to the crystallisation temperature on the chart opposite. If it is still too warm, continue to stir until it reaches the crystallisation temperature. Sometimes if I have trouble fully melting the seed, I use a stick blender to help combine it, or slightly heat the chocolate again, a few seconds at a time, stirring aggressively between each reheat.

Once the seed has entirely melted and it has reached the crystallisation temperature, your chocolate should be tempered. Hooray!

If the chocolate feels too thick for your recipe, you can heat it slightly to the working temperature on the chart. Be careful though — if you heat beyond the working temperature even by one degree Celsius, the beta crystals you've worked so hard to form will melt away, and the chocolate loses its temper. Then you will have to start the whole process from scratch again. But, at least it's good practice! You can temper your chocolate multiple times, so even if it didn't work the first time, no chocolate will ever be wasted.

40

41

42

Quick seeding

I learnt this method recently from visiting Valrhona pastry chef, Guillaume Lopvet, who learnt it from a chef he worked with in Japan. I find it is the perfect method for tempering small amounts of chocolate, as we do in this book. Quick seeding is a simplification of the original seeding technique. It adapts the same concept of seeding, where the unmelted chocolate, or the seed, is used to cool down the melted chocolate. The key difference is the seed in this method needs to be tempered, basically straight from the bar or bag. Because it's already tempered, the pre-existing beta crystals will encourage even more crystals to form.

To quick-seed your chocolate you need to melt all but two to three pieces/squares of your chocolate in a metal bowl placed over a pot of simmering water. You should be stirring the chocolate constantly, until it reaches 2–3 degrees above the working temperature given on the chart on page 24, and is completely smooth. If your chocolate gets any hotter than a few degrees over the working temperature, then allow it to cool down before continuing. If it's too hot, the chocolate will melt all the beta crystals you're about to add. Remove the bowl from the pot of simmering water, if you haven't already. Use a fine zester to grate in the squares of chocolate you set aside earlier (fig. 43). Stir to combine (fig. 44) and check the temperature. Your chocolate should now be somewhere between the crystallisation temperature and the working temperature. If it is, then it's ready to use. If it's too warm, grate in another piece or two of chocolate until the temperature is within range. If it's feeling too cold, warm your chocolate up as needed.

Tabling

Tabling to temper chocolate is more tricky. Not only does it require a marble slab to cool the chocolate down, it requires skill to control the chocolate without making a mess, and speed to ensure the chocolate doesn't set on the marble. Marble is used because it retains its cool surface when warm chocolate is spread over it, compared to metal or other surface types, which will heat up from contact with the chocolate and not cool it down. I tend to only use the tabling method at work for large quantities of chocolate, where I have a large marble table to work on. If you want to try it at home, you can purchase a marble tile. Any smooth marble or stone tile will work. Ideally it will be larger than 40 x 40cm to provide enough surface area to spread the chocolate around with metal scrapers. The larger the tile, the more room you'll have to work with, without the fear of the chocolate dripping off the side of the slab.

First, melt all of the chocolate. Once it has reached melting temperature, as per the chart on page 24, pour all bar one or two tablespoons of the chocolate onto your marble slab (fig. 45). Using a large palette knife and a small bench scraper, spread the chocolate and then immediately scrape it back into a pile (figs 46, 47, 48). Repeat this process until the crystallisation temperature is reached, checking with a thermometer. You'll need to work quickly. If you leave the chocolate on the marble without moving it, it will set. How long you have until it sets really depends on the amount of chocolate and the size of the marble slab. For a batch of chocolate that is 500g or less, the whole process shouldn't take much longer than 15 minutes from start to finish.

To remove the chocolate from the marble, hold the bowl just under the edge and use a bench scraper to scrape the chocolate in (fig. 49). This can be a bit tricky, and may take a few attempts to get right. Once in the bowl, stir the tempered chocolate to combine it with the tablespoons of warmer chocolate left in the bowl. This will raise the temperature slightly to make the tempered chocolate more workable. The chocolate is now ready to use. As with the seeding method, you can warm the chocolate slightly over a pot of simmering water if needed, just be careful not to overheat it.

A few notes on tempering chocolate

Tempered chocolate will set rapidly at room temperature. This means you need to work quickly to stop it setting in the bowl. You should have the required tools and any additional ingredients ready before starting the tempering process, so you can work with the chocolate before it sets. A hairdryer is a great tool to slightly warm chocolate as needed, with less risk of overheating it. Most pastry chefs have a dedicated chocolate hairdryer in their kitchen.

I always test chocolate to make sure it has tempered. To do this, dip a small piece of baking paper or the tip of a small knife in the chocolate and leave it to set. If it sets within 5 minutes and has no streaks on the surface, it has tempered. If it doesn't set, or it has white streaks, it hasn't properly tempered. You need to either cool it down further or start the process again.

When it comes to crystallisation, it's not just about cooling the chocolate to the crystallisation temperature, but also agitating it constantly to help the crystals form. That's why both tempering methods require constant stirring or movement on the marble.

If your chocolate doesn't temper the first, second, or even fifth try, don't worry! Tempering chocolate is an incredibly difficult skill to master, so don't be too hard on yourself. Keep trying — you can melt and re-temper your chocolate again.

Be careful not to get any water or other liquids in the chocolate. Any liquid will seize the chocolate and make it impossible to work with. If water does find its way into the chocolate bowl, use a spoon to generously scoop it out as well as the surrounding chocolate — you don't want to waste a whole bowl of chocolate if you don't have to!

Chocolate decorations

There are quite a few different chocolate decorations in this book, and while they may seem intimidating at first, they're all based on the same techniques and processes. For ease, I have split them into three types: flat decorations, curved decorations and piped decorations.

Flat and curved decorations

Both flat and curved chocolate decorations start the same way. First, you need to spread your chocolate out. Your recipe will state if you should be using an acetate sheet, baking paper, or something completely different, such as bubble wrap for the chocolate honeycomb decoration (page 50). Spreading out the tempered chocolate is a skill that might take some time to master. If your chocolate is perfectly tempered, it will set very quickly. You will only have a short timeframe to pour it onto your sheet, spread it evenly, cut it as desired and even shape it in some cases. Start by lightly spraying some spray oil onto your bench, then laying the acetate (or whatever type of sheet you're using) down on top of the oil. Wipe the top of your sheet with a clean, dry paper towel, which will remove any air bubbles from underneath. It will also prevent any fingerprints from being transferred from your sheet to the chocolate, and stop the sheet itself from moving around while you're spreading the chocolate. I like to work with the sheet in a landscape position, spreading from left to right.

Pour your chocolate down the left side of your sheet (fig. 50) and use a large palette knife to scrape it in one smooth motion to the other side (figs 51, 52), or you may want to work right to left if you're left-handed. Unless your palette knife is huge, you'll only be able to spread about half the chocolate at once. So I spread the top half of my pour first, and then go back and spread the bottom half. You want to get the chocolate as thin and even as you can — about 1mm — with only a few quick strokes. The more you manipulate it, the more you'll damage the decoration sheet. Going over the edges of the sheet with the chocolate means you'll get a nice, even layer on the sheet itself, and it'll also mean you can get as many decorations out of your sheet as possible.

50

51

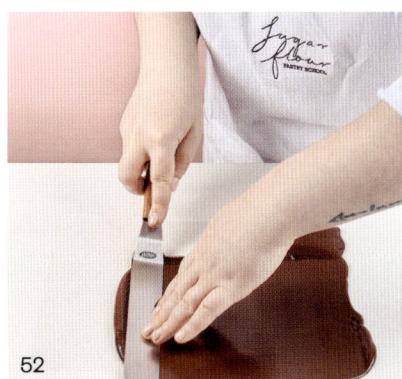
52

Once your sheet is completely covered, use a small knife or pastry scraper to find the corner of the sheet (fig. 53). Lift it up and move the sheet to a clean part of the bench (fig. 54). Once you're a chocolate master, you can use this opportunity to scrape your excess chocolate off the bench, but when you're just starting out, you can leave the cleaning for later.

Before you can start cutting your chocolate, you need to let it set slightly. Depending on the temperature of your kitchen, this can take a few seconds or up to one minute. Your chocolate needs to be slightly soft, but firm enough that you can touch it without leaving an obvious indent. If it's too soft it won't cut properly and you won't be able to get your decorations off in nice, clean-edged pieces. If you wait too long, however, it will set and you won't be able to cut it.

53
54

Once your chocolate is at the correct cutting consistency, you can use a few different techniques to make your decorations. All the decorations in this book are made by using a knife, pastry/cookie cutter, decorating comb or toothpick (or a combination of these tools) to create your shape. Occasionally you will need to use a rolling pin to roll your sheet around to create curved decorations.

Using a knife or pastry cutter follows much the same process. With a knife, use a ruler as a guide to measure out the size and shape of your decorations, and then use a pressing motion with your knife to cut the shapes (fig. 55). A cutter requires no measuring, just get in there and cut away, making sure you make your cut-outs as close together as possible to get as many decorations as you can. For any decorations requiring a more organic shape, I drag a toothpick through the chocolate to create the design I want (fig. 56).

55
56

Once you've cut your decoration as desired, you'll then either press it flat, or roll it up to make a curved decoration. To press it flat, place a sheet of baking paper on top, and then a baking tray or chopping board on top of that. As chocolate sets, it contracts. Weighing it down will stop the chocolate from contracting into an uneven curl. If you're after a curved decoration, to add volume to your gâteaux, you'll need to roll your sheet up into a tube. Use a few pieces of tape to secure it, before leaving your chocolate to set. I either roll the sheet up tightly as is, or I will roll it around a rolling pin, so the curve is more controlled and consistent. It depends on what you want the final decoration to look like. When making a rolled decoration, you need to wait for it to be just about fully set before rolling it up, to avoid your chocolate sticking to the rolling pin.

57
58

The first decoration I learnt how to make out of chocolate was a chocolate curl, which is used in two recipes in this book (passionfruit chocolate, page 148, and the symphony, page 108). To make a chocolate curl, you need to use a decorating comb, which is a small metal or plastic scraper with triangular teeth. You can buy them quite inexpensively from most cake decorating stores. Once you've spread your chocolate and it is the correct cutting consistency, you then drag your comb through the chocolate, diagonally from one corner to another (fig. 57). The more severe an angle you make your cuts, the tighter your curls will be. Repeat until the whole sheet has been cut. Roll the sheet up and tape it closed to set (figs 58, 59). The tighter you roll it, the tighter your curls will be.

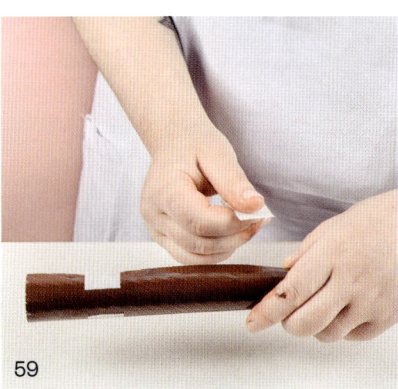

59

Removing both of these types of decorations from the sheet is my favourite part of the process. First you need to make sure you've given your chocolate enough time to fully crystallise. This will take a minimum of half an hour in a cool spot in your kitchen, but longer is better. To remove flat decorations from their sheet, take off the tray that is weighing them down and flip the sheet in one quick motion so the chocolate is touching the bench, and the sheet is facing you. Gently pull a corner of the sheet up, pulling it away from the chocolate, leaving your decorations on the bench. The side that has touched the sheet will be the shinier or more presentable side, and will be the side now facing you (fig. 60).

For curved chocolate decorations, first remove the sheet from the rolling pin (if you've used one) by gently sliding it off. Use a knife or scissors to cut the tape (fig. 61) and unfurl your decorations. They should easily come off your sheet (figs 62, 63).

You can store any chocolate decoration in an airtight container, in a cool, dry place. If the chocolate decorations are flat, I put a small piece of baking paper in between each layer to ensure the decorations don't scratch or damage each other.

Any off-cuts can be kept and reused in any way you like, melted down and re-tempered, in a mousse, or just eaten as is!

60

61

62

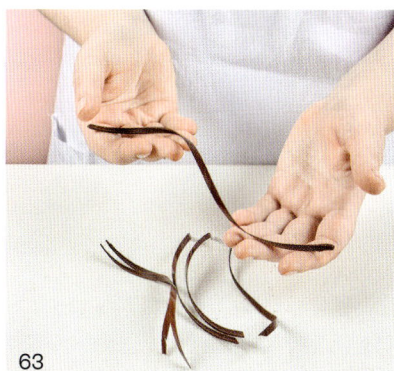
63

Piped decorations

Piped decorations are much easier to make. Simply pour your tempered chocolate into a piping bag and cut a small, 1mm opening in your bag. Test it to make sure your chocolate is flowing out consistently and evenly. If it's not, cut your hole a little bigger. Otherwise, you're ready to start piping! There are two piped chocolate decorations in this book: the chocolate flowers on the hazelnut chocolate gâteau (page 105), which are little dots piped into a flower shape straight onto the gâteau (fig. 64); and the chocolate squiggles on the tonka chocolate gâteau (page 184). These are piped onto a sheet of baking paper, left to set and then transferred onto your gâteaux with the help of a palette knife. The key to the squiggle decoration is making sure there are enough overlapping squiggles in the centre (fig. 65) to make the squiggle strong enough to be moved without breaking.

64

65

Chablon

Using a chablon, a mix of chocolate and fat, to create a shell around your gâteau is a great way to add texture and flavour. The brand of chocolate I use in all the recipes in this book, Valrhona chocolate, is a really fluid chocolate when melted, meaning it doesn't need as much oil in the chablon recipes. Other chocolate brands may be thicker, due to a smaller quantity of cocoa butter in the chocolate (this doesn't mean the chocolate is a lesser quality). This means you may need to add more oil to your chablon recipe to thin it out. Your chablon should be a smooth pouring consistency, between 30 and 35°C before you begin to use it. Make sure you keep an eye on the temperature of your chablon, reheating it as needed.

Dipping in chablon

There are two different ways I apply chablon. For both methods, first pierce each portion with a toothpick, and use the toothpick to dunk the gâteau into the chablon. The first method is to dip the entire gâteau in the chablon mix, coating the sides, top and bottom. Because your gâteau is frozen, it will immediately start to set the chablon. You will need to work quickly: dunk your gâteau in and allow any excess to drip off for a few seconds (fig. 66). Scrape the base on the edge of the bowl to get as much of the liquid chocolate off as possible. You'll then need to scrape the base across a sheet of baking paper, to allow more of the chablon to drip off (fig. 67), leaving you with as thin a layer as possible.

The second method is almost exactly the same, but instead you leave the top of the gâteau exposed, and only dip the sides and base (fig. 68). Then repeat the scraping as above (fig. 69). For both methods you may need to reheat your chablon occasionally while using it, as if it gets too cold your coating will start to become very thick. At the end of each recipe you should have a bit of chablon left over, as you always need an excess to be able to dip each gâteau. You can either store your remaining chablon in an airtight container in the pantry for up to one month, re-melting it as needed, or you can set it in the fridge and then eat it like a chocolate bar. I often do the latter, but instead of eating it I'll chop it up and use it in place of chocolate pieces in cookies.

66

67

68

69

Quenelle

A quenelle is an oval-shaped ball of cream, ice cream — or anything, really. Traditionally, a quenelle is made by moving the mixture you're shaping between two spoons until you have a three-sided oval shape. A more modern 'rocher' is created by rolling a spoon through the mixture to create a perfectly smooth oval shape. The term rocher and quenelle are used interchangeably these days, but I use the term quenelle more often, just out of habit.

To make a quenelle of cream, you need to start with the right-sized and -shaped spoon. For petits gâteaux I like to use a teaspoon that has a distinct oval shape and deep bowl. The deeper or more curved the bowl of your spoon is, the rounder your quenelle will be. As you become a master quenelle maker, you'll learn what shaped spoon you prefer working with most.

Next you need to make sure your cream is at the stiff peaks stage. If it's too soft it won't quenelle properly or hold its shape.

Set up your station so you have a mug of very hot water. I like to use water that has just about boiled, and leave my quenelle spoon sitting in it. Have your cream next to this, and then your gâteaux (frozen, portioned and ready to decorate) on a tray. I tip the bowl of cream to the side slightly, and press the cream down with a spatula so I have a nice even surface to start my quenelle on. Remove the spoon from the water and give it a few shakes or taps to get any excess water droplets off. Hold the spoon in your dominant hand, with the bowl of the spoon facing away from you. Push the bowl of the spoon through the cream until you see that it is completely filled with cream (fig. 70). With a sharp motion twist the spoon around so that it cuts through the cream, creating the quenelle shape (fig. 71). Drag the spoon back towards you to refine the shape slightly, then gently drop your quenelle onto your gâteau (figs 72, 73). This whole process needs to be done within a matter of seconds each time, as your hot spoon will be melting the cream. If your spoon isn't hot enough, you won't be able to get your quenelle off the spoon and onto your gâteaux. In between each quenelle, return your spoon to the hot water, reheating the water if needed, and level your cream into a flat surface before starting on the next quenelle.

It's almost impossible that your first quenelle will be perfect. It took me hundreds of cream quenelles to be able to do them so consistently. Like all things, the only way to get better is practice and patience. You'll just have to eat plenty of gâteaux along the way!

Piping

Piping is one of the easiest ways to make your gâteau beautiful, and is also a great way to individualise it and make it your own. It can be really hard to get your piping to look how you want it to; like everything else in this book, it takes practice.

The first step to piping is choosing the correct tip. The recipe will tell you what size and shape tip you need to put inside your bag, or what shape tip you need to cut in the bag, if not using a separate tip. Once you've got your tip in, use scissors to trim off the excess plastic of the piping bag so that the opening of the tip is clear and unobstructed. You'll then fold the opening of the bag around your hand, or around a tall jug or glass, and begin to fill it with whatever mixture you're using (fig. 74). Folding the bag like this means any spills you make while filling the bag will stay on the inside of the bag, keeping the outside of the bag clean and easy to work with. Then twist the end of the bag so that you seal in the mixture, and create enough tension in the twist to be able to push the mixture out of the tip with a gentle squeeze.

The key to getting consistent piping is to hold your bag steady. I like to wrap my fist around the mixture so that I have full control with my dominant hand (while pinching the twist closed with my thumb and index finger), and use my non-dominant hand as a guide. Now it's time to start piping!

Techniques

Piping kisses

One of the most common piping decorations I use is kisses, a basic teardrop shape that can be decorated and altered in endless ways. To pipe a kiss you need to hold your piping bag vertically, with the tip just a few millimetres away from where you want the kiss to be. Without moving the bag, squeeze the mixture out until the kiss is as wide and round as you want it to be (fig. 75). In one swift motion, stop squeezing and lift the piping bag up, leaving a perfectly peaked kiss (fig. 76). The larger the tip you use, and the more you squeeze, the larger your kiss will be, and vice versa.

Once you've piped your kisses you can either leave them as is, or you can transform them into a new decoration. For some gâteaux in this book, like the cookie caramel chip (page 182), you'll turn the kisses into little wells to hold a delicious sauce. To make a well in your kiss, dip a nice round teaspoon measure or melon baller into hot water. Shake the water off and then press the rounded base of the spoon into your kiss (fig. 77). Once your cavity is as deep as you'd like, gently slide the teaspoon measure out in an upwards motion, leaving you with a smooth, perfectly round indent (fig. 78).

For the squished kiss decoration that is used in the pandan, yuzu and coconut gâteau (page 59) and the bergamot and Earl Grey gâteau (page 159), you'll start by piping a random assortment of different-sized kisses on top of your frozen gâteau (fig. 79), leaving a few millimetres of space in between each kiss. Then take a sheet of acetate or baking paper that has been cut to the same dimensions as your tray (fig. 80), and gently press the acetate down to squash the tops of the kisses, creating an almost cobblestone-like pattern (fig. 81). Freeze your gâteau with the acetate still attached until the decoration is frozen solid. You can then remove the sheet of acetate, leaving behind your beautiful decoration (fig. 82).

75

76

77

78

79

80

81

82

Saint Honoré tip

Quite often in this book, you'll see recipes call for a Saint Honoré tip. While this is a piping tip you can buy, I actually prefer to cut the shape directly into the piping bag. All you need to do is snip the end off the bag so that the section you cut off creates a small triangle (fig. 83). If your piping bag has a seam or a more firmly pressed side, you should cut it so that the seam is the base or the longest part of the triangle. Whenever a Saint Honoré tip is asked for in this book, it will specify a size for the tip. This measurement (most commonly 1cm) refers to the length of the cut section of the bag.

When you pipe with your Saint Honoré tip, you need to hold the piping bag with the seam pointing upwards, and the bag on a bit more of an angle than if you were piping kisses. Then go back and forth in a zigzag motion to get a beautiful, ribbon-like decoration (fig. 84).

Puff pastry

There are two gâteaux in this book that use puff pastry, the mille-feuille (page 132) and the tarte tatin (page 231). You can most definitely use store-bought puff pastry, but nothing really beats the taste of homemade puff. Making puff pastry from scratch is a little bit of a process, which is why it's in the techniques section rather than with the base recipes. There are a few different methods for making puff pastry. My favourite, and the one I use here, is inverse puff pastry. This involves mixing the butter with flour to create a paste. This makes the butter much more pliable and easier to handle. You'll need:

   210g flour
   100g water
   300g cold butter
   120g flour

Mix the first measure of flour and water together until you have a just-combined, very shaggy, dry dough (figs 85, 86). Leave to rest at room temperature for half an hour. After half an hour of rest (for the dough, not just for you!), you can begin your butter paste. Dice the butter into 2cm cubes and put it in a stand mixer bowl together with the second measure of flour (fig. 87). Use the dough hook to mix the butter and flour on a low speed until they have formed a smooth, stiff paste that is a uniform colour (fig. 88). You need to make sure the butter stays cold so that the paste doesn't become too sticky.

Generously dust your bench with flour (fig. 89) and press your butter paste into a rectangle about 2cm thick (fig. 90). Press your dough that you made earlier into a rectangle, half the width of your butter paste rectangle, but the same length (fig. 91).

Dust any excess flour off the surface of your butter paste and press the dough rectangle in the centre, so that the top and bottom edges of the butter and

83

84

85

86

87

88

89

90

91

Techniques

the dough line up (approximately!) (fig. 92). Try to work quickly as being too fussy at this stage will significantly soften your butter and make it harder to work with. Fold the two edges of the butter rectangle to the centre of the dough, and pinch lightly to seal the seam (fig. 93).

Flip your dough over so that the seam is now on the bench and generously dust the bench and the dough with flour. Roll your dough into a long rectangle, rolling only in the direction of the open ends, which is where you can see the dough centre poking out of the top and bottom (figs 94, 95). Once your dough is about 2cm thick, dust any excess flour off (fig. 96). Fold the top third of the dough down to the centre third (fig. 97), and then the bottom third up over this (fig. 98). This is called a single fold, and we need to do five of these in total.

Once you've completed your first fold, rotate your dough 90 degrees, so the open ends are once again facing you (fig. 99). Repeat the rolling and folding process once more, bringing your fold total to two.

Wrap your dough in cling film and chill for 15–20 minutes before repeating the rolling and folding process to get to your total of five single folds. If your dough is getting too soft and sticky at any point, return to the fridge for a maximum of 20 minutes before continuing. Once you're finished you can use your pastry immediately or store in the fridge for up to one week, or in the freezer for up to one month. The dough may acquire a slight grey tinge after a few days in the fridge; this is due to the flour oxidising and isn't anything to worry about.

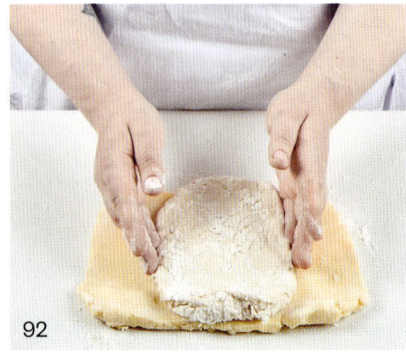
92

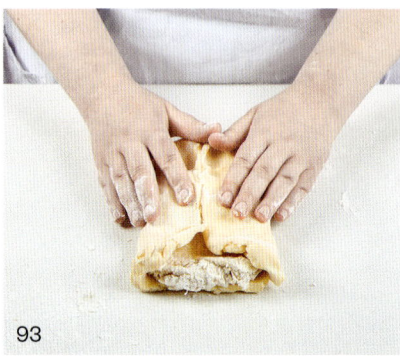
93

94

95

96

97

Troubleshooting

As I said earlier, making mistakes is one of the best ways to learn and improve. This doesn't mean it's not frustrating, though! Here are a few ways to avoid common mistakes that might happen in the gâteau-making process, and that will hopefully save you some heartache — or at least help prevent it happening again next time.

Cracking gâteau

If your gâteau is cracking when you cut it, leave it on the bench for a little longer to defrost slightly more, making it easier to cut.

98

99

Lumpy or seized caramel

When fully caramelised, the temperature of sugar is about 180°C. Adding in cream, even if it's warm, will rapidly cool the caramel down and sometimes cause it to seize or set, creating large lumps of set caramel. This is easy to fix! Turn the heat as low as it goes and simmer the mixture, stirring constantly, until the lumps of caramel have dissolved. If this takes a long time (more than 5 minutes) add a tablespoon of cream to account for the evaporation while the caramel is cooking. If you only have a few small lumps, you can just pass the caramel through a sieve. Only do this after the cream has been added; passing pure caramelised sugar through a sieve is a recipe for disaster.

Sliding layers

Sometimes once your gâteau has been portioned and defrosted, the mousse layer may slide off the layer below. This usually happens with petits gâteaux where there is a pâte de fruit layer underneath the mousse. If you don't make the mousse on the same day, or even within an hour or so, of making the pâte de fruit, it can form a layer of condensation on top. Because pâte de fruit is already a smooth layer, the condensation makes it even more difficult for the mousse to grip it. To avoid this, make your mousse as soon as the pâte de fruit is cooled, and make sure you store your pâte de fruit at room temperature only, not in the fridge or freezer, until the mousse is on top.

Split anglaise

The anglaise base that is used in bavarois recipes can overcook very easily, leaving you with a pot of scrambled eggs. This is an easy fix though. Simply strain your anglaise through a sieve, and blend with a stick blender if you have one. Then you're ready to carry on as normal.

It's summer and it's hot and everything is melting!

Pastry is always about temperature. Generally, the cooler the environment, the better. If you're baking in summer and you find recipes are splitting more easily, or not setting, then that's an indication your kitchen may be too hot. When this happens I like to take a little break. Clean up, wait until it's a bit cooler, and then get back into it. Allow things to have longer setting times and keep chilled ingredients in the fridge until the last minute, to give yourself the best chance of summer survival.

Collapsing gâteaux

The majority of the gâteaux in this book contain gelatine, which needs to be cold to set, and needs to stay cold. If it gets too warm it will start to melt and your gâteau will fall apart. Keeping your gâteaux chilled until serving will prevent this. If you're taking them to serve somewhere, I recommend transporting them while they're still frozen. Your recipe will always state at which stages a gâteau can be stored in the freezer. Most of the time, it can be frozen when it's been glazed or dipped in a chablon, so all you need to do is add the finishing touches.

Fruit and other decorations can also weigh your gâteaux down, and cause a delicate mousse to collapse under them, which is why it's best to garnish your gâteaux immediately before serving. If your gâteaux do start to fall apart, google 'Oops, I dropped the lemon tart'. If a three-Michelin-starred restaurant can serve a squashed dessert, then so can you!

Chocolate disasters

Maybe your chocolate didn't set? Or is it all white and streaky? Or you can't get it off the acetate? Don't worry! You can melt your chocolate and try again. As long as you haven't contaminated it with any water or other liquid, you can melt and temper your chocolate again. If you have contaminated it somehow, it doesn't have to go to waste — you can still use it to make mousse or ganache.

If your chocolate isn't setting, or you can't get it off your baking paper or acetate sheet, pop it into the fridge or freezer for a few minutes, and you'll be ready to go. I always remind my customers, if you've spent three days making a gâteau for someone, and they complain that the chocolate decoration isn't perfect, then you can take that gâteau straight back!

Ugly glaze or chablon

Sometimes it can take a few goes to get the hang of glazing a gâteau, or using a chablon, and the time it takes to get there can result in some not-so-beautiful products. This is where my favourite phrase comes in: tactical decoration! A touch of gold leaf or a carefully placed flower petal can hide a multitude of sins. I also urge you to remember three very important things. 1) People won't know what your gâteau is meant to look like. Unless you put it next to the book with the photo open next to it, they'll have absolutely no idea. So don't stress if it doesn't look like mine. 2) The first time I glazed a gâteau, it was a disaster. So was the second and the third time (and even more than that). But I've made a lot of them since then. 3) It will still be delicious! Which is the most important thing. Give yourself some grace.

Storing and serving

Once complete and portioned, store gâteaux in the freezer for up to one month, preferably well wrapped, or in an airtight container. Defrost gâteaux in a fridge overnight. They will keep in the fridge for up to three days.

The easiest way to move your petits gâteaux is by sliding a small offset palette knife under them and gently sliding them onto your plate. Serve chilled and enjoy!

038	Lemon meringue
041	Raspberry, beetroot and chocolate
043	Rhubarb and custard
046	Blackcurrant and violet
049	Macadamia and caramel
050	Honey bee
053	Laming-not
055	Carrot cake
056	Ispahan
059	Pandan, yuzu and coconut
060	Blueberry yuzu cheesecake
063	Matcha passionfruit opera
067	Rocky road
069	Banana, passionfruit and coconut
070	Strawberry and rhubarb
073	Passionfruit strawberry
074	Avocado and lime

Spring

Lemon meringue

Lemon meringue was my first pastry love. The crispy base, the tart lemon filling and the airy meringue makes it the most perfect combination of textures and flavours. Here I've tried to keep it simple and true to the original, while incorporating some classic French techniques. This is also a great way to showcase one of the most amazing fruits – the finger lime. It's a lime in the shape of a finger, that when cut open reveals little caviar-like pearls of citrus. They work so perfectly as a garnish on this gâteau, adding amazing pops of acidity throughout. Don't stress if you can't find any, though; the gâteau will still be delicious without them!

Makes 21

Sablé Breton base

200g sugar
4 egg yolks
110g very soft butter
200g flour, (gluten free, if desired)
3½ tsp baking powder

Preheat the oven to 160°C and line the tin. Whisk the sugar and egg yolks together until combined; this will be a very thick paste. Add the softened butter (it needs to be incredibly soft, like the texture of a thick mayonnaise) and whisk to combine. Stir in the flour and baking powder, mixing until the mixture forms a very soft dough. Spread the sablé in the tin until it's a smooth, even layer. Bake for 15–20 minutes, until it is a light golden brown. It will puff up in the oven, then shrink down again as it cools. Leave to cool at room temperature while making the crémeux.

Lemon crémeux

2 sheets gelatine
200g lemon juice
200g sugar
4 eggs
200g butter

Soak the gelatine sheets in cold water until soft. Drain and set aside. Whisk the lemon juice, sugar and eggs together in a pot and cook over a medium heat, whisking constantly, until the crémeux comes to the boil. Remove from the heat and stir in the gelatine. Allow to cool to 40–45°C. Add the butter and blend with a stick blender until the crémeux is silky smooth. Pour over the cooled sablé base and freeze overnight, or until solid.

Portioning

(page 22)

Portion the gâteau into 21 pieces that are 8 x 2cm rectangles. Store in the freezer and defrost before finishing.

Swiss meringue

Swiss meringue (recipe page 241)

Spoon the meringue into a piping bag and cut a 1cm Saint Honoré tip (page 33). Pipe the meringue on the top of each gâteau in a zigzag pattern. Do this no more than a few hours before serving, as the meringue is best when it is fresh.

To finish

1 lemon
1 finger lime
micro coriander or baby basil, if desired

Zest the lemon on top of the meringue, spoon the finger lime pearls over and top with micro coriander or baby basil, if using. Serve immediately.

Raspberry, beetroot and chocolate

Raspberry, beetroot and chocolate are a great flavour combination. Beetroot has a natural sweetness that works perfectly in desserts, and when balanced with the dark chocolate and fruity raspberry — it's a match made in heaven.

Makes 20

Chocolate cake

chocolate cake (recipe page 239)

Once baked, leave to cool completely.

Raspberry compote

raspberry compote (recipe page 240)

Reserve 50g of compote in the fridge for finishing, before pouring the remaining compote over the cake and store in the freezer for at least 30 minutes before making the beetroot mousse.

Beetroot mousse

3¼ sheets gelatine
200g beetroot juice (store-bought apple and beetroot will work, or juice a beetroot yourself with a juicer)
200g cream
2 egg whites
90g sugar

Soak the gelatine sheets in cold water until soft. Drain and put in a pot with 20g of the beetroot juice. Cook over a low heat until the gelatine has fully melted. Remove from the heat and stir in the remaining beetroot juice. Set aside while you whip the cream to soft peaks. Set the cream aside while you make the Swiss meringue (page 18). Whisk the egg whites and sugar together over a pot of simmering water until the mixture is hot to the touch, or 75°C. Whisk with a handheld electric mixer or with a stand mixer until the meringue reaches stiff peaks. Gently fold the beetroot mixture into the meringue. Fold in the cream until just combined. Pour over the frozen raspberry compote and level off with a palette knife. Freeze overnight, or until solid.

Portioning

(page 22)

Portion the gâteau into 20 pieces that are 6 x 3cm rectangles. Store frozen and defrost fully before finishing.

To finish

200g fresh raspberries
50g reserved raspberry compote
micro coriander, or other micro herbs/edible flowers

Decorate each gâteau with a mixture of cut and whole raspberries. Fill the centre of the whole raspberries with the reserved raspberry compote and finish with micro coriander or edible herbs/flowers. Serve immediately.

Rhubarb and custard

Rhubarb and custard is a classic English pairing and with the addition of elderflower, this gâteau has a lovely floral flavour. Using a choux pastry sponge not only gives you a super light sponge base, but it also has a slight eggy flavour that helps enhance the custard tones.

Makes 24

Choux pastry sponge

35g milk
25g butter
35g flour
3 egg yolks
3 egg whites
30g sugar

Preheat the oven to 180°C and line the tin. Bring the milk and butter to a boil. Remove from the heat and stir in the flour. Mix thoroughly until you have a thick paste and return to a low heat, stirring constantly until a thin film coats the base of the pot, and the choux has formed a rough ball. This won't take more than a minute. Remove from the heat and leave to stand for a minute or two until the choux base cools down slightly. It can still be warm to the touch, but should not feel hot. Using a stand mixer with the paddle attachment, or by hand, mix in the egg yolks, one at a time, until fully combined. Set this aside. Whisk the egg whites in a stand mixer or with an electric whisk, until they have doubled in size. Add the sugar and continue whisking until the meringue forms stiff peaks. Stir a third of the meringue into the choux pastry base to loosen it slightly. Fold in the remaining meringue until just combined. Pour into the lined tin and level off with a palette knife. Bake for 10–12 minutes, until lightly golden brown and the sponge is just set to the touch. Allow to cool while you make the rhubarb compote.

Candied rhubarb

2 stalks rhubarb, cut into approximately 10cm lengths
100g sugar
100g water
⅛ tsp vanilla bean paste
1 drop red colouring

Preheat the oven to 90°C and line a baking tray with baking paper. Use a mandolin or a vegetable peeler to slice 0.5–1mm thin slices of rhubarb so you have long, thin strips, the same length and width as the rhubarb stalks. Reserve any pieces that aren't thin enough for the compote. Bring the sugar, water, vanilla and colouring to a boil. Remove from the heat and allow to cool for 5 minutes. Put the rhubarb strips in the syrup and stir them around so they are fully coated. Working one piece at a time, remove the rhubarb from the syrup and lay it down flat on the lined baking tray. The rhubarb can be placed very close together, but do not overlap them. Once you have arranged all the rhubarb, put the tray in the oven and bake for 4 hours, or until the rhubarb is dry and crisp. Allow to cool before storing in an airtight container with a piece of baking paper separating each layer to stop the rhubarb strips from sticking to each other. Store for up to two weeks in the pantry.

Rhubarb elderflower compote

1½ sheets gelatine
250g diced fresh or frozen rhubarb
150g elderflower cordial
½ tsp vanilla bean paste
red colouring, if desired

Soak the gelatine sheets in cold water until soft. Drain and set aside. In a medium-sized pot, mix the rhubarb, elderflower and vanilla together. Cook over a low heat, stirring every few minutes to prevent scorching, until the rhubarb has completely broken down. Depending on the colour of the rhubarb, you may want to add a drop or two of red colouring to enhance it. Remove from the heat and stir in the gelatine until it melts in. Pour over the cooled sponge, level off with a palette knife and freeze while you make the bavarois.

Continued overleaf

Vanilla bavarois

3 sheets gelatine
90g milk
½ tsp vanilla bean paste
3 egg yolks
30g sugar
210g cream
45g mascarpone

Soak the gelatine sheets in cold water until soft. Drain and set aside. First make an anglaise by bringing the milk and vanilla to a boil. In a bowl, whisk the egg yolks and sugar together. Pour a third of the hot milk into this and whisk thoroughly. Return this to the pot with the rest of the milk and whisk to combine. Cook over a low heat, stirring constantly with a spatula, until the foam on the top disappears and the mixture thickens slightly, or it reaches 75°C. Remove from the heat, whisk in the gelatine until melted, then pour through a sieve to remove any eggy lumps. Leave to cool to about 30–35°C, or body temperature, stirring every 5 minutes. This will take a while, so you can put it in a bowl over ice water to speed up the process. While you're waiting, whisk the cream to medium peaks, and set aside. Once the anglaise base has cooled, whisk in the mascarpone, then fold in the cream until just combined. Pour over the rhubarb compote, spread evenly with a palette knife and freeze overnight, or until solid.

Glaze

coloured glaze (recipe page 239), coloured white if desired

Follow the method on page 21 for glazing the gâteau. Return to the freezer for a few minutes to allow the glaze to set before portioning.

Portioning

(page 22)

Portion the gâteau into 24 pieces that are 4 x 4cm squares. Store in the freezer and defrost fully before finishing.

To finish

candied rhubarb
edible flowers

Snap the candied rhubarb into shards of random sizes and place on the top and sides of the gâteaux. Finish with edible flowers and serve immediately.

Blackcurrant and violet

This is a flavour combination I first discovered when working in Paris. Interestingly, I don't like blackcurrant or violet separately, but I find when they are together they create a beautiful harmony. The floral violet that can sometimes be soapy is toned down by the blackcurrant, while the bitterness of the blackcurrant is mellowed by the violet. Blackcurrant purée can be a pain to get seeds out of, so I blend the defrosted blackcurrants with a bit of water to help loosen the purée up a bit.

Makes 24

Vanilla cake

vanilla cake
(recipe page 242)

Once baked, leave to cool completely.

Blackcurrant mousse

2 ½ sheets gelatine
200g seedless blackcurrant purée (page 12)
60g sugar
200g cream
3 tbsp violet liqueur

Soak the gelatine sheets in cold water until soft. Drain and put in a small pot with 20g of the blackcurrant purée and the sugar. Cook over a low heat, stirring constantly until the gelatine has completely melted. Remove from the heat and stir in the remaining purée. Whip the cream and liqueur together until medium peaks form. Once the temperature of the blackcurrant and gelatine reaches about 30°C, or body temperature, fold in the whipped cream until just combined. Pour over the cake and level off with a palette knife. Freeze for at least 2 hours or until solid.

Blackcurrant compote

½ sheet gelatine
300g blackcurrants, fresh or frozen
120g sugar
2 tbsp violet liqueur

Soak the gelatine sheet in cold water until soft. Drain and set aside. Put the blackcurrants and sugar together into a pot and cook over a low heat until boiling. Turn the heat down and simmer for 5 minutes. Remove from the heat and stir in the gelatine and the violet liqueur. Allow to cool to room temperature before pouring over the frozen mousse. Spread with a palette knife and return to the freezer until solid.

Portioning

(page 22)

Portion the gâteau into 24 pieces that are 4 x 4cm squares and return to the freezer until ready to finish.

Blackcurrant chablon

300g white chocolate
50g canola or other flavourless oil
1 tbsp freeze-dried blackcurrant powder

Melt the chocolate and oil together either in a microwave or over a pot of simmering water. Whisk in the blackcurrant powder. Follow the instructions on page 30 for dipping the gâteaux in chablon, leaving the top exposed. Store in the freezer and defrost before finishing.

To finish

edible flowers

Finish the gâteaux with edible flowers and serve.

Macadamia and caramel

This gâteau is a great example of sweet and salty. Macadamia nuts can be quite rich, but the crushed potato chips in the praline layer add a great contrast to this, not only with the texture, but also with the salt. Making the macadamia praline does require a food processor, but the effort is worth it. I like to buy roasted, salted macadamias from the supermarket, and then roast them for another 10 minutes or so until they're a deeper golden brown.

Makes 20

Brown sugar cake

¼ tsp instant coffee powder
100g water
1 egg
100g brown sugar
80g golden syrup
60g canola or other flavourless oil
110g flour (gluten free, if desired)
¼ tsp baking soda

Preheat the oven to 170°C and line the tin. In a large bowl, whisk the instant coffee with the water until dissolved, then whisk in the egg, sugar, golden syrup and oil until fully combined. Whisk in the flour and baking soda and pour into the lined tin. Bake for 12–15 minutes, until lightly golden and the cake is just set to the touch. Leave to cool while making the macademia praline.

Macadamia praline

100g roasted, salted macadamias
75g caramelised white chocolate
25g thin-cut ready salted chips, crushed into a rough crumb

In a food processor, blend the macadamias until they turn into a smooth paste. You may need to scrape the food processor down every now and then to help it blend. Melt the chocolate in a bain-marie, stirring constantly until the chocolate is fully melted. Remove from the heat and stir in the macadamia paste and the crushed chips. Pour on top of the cooled cake and leave to set at room temperature.

Caramel mousse

2 sheets gelatine
50g sugar
80g cream, boiled then set aside to cool
2 egg yolks
60g sugar
100g cream

Soak the gelatine sheets in cold water until soft. Drain and set aside. Make a dry caramel (page 19) by cooking the first measure of sugar in a pot over a high heat, stirring constantly until it forms a deep amber caramel. Deglaze with the first measure of cream, allowing it to bubble up before stirring (to avoid being burnt by steam) and scraping the base of the pot to incorporate all of the caramel goodness. Remove from the heat and stir in the gelatine. Set aside while making the pâte à bombe base (page 18). To do this, whisk the egg yolks and the second measure of sugar together in a bain-marie. Whisk constantly until the mixture is hot to the touch or has reached 75°C. Remove from the heat and whisk in the caramel mixture. Set aside to cool while you whip the second measure of cream to medium peaks. Once the base has cooled to about 30°C, or body temperature, fold in the cream. Pour the mousse over the praline and freeze overnight, or until solid.

Caramel glaze

2 sheets gelatine
100g sugar
10g water
100g cream

Soak the gelatine sheets in cold water until soft. Drain and set aside. Make a wet caramel (page 19) by cooking the sugar and water together in a pot over a medium-high heat, without stirring. Once the caramel reaches a light amber colour, remove from the heat and immediately add the cream. Leave to bubble up before stirring. Whisk in the gelatine sheets, then pour through a sieve to remove any potential caramel lumps. Leave to cool to 25°C before using this to glaze the top of the gâteau, following the guide on page 21. Allow to set before portioning. This glaze is one of the hardest to work with, as it will set very quickly. As always, you can omit the glaze, but this one is delicious, and worth the effort.

Portioning

(page 22)

Portion the gâteau into 20 pieces that are 2.5 x 7cm rectangles and store in the freezer and defrost before finishing.

To finish

gold leaf
roasted salted macadamias

Finish each gâteau with a macadamia and a touch of gold leaf, and serve.

Honey bee

Inspiration for new pastries comes from so many different places. This gâteau was inspired by the decoration technique of spreading tempered chocolate on bubble wrap to make an adorable honeycomb decoration. This decoration obviously had to go with a honey gâteau, and the addition of passionfruit helps to cut through the sweetness of the honey and the chocolate.

Makes 20

Honey cake

75g very soft butter
80g honey
30g sugar
¼ tsp vanilla bean paste
1 egg
20g canola or other flavourless oil
100g flour (gluten free, if desired)
1 tsp baking powder

Preheat the oven to 160°C and line the tin. Whisk the butter, honey, sugar and vanilla together until smooth. Whisk in the egg, followed by the oil. Once well combined, whisk in the flour and baking powder. Pour into the lined tin and spread out with a palette knife. Bake for 10–12 minutes, until the cake is just set to the touch. Allow to cool completely while you make the mousse.

Honey yoghurt mousse

1 sheet gelatine
¼ tsp vanilla bean paste
10g honey
80g natural yoghurt
40g cream
1 egg white
25g sugar

Soak the gelatine sheet in cold water until soft. Drain and put in a pot with the vanilla, honey and 20g of the yoghurt. Cook over a low heat, stirring constantly, until the gelatine has fully melted. Remove from the heat and whisk in the remaining yoghurt. Set aside to cool. Whip the cream to soft peaks and set aside. Make a Swiss meringue (page 18) by whisking the egg white and sugar together in a bain-marie. Whisk constantly until the mixture is hot to the touch or reaches 75°C. With an electric whisk or stand mixer, whisk the meringue until it reaches stiff peaks. Fold the yoghurt mixture into the meringue until almost fully combined, then fold in the cream until just combined. The mousse will look slightly split at this point, but it will come together as it sets. Pour over the cooled cake and level off with a palette knife. Freeze overnight, or until solid.

Passionfruit gel

2 sheets gelatine
80g sugar
1 tsp pectin
160g passionfruit juice

Soak the gelatine sheets in cold water until soft. Drain and set aside. Whisk the sugar and pectin together. In a pot, bring the passionfruit juice to a boil. Whisk in the pectin sugar mixture and boil, while whisking constantly, for one minute. Remove from the heat and whisk in the gelatine. Allow to cool to room temperature before pouring over the frozen mousse. Freeze for at least an hour, or until solid.

Portioning

(page 22)

Portion the gâteau into 20 pieces that are 2.5 x 7cm rectangles and store frozen until finishing.

Chocolate honeycomb

200g white chocolate, coloured yellow (page 24)
1 A4-sized piece bubble wrap

Temper and colour the chocolate following the instructions on page 24. Using the guide for making flat decorations on page 27, spread the chocolate onto the bubble wrap. Use a 3cm circle cutter to cut out the decorations. Store in an airtight container in the pantry for up to 1 month.

Chablon

white chocolate chablon (recipe page 239), coloured honey bee yellow (page 24)

Follow the instructions on page 30 for dipping the gâteau in chablon, leaving the base exposed. Store in the freezer and defrost before finishing.

To finish

100g dark chocolate, melted at 30°C

Use a piping bag with a 0.5mm hole to drizzle lines of melted dark chocolate widthways over the gâteau. Use a little dark chocolate to stick a honeycomb chocolate decoration on each gâteau. Allow to defrost fully before serving.

Laming-not

A sponge with a raspberry jam centre, covered with a raspberry soak and desiccated coconut, the lamington is a real classic Kiwi treat. I've tried to add my touch to it by turning it into a petit gâteau while still focusing on the raspberry and coconut flavours. The white desiccated coconut on the outside of the gâteau looks beautiful, but you can also toast it for a golden-brown colour and flavour if you prefer.

Makes 24

Coconut cake

60g soft butter
120g sugar
3 egg whites
100g flour (gluten free, if desired)
¾ tsp baking powder
30g desiccated coconut
90g coconut cream

Preheat the oven to 170°C and line the tin. In a bowl, whisk the butter and sugar together until smooth. Whisk in the egg whites until fully combined. Add the flour, baking powder and desiccated coconut and whisk until smooth, followed by the coconut cream. Pour into the lined tin and bake for 10–12 minutes, until the cake is just set to the touch, but not yet starting to get any colour on it. Leave to cool while you make the compote.

Raspberry compote

raspberry compote (recipe page 240)

Pour over the coconut cake and level off with a palette knife. Freeze for at least an hour before making the raspberry mousse.

Raspberry mousse

2½ sheets gelatine
200g seedless raspberry purée (page 12)
20g sugar
200g cream

Soak the gelatine sheets in cold water until soft. Drain and put in a small pot with 20g of raspberry purée and the sugar. Cook over a low heat, stirring constantly until the gelatine has completely melted into the purée. Remove from the heat and stir in the remaining purée. Whip the cream to medium peaks. Once the raspberry base has cooled to about 30°C, or body temperature, fold in the cream until just combined. Pour over the frozen compote and level off with a palette knife. Freeze overnight, or until solid.

Portioning

(page 22)

Portion the gâteau into 24 pieces that are 4 x 4cm squares and store frozen until ready to finish.

Whipped coconut cream

100g cream
50g coconut cream
20g icing sugar
¼ tsp vanilla bean paste

Whisk everything together until it forms stiff peaks. Use immediately to finish the gâteaux, as below.

To finish

200g desiccated coconut
whipped coconut cream
freeze-dried raspberries, crushed

Place the coconut in a shallow tray or bowl. Leave the portioned frozen gâteaux out at room temperature for 5 minutes. Press each side of the gâteaux and the top into the coconut to coat the mousse. Use a teaspoon to create a quenelle of cream to add on top of each gâteau, following the guide on page 30. Top with a few pieces of crushed freeze-dried raspberry and allow to defrost fully before serving.

Spring

Carrot cake

Carrot cake is one of the first recipes I ever mastered. I used to make carrot cake cupcakes with cream cheese icing and take them into my work experience job at Logan Brown Restaurant in Wellington. Eventually the cakes made it onto the high tea menu in mini form – which was the first time something of mine featured on a restaurant menu. The carrot cake recipe here is derived from that original one, but has changed so much over the years that it's truly my own.

Makes 20

Carrot cake

50g sugar
50g brown sugar
1 egg
15g milk
50g canola or other flavourless oil
½ tsp vanilla extract
65g flour (gluten free, if desired)
½ tsp ground cinnamon
¼ tsp baking powder
¼ tsp baking soda
75g coarsely grated carrot

Preheat the oven to 160°C and line the tin. Whisk both sugars, egg, milk, oil and vanilla together until smooth. Whisk in the flour, cinnamon, baking powder and baking soda until well combined, then stir in the grated carrot. Pour into the lined tin and level off with a palette knife. Bake for 12–15 minutes, until lightly golden and the cake is just set to the touch. Allow to cool completely while you make the soft cheesecake.

Soft cheesecake

250g cream cheese
100g sugar
½ tsp vanilla bean paste
2 egg yolks
30g milk
1 tbsp cornflour

Preheat the oven to 150°C. Mix the cream cheese with a spatula until smooth. Stir in the sugar and vanilla. Whisk the egg yolks, milk and cornflour together in a separate bowl, then pour this into the cream cheese mix. Whisk until fully combined. Pour into a tin or baking dish the same or similar size to the tin and bake for 15 minutes, until starting to puff around the edges. Remove from the oven and allow to cool for 10–15 minutes. Scrape into a bowl and use a stick blender to blend until you have a smooth cheesecake mix. Spread over the cooled carrot cake and level off with a palette knife. Freeze overnight, or until solid.

Portioning

(page 22)

Portion the gâteau into 20 pieces that are 2.5 x 7cm rectangles. Store in the freezer until ready to finish.

Caramelised white chocolate chablon

caramelised white chocolate chablon (recipe page 239)

Dip each gâteau in the chablon, following the instructions on page 30 for fully coating. Store in the freezer and defrost fully before finishing.

Whipped cheesecake

whipped cheesecake (recipe page 242)

Spoon the whipped cheesecake into a piping bag with a 1cm round tip and pipe three kisses on top of each gâteau, following the instructions on page 32.

To finish

1 orange
fresh thyme

Zest the orange over the gâteaux and finish with a few thyme leaves just before serving.

Ispahan

Ispahan is the name for the classic pastry combination of raspberry, rose and lychee. Invented by French chef Pierre Hermé, ispahan is now synonymous with French pâtisserie. Mixed together, these flavours are floral, delicate and fruity. Fresh lychees for the purée tend to be hard to find, but tinned lychees work perfectly well in their place.

Makes 28

Shortcake sponge

shortcake sponge (recipe page 241)

Once baked, leave to cool completely.

Raspberry mousse

1¾ sheets gelatine
150g seedless raspberry purée (page 12)
15g sugar
150g cream
1 tsp rose water

Soak the gelatine sheets in cold water until soft. Drain and put in a pot with 20g of the raspberry purée and the sugar. Melt over a low heat, stirring constantly, until the gelatine is fully melted. Remove from the heat and stir in the remaining purée. Set aside to cool to about 30°C, or body temperature. In the meantime, whisk the cream and rose water together until stiff peaks form. Fold the cream into the mousse base until just combined. Pour over the cooled sponge and level off with a palette knife. Freeze overnight, or until solid.

Lychee gel

2 sheets gelatine
200g lychee purée (page 12)
10g sugar
2 tsp pectin
¼ tsp citric acid

Soak the gelatine sheets in cold water until soft. Drain and set aside. Bring the lychee purée to a boil. Whisk the sugar, pectin and citric acid together in a bowl to combine. Whisk this into the boiling purée and cook for 30 seconds, whisking constantly. Remove from the heat and whisk in the gelatine. Allow to cool to room temperature before pouring over the frozen mousse. Freeze for at least one hour or until solid.

Portioning

(page 22)

Portion the gâteau into 28 pieces that are 3.5 x 3.5cm squares. Store in the freezer and defrost fully before finishing.

To finish

50g rose or vanilla pashmak
dried rose petals
freeze-dried raspberries, crushed

Place a small ball of pashmak on top of each defrosted gâteau. Sprinkle a few dried rose petals on top, followed by a sprinkle of freeze-dried raspberries. Serve immediately — the pashmak will dissolve like cotton candy, so this step really needs to be done at the last moment.

Pandan, yuzu and coconut

Pandan is a fragrant leaf used in both sweet and savoury dishes in many Southeast Asian cuisines. It has a slightly grassy but floral flavour, that works incredibly well with the yuzu and coconut. Pandan comes in many different forms. Here I have used pandan essence, which gives the crémeux its vibrant green colour – a signature of any pandan-flavoured treat.

Makes 24

Pandan cake

60g melted butter
100g sugar
2 eggs
40g canola or other flavourless oil
40g coconut cream
2 tsp pandan essence
100g flour (gluten free, if desired)
1 tsp baking powder

Preheat the oven to 170°C and line the tin. Whisk the butter and sugar together in a bowl until smooth. Whisk in the eggs, one at a time, followed by the oil, coconut cream and pandan essence. Once smooth, whisk in the flour and baking powder until well combined. Pour into the lined tin and level off with a palette knife. Bake for 12–15 minutes, until just set to the touch. Remove from the oven and allow to cool fully before making the coconut mousse.

Pandan yuzu crémeux

2 sheets gelatine
150g yuzu juice
150g sugar
3 eggs
1½ tbsp pandan essence
150g butter, cubed

Soak the gelatine sheets in cold water until soft. Drain and set aside. Whisk the yuzu juice, sugar, eggs and pandan essence together in a medium-sized pot. Cook over a medium heat, whisking constantly, until the crémeux boils. Remove from the heat and whisk in the gelatine. Allow to cool to 45°C, then blend the butter in with a stick blender. Pour into a bowl or container, cover with cling film touching the surface of the crémeux to avoid a skin forming, and chill overnight. The next day, follow the instructions on page 32 for a squished kiss decoration. Freeze the gâteau until solid before portioning.

Coconut mousse

2½ sheets gelatine
200g coconut cream
60g sugar
200g cream

Soak the gelatine sheets in cold water until soft. Drain and put in a pot with 20g of the coconut cream and the sugar. Cook over a low heat, stirring constantly, until the gelatine has completely melted. Remove from the heat and stir in the remaining coconut cream. Set aside to cool while you whip the cream to medium peaks. Once the base has cooled to about 30°C, or body temperature, fold the cream in until just combined. Pour over the cooled cake and freeze for at least two hours or overnight until solid.

Portioning

(page 22)

Portion the gâteau into 24 pieces that are 4 x 4cm squares. Store in the freezer and defrost fully before serving.

To finish

Nothing! The texture of the crémeux is all the decoration these gâteaux need.

Blueberry yuzu cheesecake

Growing up, my mum always made the best cheesecake. I never thought I could make one as good as hers, but this comes pretty close! This recipe is adapted from one I learnt to make when working in Paris. Baking it at such a low temperature results in the smoothest cheesecake ever, and makes it almost impossible to over-bake, too.

Makes 22

Brown sugar base

70g melted butter
100g brown sugar
140g flour (gluten free, if desired)

Preheat the oven to 160°C and line the tin. In a bowl, mix the butter, sugar and flour together until you have a crumbly dough. Press this into the lined tin and bake for 12 minutes. Remove from the oven and allow to cool while you make the cheesecake.

Blueberry compote

250g frozen blueberries
15g yuzu juice
¼ tsp vanilla bean paste
50g sugar
½ tbsp cornflour

Mix the blueberries, yuzu juice and vanilla together in a medium-sized pot. Begin to cook over a low heat. Whisk the sugar and cornflour together, then add this into the blueberries. Turn the heat up to medium and bring to the boil, stirring constantly, until you have a thick compote. Remove from the heat and allow to cool before storing in the fridge.

Cheesecake

400g cream cheese
50g icing sugar
1 egg yolk
2 eggs
50g cream
30g yuzu juice
1 tsp vanilla bean paste

Preheat the oven to 110°C. Mix the cream cheese with a spatula until softened and smooth, then stir in the icing sugar. Whisk the egg yolk in, followed by the whole eggs, one at a time. Once well combined, whisk in the cream, then the yuzu juice and the vanilla until you have a smooth mix. Pour on top of the base and level off with a palette knife. Bake for 1 hour, rotating halfway through, until the cheesecake has only the slightest jiggle in the middle. Remove from the oven and allow to cool for an hour at room temperature before freezing. Freeze overnight, or until solid before portioning.

Yuzu gel

100g yuzu juice
¼ tsp vanilla bean paste
50g sugar
1 tsp agar-agar

Bring the yuzu juice and vanilla bean paste to a boil. In a bowl, whisk the sugar and agar-agar together, then whisk this into the boiling yuzu. Boil for one minute, whisking constantly. Pour into a bowl or container and leave to chill for an hour, or until set solidly. Blend with a stick blender or in a food processor until you have a smooth gel. You can add water, or yuzu juice (or even gin if you feel adventurous!) as needed to thin out the gel to help it blend more smoothly. Reserve in a piping bag in the fridge.

Portioning

(page 22)

Portion the cheesecake into 22 pieces that are 4 x 7 x 7cm triangles. Store in the freezer and defrost before finishing.

To finish

blueberry compote
yuzu gel
freeze-dried blueberry slices
dried edible flowers

Place the blueberry compote in a sieve to drain any excess liquid. Spoon the compote on top of each cheesecake. Pipe dots of yuzu gel on top of the compote, sprinkle with freeze-dried blueberry slices and dried flowers. Serve immediately.

Matcha passionfruit opera

This recipe is inspired by the traditional opera cake. Layers of almond sponge, or joconde, coffee buttercream and chocolate ganache make it one of the most classic French pastries around. Here I've given it a twist by replacing the coffee and chocolate with passionfruit and matcha. The acidity of the passionfruit is a great contrast to the earthy matcha tea.

Makes 28

Matcha joconde

60g icing sugar
60g ground almonds
20g flour (gluten free, if desired)
1 tbsp matcha tea powder
1 egg yolk
1 egg
15g melted butter
4 egg whites
30g sugar

Preheat the oven to 190°C and line the tin. Whisk the icing sugar, almonds, flour and matcha together in a medium-sized bowl until combined. Whisk in the egg yolk and whole egg until combined, followed by the butter. It will be a very stiff mixture. In a stand mixer bowl, or with an electric whisk, whisk the egg whites and sugar on medium speed until doubled in size and stiff peaks have formed. Whisk about a quarter of the egg whites into the base matcha mix to loosen it up. Add the remaining egg whites and fold gently until the mix is just combined and no streaks of egg white remain. Bake the joconde in two batches. Spread half the mixture in the lined tin, and the other half over another sheet of baking paper to the same size as the baking tin. You don't want to leave the second half in the bowl and spread it after the first half is baked, as you'll end up with a more deflated sponge. Bake the first half for 8–10 minutes, until the cake is just set to the touch and just starting to brown at the edges. Remove from the tin, insert the baking paper with the other half of the mixture on it into the tin, and bake the second half the same way. Of course, if you do happen to have two tins then you can bake them both at the same time. Leave the joconde bases to cool completely before making the matcha mousse.

Matcha mousse

¾ sheet gelatine
45g white chocolate
1 tsp matcha tea powder
20g water
10g sugar
80g cream

Line the tin with a fresh sheet of baking paper. Place one layer of cooled joconde in the base. Soak the gelatine sheet in cold water until soft. Drain and place in a bowl with the chocolate and matcha. Bring the water and sugar to a boil in a small pot. Pour over the gelatine, chocolate and matcha and whisk together until smooth. Leave this to cool while you whip the cream to medium peaks. Once the base has reached 30°C, or body temperature, fold in the cream until just combined. Pour the mousse on top of the joconde and level out with a palette knife. Freeze for at least 30 minutes before putting the second joconde layer on top of the mousse and freezing again. You can make the passionfruit crémeux during this half hour.

Passionfruit crémeux

¾ sheet gelatine
50g passionfruit purée (page 12)
50g sugar
1 egg
50g butter

Soak the gelatine sheet in cold water until soft. Drain and set aside. Whisk the passionfruit purée, sugar and egg together in a small pot. Bring to a boil, whisking constantly. Remove from the heat and leave to cool to 45°C. Add the gelatine and butter. Blend in the butter using a stick blender until the mixture has lightened in colour and is silky smooth. Pour this on top of the second joconde layer, level out with a palette knife and return to the freezer for at least 1 hour or until solid.

Matcha passionfruit ganache

30g passionfruit purée (page 12)
5g liquid glucose
10g cream
75g white chocolate
5g cocoa butter, finely chopped
½ tsp matcha tea powder

Put the passionfruit purée, glucose and cream into a pot and bring to a boil. Pour this over the chocolate, cocoa butter and matcha. Whisk until everything is melted and well combined. You can hold the bowl over a pot of simmering water, or microwave it in 10-second bursts if needed, to help the chocolate fully melt. Pour this over the frozen crémeux and level off with a palette knife. Freeze overnight, or until solid.

Continued overleaf

Portioning

(page 22)

Use a large knife to portion the opera into 28 pieces that are 3.5 x 3.5cm squares. Store in the freezer and defrost fully before finishing.

Matcha chocolate plaques

200g white chocolate
1 tsp matcha tea powder

Scrunch an A4-sized sheet of baking paper up into a ball. Unfurl the sheet of baking paper and set aside. Melt the chocolate and matcha together and temper as per the instructions on page 24. Follow the guide for making flat chocolate decorations on page 27, spreading the chocolate over the crumpled sheet of baking paper to create texture. Cut the chocolate into 3 x 3cm plaques.

To finish

matcha tea powder
matcha chocolate plaques

Just before serving, dust with a touch of matcha powder and finish with a matcha chocolate plaque in each corner.

Rocky road

One of my favourite things about rocky road is the combination of textures — the gummy lollies, soft marshmallow, crisp biscuit and smooth chocolate. In this pastry, I've embodied all of these things in a fresh, vibrant petit gâteau — it has all the texture of rocky road, paired with fresh berries and fruity flavours to make it sing. If you can't get your hands on freeze-dried marshmallows, you can replace them with mini meringues from the Mont Blanc recipe (page 177) for a similar flavour and crunch.

Makes 24

Chocolate cake

chocolate cake (recipe page 239)

Once baked, leave to cool completely while you make the chocolate delice.

Chocolate delice

50g cream
30g butter
110g dark chocolate
40g warm water (about 50°C)
2 egg yolks
30g sugar

Bring the cream and butter to a boil in a small pot. Pour this over the chocolate and whisk until well combined. Add the water and whisk until the ganache is smooth. Make a pâte à bombe base (page 18). To do this, whisk the egg yolks and sugar together in a bowl, and place over a pot of simmering water. Whisk constantly until the mixture reaches 75°C. Remove from the heat and transfer to the bowl of a stand mixer, or use an electric whisk, to whip the egg yolks to ribbon stage (page 18) and almost cool to the touch. Fold the egg yolks into the ganache base. Pour on top of the cooled cake and level off with a palette knife. Freeze for at least an hour before making the raspberry mousse.

Raspberry mousse

1½ sheets gelatine
125g seedless raspberry purée (page 12)
10g sugar
125g cream

Soak the gelatine sheets in cold water until soft. Drain and put in a small pot with 25g of the raspberry purée and the sugar. Cook over a low heat, stirring constantly, until the gelatine has fully melted. Remove from the heat and stir in the remaining purée. Set aside to cool to about 30°C, or body temperature. Whip the cream to medium peaks, then fold this into the cooled raspberry base. Pour on top of the frozen delice and spread out with a palette knife. Freeze overnight, or until solid.

Portioning

(page 22)

Portion the gâteau into 24 pieces that are 7 x 2cm rectangles. Store in the freezer and defrost before finishing.

Chocolate discs

300g dark chocolate

Temper the dark chocolate following the instructions on page 24. Spread half the chocolate over an A4 sheet of acetate and follow the directions for cut-out chocolate shapes on page 27. Repeat with the remaining chocolate and second acetate sheet. Use a 3cm and a 2cm round cutter to cut 24 discs of each size, one of each size per gâteau.

To finish

20g freeze-dried mini marshmallows, or approximately 48 mini meringue kisses
100g fresh raspberries
150g fresh strawberries
100g drained Amarena cherries, or fresh pitted cherries
chocolate discs

At the end of each gâteau, push a larger chocolate disc standing up in the mousse, then a smaller disc slightly in front of it. Cut the strawberries into eighths lengthways and cut the cherries in half. Decorate each gâteau with a mix of fruit and the mini marshmallows or meringues just before serving.

Spring

Banana, passionfruit and coconut

This gâteau may appear simple, but it really packs a punch in terms of flavour. The banana, passionfruit and coconut combination creates a tropical dream that's beautifully light and fresh. Freeze-dried lime leaf powder is easily available online, but you can replace it with fresh lime zest if you can't get hold of it.

Makes 16

Banana cake

banana cake (recipe page 238)

Once baked, leave to cool completely while you make the passionfruit crémeux.

Passionfruit crémeux

1 sheet gelatine
100g passionfruit purée (page 12)
100g sugar
2 eggs
100g butter

Soak the gelatine sheet in cold water until soft. Drain and set aside. Whisk the passionfruit purée, sugar and eggs together in a small pot. Bring to a boil, whisking constantly. Remove from the heat, add the gelatine, and mix until the gelatine is melted. Allow to cool to 45°C and blend the butter in using a stick blender. Pour over the cooled banana cake and level off with a palette knife. Freeze for at least an hour before making the coconut mousse.

Coconut mousse

1½ sheets gelatine
125g coconut cream
20g sugar
125g cream

Soak the gelatine sheets in cold water until soft. Drain and put in a pot with 20g of the coconut cream and the sugar. Cook over a low heat, stirring constantly, until the gelatine is fully melted. Stir in the remaining coconut cream and set aside to cool to about 30°C, or body temperature. Whip the cream to stiff peaks and fold this into the cooled coconut base until just combined. Pour over the frozen passionfruit crémeux and freeze overnight, or until solid.

Portioning

(page 22)

Portion the gâteau into 16 pieces that are 7 x 3cm rectangles. Store in the freezer and defrost before finishing.

To finish

freeze-dried lime leaf powder, or fresh lime zest
dried edible flowers

Dust each gâteau with freeze-dried lime leaf powder, or sprinkle with fresh lime zest. Finish with dried edible flowers and serve.

Strawberry and rhubarb

Strawberries and rhubarb are a match made in heaven. In New Zealand, we're lucky that rhubarb is available all year round, so we can make use of this pairing throughout the strawberry season.

Makes 24

Vanilla pound cake

75g soft butter
75g sugar
¼ tsp vanilla bean paste
1 egg
75g self-raising flour (gluten free, if desired)

Preheat the oven to 170°C and line the tin. Whisk the butter, sugar and vanilla together until smooth. Whisk in the egg until well combined, then whisk in the flour to create a smooth batter. Pour into the lined tin and level off with a palette knife. Bake for 8–10 minutes until just set to the touch. Remove from the oven and allow to cool completely while you make the compote.

Rhubarb compote

2½ sheets gelatine
250g roughly chopped rhubarb
75g sugar
50g strawberries
¼ tsp vanilla bean paste
1 drop red colouring, if desired

Soak the gelatine sheets in cold water until soft. Drain and set aside. Mix the rhubarb, sugar, strawberries, vanilla and colouring in a medium-sized pot. Cook over a low heat, stirring constantly, until the rhubarb has completely broken down into a thick compote. Remove from the heat, stir in the gelatine and pour over the cooled cake. Level off with a palette knife and freeze for at least 2 hours before making the mousse.

Strawberry mousse

strawberry mousse (recipe page 241)

Pour the strawberry mousse over the frozen compote and smooth off with a palette knife. Freeze overnight, or until solid.

Portioning

(page 22)

Portion the gâteau into 24 pieces that are 4 x 4cm squares. Store in the freezer and defrost fully before finishing.

Poached rhubarb

200g rhubarb
200g sugar
100g water
¼ tsp vanilla bean paste
30g strawberry purée (page 12)

Slice the rhubarb into 5mm pieces. Bring the sugar, water, vanilla and strawberry purée to a boil. Add the rhubarb and cover the pot with a lid or a sheet of cling film. Remove from the heat and leave to cool at room temperature before transferring to the fridge. (The rhubarb is thin enough that it will cook in the residual heat.)

To finish

10 fresh strawberries
poached rhubarb
edible flowers

Trim the stalks off the strawberries and cut them lengthways into eight pieces. Drain the poached rhubarb using a sieve and place pieces of poached rhubarb and strawberry on top of each gâteau. Finish with a few edible flower petals and serve.

Spring

Passionfruit strawberry

You may have noticed – by how often they appear in this book – that passionfruit and strawberry are two of my favourite flavours, and they also work perfectly together. The decoration for this pastry is inspired by the incredible pastry chef Frank Haasnoot, and I think it is such a fun way to finish this colourful gâteau.

Makes 24

Passionfruit cake

90g melted butter
75g sugar
1 egg
1 egg yolk
30g canola or other flavourless oil
30g passionfruit juice
75g flour (gluten free, if desired)
¾ tsp baking powder

Preheat the oven to 170°C and line the tin. Whisk the butter and sugar together until well combined, followed by the egg and egg yolk. Whisk in the oil and passionfruit juice, then whisk in the flour and baking powder until you have a smooth batter. Pour into the lined tin and smooth out with a palette knife. Bake for 10–12 minutes, until the cake is just set to the touch. Allow to cool before making the strawberry mousse.

Strawberry mousse

strawberry mousse (recipe page 241)

Pour over the cake and level off with a palette knife. Freeze for at least 2 hours or overnight before making the passionfruit crémeux.

Passionfruit crémeux

passionfruit crémeux (recipe page 240)

Pour over the frozen strawberry mousse, level off with a palette knife and freeze overnight, or until solid.

Portioning

(page 22)

Portion the gâteau into 24 pieces that are 7 x 2cm rectangles. Store in the freezer and defrost before finishing.

Chocolate plaques

300g white chocolate, coloured yellow (page 24)

Temper the chocolate following the instructions on page 24. Follow the guide on page 27 for making flat chocolate decorations, spreading half the chocolate on an A4 sheet of acetate. Use a large knife to cut 6cm wide strips the length of the acetate sheet. Use a toothpick to drag a wave pattern through the middle of the 6cm strips. Use the knife to then cut these into 7cm long pieces. Repeat with the remaining chocolate on a second sheet of acetate. Allow to set fully before removing from the acetate.

To finish

chocolate plaques
black sesame seeds

Press a wavy chocolate plaque into both long sides of the gâteaux. Sprinkle the top with a few black sesame seeds and serve.

Avocado and lime

This one sounds a bit odd, especially as we tend to know avocado as a savoury food, but in many countries it's served as a sweet, often dressed in condensed milk. Here I've used avocado in that sweet sense, without it being overwhelming. The lime balances the avocado out beautifully, making a pastry that's surprisingly delicious.

Makes 28

Lime cake

45g melted butter
75g sugar
1 egg
1 egg yolk
30g canola or other flavourless oil
30g lime juice
75g flour (gluten free, if desired)
¾ tsp baking powder

Preheat the oven to 170°C and line the tin. Whisk the butter and sugar together until smooth, then whisk in the egg and egg yolk, followed by the oil and lime juice. Finish by whisking in the flour and baking powder until you have a smooth batter. Pour into the lined tin and level off with a palette knife. Bake for 10–12 minutes, until the cake is just set to the touch. Leave to cool completely while you make the lime mousse.

Lime mousse

1½ sheets gelatine
100g lime juice
100g cream
1 egg white
60g sugar

Soak the gelatine sheets in cold water until soft. Drain and put into a pot with 20g of the lime juice. Cook over a low heat, stirring constantly, until the gelatine is fully melted. Add the remaining lime juice and leave to cool. Whip the cream to medium peaks and set aside. Make a Swiss meringue (page 18) by whisking the egg white and sugar together in a bowl, over a small pot of simmering water. Whisk constantly until the meringue mixture reaches 75°C. Remove from the heat and whisk with an electric whisk or using a stand mixer until the meringue reaches stiff peaks. Whisk the lime juice base into the meringue. Once combined, fold in the cream until just combined. Pour over the cooled cake and level off with a palette knife. Freeze for at least 2 hours before making the avocado cream.

Avocado cream

1 sheet gelatine
35g lime juice
350g avocado flesh
60g condensed milk

Soak the gelatine sheet in cold water until soft. Drain and put into a pot with the lime juice. Cook over a low heat, stirring constantly, until the mix is warm to the touch and the gelatine is fully melted. Using a stick blender or food processor, blend the avocado and condensed milk until smooth. Blend in the lime and gelatine mixture until just combined. Pour over the frozen mousse and level off with a palette knife. Return to the freezer and freeze overnight, or until solid.

Portioning

(page 22)

Portion the gâteau into 28 pieces that are 3.5 x 3.5cm squares. Store in the freezer and defrost fully before finishing.

Chocolate splats

300g white chocolate, coloured green (page 24)

Temper and colour the chocolate following the instructions on page 24. Follow the guide for making flat chocolate decorations on page 27. Spread half the chocolate over an A4 sheet of acetate and use a toothpick to create splat-shaped decorations. Repeat with other half of chocolate and another acetate sheet. Allow to set before removing from the acetate and store in an airtight container in the pantry.

To finish

100g icing sugar
1 tsp cornflour
1 tsp powdered green colouring
chocolate splats

Whisk everything together and use a sieve to dust over the chocolate splats. Place a splat on top of each defrosted gâteau and serve immediately.

078	Grapefruit and gin
081	Blueberry pancake
082	Jelly tip
084	Mango and lime
087	Boysenberry and elderflower
089	PB&J
090	Pimm's
093	Hokey pokey
094	Black Forest
096	Lemon, poppy and blackberry
099	Peach Melba
101	Sweetcorn and caramel
102	Mango and sake
105	Hazelnut chocolate
107	Strawberry shortcake
108	The symphony
110	Peach and sweet wine

Summer

Grapefruit and gin

I love pairing gin with pastries. Finding different gins with varying flavour profiles is such a fun way to alter the taste of a pastry while using the same recipe. Grapefruit and gin are a flavour match made in heaven, and create a pretty pink gâteau at the same time.

Makes 20

Grapefruit cake

30g melted butter
50g sugar
1 egg
20g canola or other flavourless oil
20g pink or ruby red grapefruit juice
50g flour (gluten free, if desired)
½ tsp baking powder

Preheat the oven to 170°C and line the tin. Whisk the butter and sugar together in a bowl until well combined, then whisk in the egg. Whisk the oil and grapefruit juice in, followed by the flour and baking powder. Once smooth, pour into the lined tin and bake for 10–12 minutes, until the cake is just set to the touch. Remove from the oven and allow to cool completely.

Grapefruit gin crémeux

¾ sheet gelatine
50g pink or ruby red grapefruit juice
50g sugar
1 egg
1 tiny drop red colouring
15g gin
50g butter

Soak the gelatine sheet in cold water until soft. Drain and set aside. Whisk the grapefruit juice, sugar, egg, red colouring and gin together in a small pot. Cook over a medium heat, whisking constantly, until the mixture boils. Remove from the heat and whisk in the gelatine sheet. Allow to cool to 45°C, then blend in the butter with a stick blender. Once fully combined, pour over the cooled cake, level off with a palette knife and freeze for at least an hour before making the grapefruit and gin mousse.

Grapefruit and gin mousse

3 sheets gelatine
175g pink or ruby red grapefruit juice
25g gin
1 tiny drop red colouring
200g cream
2 egg whites
90g sugar

Soak the gelatine sheets in cold water until soft. Drain and put in a pot with 20g of the grapefruit juice. Cook over a very low heat, stirring constantly, until the gelatine is fully melted. Remove from the heat and stir in the remaining grapefruit juice, gin and red colouring. Set aside while you whip the cream to medium peaks. Set the cream aside and make the Swiss meringue (page 18). Put the egg whites and sugar together in a bain-marie. Whisk constantly until the mixture is hot to the touch, or has reached 75°C. Remove from the heat and whisk with an electric whisk or a stand mixer until you have a stiff-peaked meringue. Whisk the grapefruit mixture into this, then fold in the cream until just combined. Pour over the frozen crémeux and level off with a palette knife. Freeze overnight, or until solid.

Portioning

(page 22)

Portion the gâteau into 20 pieces that are 7 x 2.5cm rectangles. Store in the freezer and defrost fully before finishing.

To finish

1 pink or ruby red grapefruit
baby basil
edible flowers

Use a fine zester to zest the grapefruit over the gâteaux. Decorate with a few leaves of baby basil and edible flowers.

Blueberry pancake

I know that I should start the morning with something healthy, but my sweet tooth runs my life 24/7, so this pastry is one that is totally acceptable (in my mind) to eat for breakfast!

Makes 24

Pancake cake

30g melted butter
250g milk
½ tsp white vinegar
1 egg
½ tsp vanilla bean paste
1 tsp vanilla extract
40g icing sugar
150g flour
50g cornflour

Preheat the oven to 200°C and line the tin. Whisk the butter, milk, vinegar, egg, vanilla paste and extract together until well combined. Whisk in the icing sugar, flour and cornflour until smooth. Pour 160g of the batter into the tin and bake for 6–8 minutes, until the cake is just set to the touch. Remove from the tin and repeat twice more with the remaining mixture so that you have three pancake layers.

Blueberry compote

2½ sheets gelatine
50g sugar
3 tsp pectin
1 tsp citric acid
250g blueberry purée (page 12)
¼ tsp vanilla bean paste

Soak the gelatine sheets in cold water until soft. Drain and set aside. Whisk the sugar, pectin and citric acid together. Bring the blueberry purée and vanilla to a boil. Whisk in the sugar pectin mixture and boil, for 1 minute, while whisking constantly. Remove from the heat and whisk in the gelatine. Allow to cool to room temperature. Line the tin with a fresh sheet of baking paper and place one pancake layer in it. Spread the blueberry compote on top and level off with a palette knife. Freeze for about an hour, or until the compote has set, and top with another pancake layer. Return to the freezer while you make the mascarpone mousse.

Mascarpone mousse

1 sheet gelatine
35g sugar
zest of 2 lemons
¼ tsp vanilla bean paste
85g mascarpone
120g cream

Soak the gelatine sheet in cold water until soft. Drain and put in a small pot with the sugar, lemon zest, vanilla and 20g of the mascarpone. Cook over a low heat, stirring constantly, until the gelatine is fully melted. Remove from the heat and set aside to cool. Whip the remaining mascarpone and the cream together to medium peaks. Check the temperature of the gelatine base; once it has reached 30°C, or body temperature, fold in the whipped cream until just combined. Pour on top of the gâteau, level off with a palette knife and freeze for an hour before placing the final pancake layer on top. Freeze overnight, or until solid.

Portioning

(page 22)

Portion the gâteau into 24 pieces that are 4 x 4cm squares. Store frozen and defrost before finishing.

Mascarpone whip

10g icing sugar
50g mascarpone
¼ tsp vanilla bean paste
75g cream

Whisk everything together until you have a stiff-peaked cream. Spoon into a piping bag with a 1cm round piping tip. Use immediately to finish the gâteaux.

To finish

250g blueberries
mascarpone whip
edible flowers

Pipe a large tablespoon-sized kiss (page 32) of mascarpone whip on top of each gâteau. Finish with blueberries and edible flowers. Serve immediately.

Jelly tip

The jelly tip is a classic summertime favourite. Here I've reinvented the vanilla ice cream with raspberry jelly and chocolate shell into a petit gâteau made of a chocolate cake, vanilla mousse, raspberry jelly, fresh raspberries and a thin tempered chocolate decoration. A delicious, classic and beautiful dessert.

Makes 24

Chocolate cake

chocolate cake (recipe page 239)

Once baked, leave to cool completely while you make the vanilla yoghurt mousse.

Vanilla yoghurt mousse

2½ sheets gelatine
160g natural unsweetened yoghurt
¼ tsp vanilla bean paste
30g sugar
80g cream
2 egg whites
50g sugar

Soak the gelatine sheets in cold water until soft. Drain and put into a pot with 40g of the yoghurt, vanilla and the first measure of sugar. Cook over a low heat until the gelatine is fully melted. Remove from the heat and whisk in the remaining yoghurt. Set aside to cool and whip the cream to soft peaks. Make a Swiss meringue (page 18) by whisking the egg whites and the second measure of sugar together in a bain-marie. Whisk constantly until the meringue mixture reaches 75°C, or feels hot to the touch. Remove from the heat and whisk with either a stand mixer or an electric whisk until you have a stiff-peaked meringue. Check the temperature of the yoghurt base, and once it is around 30°C, or body temperature, fold it into the meringue until almost fully combined. Fold in the cream until just combined, then pour over the chocolate cake. Level off with a palette knife and freeze overnight, or until solid.

Raspberry jelly

2 sheets gelatine
200g seedless raspberry purée (page 12)
80g sugar
1 tsp pectin
½ tsp citric acid

Soak the gelatine sheets in cold water until soft. Drain and set aside. Put the raspberry purée in a pot and bring to a boil. Whisk the sugar, pectin and citric acid together and whisk this into the boiling purée. Cook for 1 minute, whisking constantly. Remove from the heat and whisk in the gelatine. Allow to cool to room temperature before pouring over the frozen mousse and spreading out with a palette knife. Freeze for at least 1 hour, or until solid.

Portioning

(page 22)

Portion the gâteau into 24 pieces that are 7 x 2cm rectangles. Store frozen and defrost before finishing.

Chocolate plaques

200g dark chocolate

Temper the chocolate following the instructions on page 24. Following the guide on page 27 for making flat chocolate decorations, spread the chocolate over an A4 sheet of acetate and cut it into 7 x 2cm rectangles, ensuring you have at least 24. Allow to set fully before removing from the acetate, and storing in an airtight container in the pantry.

To finish

300g fresh raspberries
chocolate plaques

Place four fresh raspberries on top of each gâteau. Top with a chocolate plaque and serve immediately. The weight of the raspberries will cause this gâteau to droop, so make sure you put them on only just before serving.

Mango and lime

Mangoes are such an incredible summer fruit, and their rich flavour makes for a beautiful mousse that pairs so well with the sharp lime. You can buy tinned kesar mango purée from spice stores and Indian supermarkets for an incredibly affordable price, or make your own with fresh mango.

Makes 16

Mango mousse

3 sheets gelatine
240g mango purée (page 12)
240g cream

Line the tin. Soak the gelatine sheets in cold water until soft. Drain and place in a small pot with 20g of the mango purée. Heat over a low heat, stirring constantly until the gelatine has melted. Pour this into a bowl with the remaining purée and whisk to combine. Set aside while you whip the cream to medium peaks. Check the temperature of the mango base. Once it's reached 30°C, or body temperature, fold in the cream until just combined. Pour this into the lined tin and freeze for 1 hour or until solid before making the lime mousse.

Lime mousse

2 sheets gelatine
100g lime juice
100g cream
1 egg white
40g sugar

Soak the gelatine sheets in cold water until soft. Drain and place in a pot with 20g of the lime juice. Cook over a low heat, stirring constantly, until the gelatine has completely melted. Remove from the heat, stir in the remaining lime juice and set aside. Whip the cream to firm peaks and set aside. Make a Swiss meringue (page 18) by mixing the egg white and sugar together in a bain-marie using a metal bowl. Whisk constantly until the mixture is hot to the touch, or reaches 75°C. Transfer to a stand mixer bowl, or use an electric whisk, to whip the meringue until it reaches stiff peaks. Use a whisk to gently fold your cooled lime mixture into the meringue, then gently fold in the cream with a spatula until just combined. The liquid in this mousse will sink to the bottom of the bowl so make sure to scrape the base of the bowl as you fold. Pour this mousse on top of the frozen mango mousse and freeze overnight, or until solid.

Portioning

(page 22)

Portion the mousse into 16 pieces that are 7 x 3cm rectangles. You want to portion this mousse by cutting it in half longways and trimming the sides to make each half 7cm wide, and then portioning these into 3cm thick slices. This will give you 16 pieces. Portioning this way will mean that when you turn the gâteau on the side you will see the layers of mango and lime mousse, and this will become the tops of the gâteaux. Store in the freezer until ready to finish.

Yellow chablon

white chocolate chablon (recipe page 239), coloured yellow (page 24)

Follow the instructions on page 30 for dipping the gâteaux in chablon, leaving the top exposed so you can see both mousses easily. Store in the freezer and defrost before finishing.

To finish

2 ripe mangoes
1 lime
micro coriander

Peel and dice the mangoes into 1cm cubes. Place a heaped teaspoon of mango dice onto one end of each gâteau. Finish with a shaving of lime zest and a sprig of micro coriander.

Boysenberry and elderflower

This gâteau is a combination of my favourite things. Floral sweet elderflower, zingy fresh berries and creamy boysenberry mousse. The mousse is deliciously soft, so it's important that you put the berries on top only just before serving, as the weight of the berries will cause the mousse to collapse.

Makes 24

Boysenberry cake

boysenberry cake (recipe page 238)

Once baked, allow the cake to cool completely while you make the mousse.

Boysenberry elderflower mousse

3¼ sheets gelatine
80g elderflower cordial
200g seedless boysenberry purée (page 12)
240g cream

Soak the gelatine sheets in cold water until soft. Drain and put in a small pot with the elderflower cordial and 20g of the boysenberry purée. Cook over a low heat, stirring constantly, until the gelatine is fully melted. Remove from the heat and stir in the remaining purée. Set aside to cool to 30°C, or body temperature, while you whip the cream to medium peaks. Fold the cream into the boysenberry base until just combined. Pour over the cake, level off with a palette knife and freeze overnight, or until solid.

Boysenberry gel

2 sheets gelatine
220g fresh or frozen boysenberries
80g elderflower cordial
⅛ tsp vanilla bean paste
10g sugar
2 tsp pectin
⅛ tsp citric acid

Soak the gelatine sheets in cold water until soft. Drain and set aside. Put the boysenberries, elderflower cordial and vanilla into a small pot and cook over a medium heat, until the berries have started to break down and the mix starts to boil. Whisk the sugar, pectin and citric acid together, then whisk this into the boiling berry mix. Boil for 2 minutes, whisking constantly. Remove from the heat and whisk in the gelatine. Allow to cool to room temperature before spreading over the frozen mousse. Return the gâteau to the freezer for at least 1 hour, or until solid.

Portioning

(page 22)

Portion the gâteau into 24 pieces that are 7 x 2cm rectangles. Store in the freezer and defrost fully before finishing.

To finish

36 fresh boysenberries
edible flowers
baby basil

Cut the boysenberries in half lengthways. Place three halves, cut side up, on each gâteau. Finish with edible flowers and a few baby basil leaves. Serve immediately.

PB&J

This petit gâteau is inspired by the classic flavour combination that is peanut butter and jelly. The sharp raspberry compote contrasts perfectly with the smooth, rich peanut butter mousse. Finished with a mirror glaze and a tempered chocolate decoration, this is a great petit gâteau to practise pâtisserie skills.

Makes 28

Peanut financier

90g butter
45g smooth peanut butter
90g icing sugar
45g ground almonds
25g flour (gluten free, if desired)
60g egg whites

Preheat the oven to 180°C and line the tin. Melt the butter in a small pot over a medium heat — once it's melted, begin to whisk and turn the heat up slightly. Whisk continuously until the butter is a deep, nutty brown. It will be incredibly hot at this point so be careful. Pour into a metal bowl and add the peanut butter. Whisk until the mix is fully emulsified, then whisk in the icing sugar, almonds and flour. Once combined, whisk in the egg whites and pour into the lined tin. Bake for 8–10 minutes, until lightly golden and the cake is just set to the touch. Leave to cool at room temperature.

Raspberry compote

raspberry compote (recipe page 240)

Pour the compote over the financier and freeze while you make the peanut mousse.

Peanut mousse

½ sheet gelatine
40g caramelised white chocolate
15g water
10g sugar
40g smooth peanut butter
75g cream

Soak the gelatine sheet in cold water until soft. Drain and put in a small bowl with the chocolate. Bring the water and sugar to a boil. Pour this over the chocolate and mix until the chocolate is fully melted and the mixture is smooth. Whisk the peanut butter into the chocolate mixture. Whip the cream to medium peaks. Check the temperature of the peanut base is around 30–35°C, or body temperature, then fold in the cream. Pour the mousse on top of the raspberry compote and smooth it out with a palette knife. Freeze overnight, or until solid.

Caramelised white chocolate glaze

1 sheet gelatine
50g caramelised white chocolate
55g white chocolate
50g milk
15g liquid glucose

Soak the gelatine sheet in cold water until soft. Drain and put in a bowl with both the chocolates. Bring the milk and glucose to a boil and pour over the chocolate and gelatine. Use a spatula to mix together until fully emulsified. Leave to cool to 35°C before using to glaze the frozen gâteau, following the instructions on page 21 for glazing. Allow the glaze to set fully — this should take 5–10 minutes — before portioning.

Portioning

(page 22)

Portion the gâteau into 28 pieces that are 3.5 x 3.5cm squares. Store in the freezer and defrost before finishing.

Raspberry peanut chocolate discs

200g caramelised white chocolate
chopped roasted peanuts
freeze-dried raspberries

Temper the chocolate following the instructions on page 24. Follow the guide for making flat chocolate decorations on page 27. Spread the chocolate onto an A4 sheet of acetate. As soon as you spread the chocolate out, sprinkle the raspberries and peanuts on top, pressing down on them slightly to help them adhere to the chocolate. Use a 3cm round cutter to cut the chocolate decorations. Allow to set before removing from the acetate and storing in an airtight container in the pantry for up to 1 month.

To finish

raspberry peanut chocolate discs

Finish each gâteau with a raspberry peanut chocolate disc.

Pimm's

There's nothing quite as reminiscent of British summer as a glass of Pimm's, filled to the brim with different summer fruits. I wanted this gâteau to taste like the summers I spent in London, and it does just that. As with some of the other fruit-loaded gâteaux, you want to put the fruit garnishes on only just before serving, so as to stop your gâteau collapsing under the fruit's weight.

Makes 16

Lemon cake

30g melted butter
50g sugar
zest of 1 lemon
1 egg
20g canola or other flavourless oil
20g lemon juice
¼ tsp vanilla bean paste
50g flour (gluten free, if desired)
½ tsp baking powder

Preheat the oven to 170°C and line the tin. Whisk the butter, sugar and lemon zest together in a bowl until well combined. Whisk in the egg, followed by the oil, lemon juice and vanilla until smooth. Whisk in the flour and baking powder and pour the batter into the lined tin. Level off with a palette knife and bake for 8–10 minutes, until the cake is just set to the touch. Remove from the oven and allow to cool completely while you make the Pimm's mousse.

Pimm's mousse

1½ sheets gelatine
50g orange juice
40g lemon juice
20g Pimm's
100g cream
1 egg white
45g sugar

Soak the gelatine sheets in cold water until soft. Drain and put in a pot with 25g of the orange juice. Cook over a low heat until the gelatine has melted into the orange juice. Remove from the heat and whisk in the remaining orange juice, lemon juice and Pimm's. Set aside to cool. Whip the cream to soft peaks and set aside while you make a Swiss meringue (page 18). Whisk the egg white and sugar together in a bain-marie. Whisk constantly until the mixture reaches 75°C or feels hot to the touch. Remove from the heat and whisk with an electric whisk or using a stand mixer until you have a stiff-peaked meringue. Fold the Pimm's mixture into the meringue, then gently fold in the whipped cream until just combined. Pour over the cooled lemon cake. Spread the mousse out evenly with a palette knife and freeze overnight, or until solid.

Pimm's gel

1½ sheets gelatine
10g sugar
1 tsp pectin
50g Pimm's
100g lemonade
30g lemon juice

Soak the gelatine sheets in cold water until soft. Drain and set aside. Whisk the sugar and pectin together in a small bowl. In a pot, bring the Pimm's, lemonade and lemon juice to a boil and whisk in the pectin sugar mix. Boil for 1 minute, whisking constantly. Remove from the heat and whisk in the gelatine. Allow to cool to room temperature before spreading over the frozen mousse. Freeze for at least 1 hour, or until solid.

Portioning

(page 22)

Portion the gâteau into 16 pieces that are 7 x 3cm rectangles. Store frozen and defrost before serving.

To finish

250g fresh strawberries
1 orange
1 blood orange or grapefruit
¼ telegraph cucumber
1 bunch basil

Cut the strawberries into eighths and segment the citrus fruit. Use a vegetable peeler to slice thin ribbons of cucumber. Place the fruit and cucumber decoratively on top of each gâteau and finish with a few pieces of ripped basil leaves. Serve immediately.

Hokey pokey

There's nothing quite as classic for Kiwis as hokey pokey ice cream — vanilla ice cream studded with chunks of hokey pokey, which melts into the ice cream over time. The ginger cake in this pastry compliments the hokey pokey perfectly, and the chablon coating with the honeycomb pieces gives it a great crunch. The large chunk of hokey pokey on top will get sticky quite quickly, so put it on top of your gâteaux just before serving.

Makes 20

Ginger cake

60g butter
115g golden syrup
125g milk
½ tsp vanilla bean paste
1 egg yolk
60g brown sugar
110g flour (gluten free, if desired)
1 tsp baking powder
½ tsp baking soda
1 tsp ground ginger

Preheat the oven to 150°C and line the tin. In a small pot, melt the butter and golden syrup together until liquid. Pour into a bowl and whisk in the milk, vanilla, egg yolk and sugar until well combined. Whisk in the flour, baking powder, baking soda and ginger until smooth. Pour into the lined tin and bake for 15–20 minutes, until the cake is just set to the touch. Remove from the oven and leave to cool completely.

Hokey pokey

hokey pokey (recipe page 239)

Once the hokey pokey is set, break it into pieces and reserve 120g for the bavarois. Put 16 larger chunks about 2cm diameter in an airtight container in the pantry and reserve for decoration. Crush 40g of hokey pokey into a fine crumb and save this for the chablon. Eat the rest!

Hokey pokey bavarois

4 sheets gelatine
120g milk
4 egg yolks
120g hokey pokey
280g cream
60g mascarpone

Soak the gelatine sheets in cold water until soft. Drain and set aside. Bring the milk to a boil. In a bowl, whisk the egg yolks until loosened. Add 2 tablespoons of the hot milk to the egg yolks and whisk to combine. Pour this back into the pot and whisk together. Swap to a spatula and cook over a very low heat, stirring constantly, until this thickens slightly, or reaches 75°C. Remove from the heat and stir in the gelatine, then the hokey pokey. Allow to cool, stirring every 5 minutes, until the hokey pokey has all dissolved and the mixture is cool to the touch. Whip the cream and mascarpone to medium peaks, then fold into the hokey pokey base until just combined. Pour over the cooled ginger cake and freeze overnight, or until solid.

Portioning

(page 22)

Portion the gâteau into 20 pieces that are 7 x 2.5cm rectangles. Store in the freezer until ready to finish.

Hokey pokey chablon

40g hokey pokey crumbs
white chocolate chablon (recipe page 239)

Mix the hokey pokey crumbs into the chablon and use immediately. Dip each gâteau in the chablon, following the instructions on page 30 for fully coating. Store frozen and defrost before finishing.

To finish

50g white chocolate
hokey pokey pieces

Just before serving, melt the chocolate to 30°C, or body temperature. Use the chocolate as glue to stick the hokey pokey pieces to the top of the gâteaux, by dipping a small section of the hokey pokey chunk into the chocolate and pressing this section onto the gâteau.

Summer

Black Forest

Traditionally a chocolate sponge cake layered with whipped cream and cherries, I've made a more modern version of a Black Forest here. The richness of the dark chocolate is offset by the acidity in the cherry compote, making for the perfect bite. If you're making this in cherry season you can top each gâteau with a fresh cherry, or you can use Amarena cherries with a vanilla pod as the stalk, just like I have in the photo. Kirsch is the traditional liqueur used in Black Forest gâteau, but can be omitted to make this alcohol-free.

Makes 22

Chocolate cake

chocolate cake (recipe page 239)

Once baked, allow the cake to cool while you make the cherry compote.

Cherry compote

300g fresh or frozen pitted cherries
1 tbsp Kirsch
100g sugar
1 tsp pectin
¾ tsp citric acid

Heat the cherries and Kirsch up in a small pot over a low heat. Whisk the sugar, pectin and citric acid together in a bowl. Once the cherries are steaming, stir in the sugar mixture and cook, stirring constantly, for about 2–3 minutes, until the cherries have softened and any juice that has leached out of them has thickened. Pour over the chocolate cake and spread out with a palette knife. There will be larger lumps of whole cherry, so the compote will not be completely flat. Freeze for an hour before making the mousse.

Dark chocolate mousse

1 sheet gelatine
100g dark chocolate
80g milk
150g cream
1 tbsp Kirsch

Soak the gelatine sheet in cold water until soft. Drain and put in a bowl with the chocolate. Bring the milk to a boil and pour over the chocolate and gelatine. Whisk until the chocolate is melted, smooth and well combined. Set aside to cool to about 30°C, or body temperature. Whip the cream and Kirsch to medium peaks and fold into the chocolate base until just combined. Pour over the frozen cherry compote, level off with a palette knife and return to the freezer. Freeze overnight, or until solid.

Glaze

black glaze (recipe page 238)

Using the instructions on page 21, glaze the top of the gâteau. Leave the glaze to set in the freezer for a few minutes before portioning.

Portioning

(page 22)

Portion the gâteau into 22 pieces that are 4 x 7 x 7cm triangles. Store in the freezer and defrost fully before finishing.

To finish

22 fresh cherries or 22 drained Amarena cherries + 1 vanilla pod

If using the fresh cherries, trim the top of the stalk with scissors so they're nice and neat. Place one cherry on the wide end of each gâteau. If using Amarena cherries, place one cherry on the wide end of each gâteau. Scrape the seeds out of the vanilla pod and reserve the seeds for another use. Use a small paring knife to cut thin strips of vanilla pod to use as the stalks. Press one into the hole of each Amarena cherry.

Lemon, poppy and blackberry

I wanted to create a pastry inspired by a lemon poppy cake, but with something a bit extra. When blackberries came into season I knew they would be the perfect flavour to tie this gâteau together.

Makes 28

Lemon poppy cake

30g melted butter
50g sugar
1 egg
20g canola or other flavourless oil
20g lemon juice
¼ tsp vanilla bean paste
50g flour (gluten free, if desired)
½ tsp baking powder
1 tbsp black poppy seeds

Preheat the oven to 160°C and line the tin. Whisk the butter and sugar together until well combined, then whisk in the egg until smooth. Whisk in the oil, lemon juice and vanilla, followed by the flour and baking powder. Once you have a well combined mixture, stir in the poppy seeds and pour into the lined tin. Level off with a palette knife and bake for 10–12 minutes, until the cake is just set to the touch. Allow to cool completely while you make the blackberry mousse.

Blackberry mousse

3 sheets gelatine
240g blackberry purée (page 12)
40g sugar
240g cream

Soak the gelatine sheets in cold water until soft. Drain and put in a small pot with 40g of the blackberry purée and the sugar. Cook over a low heat, stirring constantly, until the gelatine has fully melted. Remove from the heat and stir in the remaining purée. Leave to cool to about 30°C, or body temperature. Whip the cream to soft peaks, then fold the blackberry base into it, until just combined. Pour on top of the cooled cake and freeze overnight, or until solid.

Lemon crémeux

1½ sheets gelatine
100g sugar
100g lemon juice
2 eggs
100g butter

Soak the gelatine sheets in cold water until soft. Drain and set aside. Whisk the sugar, lemon juice and eggs together until well combined in a small pot. Cook over a medium heat, whisking constantly until boiling. Remove from the heat and allow to cool to 45°C, whisking every 5 minutes to prevent a skin forming on the top. Use a stick blender to blend the butter in. Pour into a container and cover with cling film pressed onto the surface to stop a skin forming. Chill at least overnight or up to 3 days before using.

Portioning

(page 22)

Portion the gâteau into 28 pieces that are 3.5 x 3.5cm squares. Store in the freezer until ready to finish.

Chablon

white chocolate chablon (recipe page 239), coloured yellow (page 24)

Colour the chablon the same shade of yellow as the crémeux. Dip each gâteau in the chablon, following the instructions on page 30 for fully coating. Store in the freezer and defrost fully before finishing.

To finish

7–8 fresh blackberries
1 tbsp black poppy seeds
lemon crémeux

Use a small round piping tip to pipe nine small kisses (page 32) of crémeux on top of each gâteau. Decorate with a sprinkle of poppy seeds. Cut each blackberry into 3–4 rounds (depending on size) and place a round on each gâteau. Serve immediately.

Peach Melba

A peach Melba is a traditional dessert made of vanilla ice cream with a raspberry sauce and fresh peaches. It's light and fresh, perfect for the summer days when stone fruit is ripe and plentiful. I've used those flavours and textures as the inspiration for this gâteau.

Makes 20

Shortcake sponge

shortcake sponge (recipe page 241)

Once baked, trim and place in the freezer for at least 30 minutes while you make the raspberry compote.

Raspberry compote

raspberry compote (recipe page 240)

Once made, allow to cool to room temperature before pouring over the frozen sponge and levelling off with a palette knife. Return to the freezer to set while you make the vanilla mousse.

Vanilla mousse

1 sheet gelatine
10g sugar
¼ tsp vanilla bean paste
80g plain yoghurt
40g cream
1 egg white
25g sugar

Soak the gelatine sheet in cold water until soft. Drain and put in a small pot with the sugar, vanilla and 20g of the yoghurt. Cook over a low heat, stirring constantly, until the gelatine has fully melted. Remove from the heat and stir in the remaining yoghurt. Set aside to cool to about 30°C, or body temperature. Whip the cream to medium peaks and set aside. To make the Swiss meringue (page 18), whisk the egg white and sugar together in a bain-marie using a metal bowl. Whisk constantly until the mixture reaches 75°C, or is hot to the touch. Remove the bowl from the heat and whisk with an electric whisk or a stand mixer until you have a stiff-peaked meringue. Fold the yoghurt mixture into the meringue with a whisk. Once almost fully combined, swap to a spatula and fold in the cream until just combined. Pour over the raspberry compote and spread out with a palette knife. Freeze overnight, or until solid.

Peach gel

1 sheet gelatine
150g yellow peach juice or purée (page 12)
¼ tsp vanilla bean paste
20g sugar
1 tsp pectin

Soak the gelatine sheet in cold water until soft. Drain and set aside. In a small pot, bring the peach juice or purée and the vanilla to a boil. Whisk the sugar and pectin together in a bowl and whisk them into the boiling purée. Boil for 1 minute, whisking constantly. Remove from the heat and whisk in the gelatine. Allow to cool to room temperature before pouring over the frozen vanilla mousse and levelling out with a palette knife. Freeze for at least 1 hour or until set before portioning.

Portioning

(page 22)

Portion the gâteau into 20 pieces that are 7 x 2.5cm rectangles. Store in the freezer and defrost fully before finishing.

To finish

3 fresh peaches
125g fresh raspberries
edible flowers

Cut the fresh peaches into small wedges. Decorate each gâteau with a mix of peach wedges, raspberries and edible flowers. Serve immediately.

Sweetcorn and caramel

This gâteau is inspired by the delicious sweetness of fresh summer corn. The corn flavour here isn't overwhelming, but adds a rather lovely background note and subtle sweetness. Freeze-dried corn kernels blended into a powder create a great depth of flavour in the cake base, and are surprisingly easy to get hold of, too!

Makes 16

Sweetcorn cake

55g soft butter
150g sugar
1 egg
60g milk
40g canola or other flavourless oil
1 tsp white vinegar
30g freeze-dried corn kernels, ground into a powder
100g flour (gluten free, if desired)
1 tbsp cornflour
¾ tsp baking powder

Preheat the oven to 160°C and line the tin. Whisk the butter and sugar together until smooth, then whisk in the egg until well combined. Whisk the milk, oil and vinegar in, followed by the freeze-dried corn kernel powder, flour, cornflour and baking powder until you have a smooth batter. Pour into the lined tin and level off with a palette knife. Bake for 10–12 minutes, until the cake is just set to the touch. Remove from the oven and allow to cool completely while you make the caramel crémeux.

Caramel crémeux

caramel crémeux (recipe page 238)

Pour over the cooled sweetcorn cake and freeze while you make the sweetcorn custard.

Sweetcorn custard

2½ sheets gelatine
320g fresh or defrosted frozen corn kernels
500g milk
125g cream
½ tsp vanilla bean paste
3 egg yolks
60g sugar
1½ tbsp cornflour

Soak the gelatine sheets in cold water until soft. Drain and set aside. Put the corn, milk, cream and vanilla together in a large pot. Bring to the boil and then turn down to a simmer. Simmer for 5 minutes. Remove from the heat and allow to cool slightly before pulsing with a stick blender to break up the corn. Pour through a sieve, pressing down with a ladle to extract as much liquid as possible. Discard the corn solids then pass the mixture through the sieve again, without pressing, so you get a smoother mix. Pour the corn liquid into a medium-sized pot and discard any other solids in the sieve. Bring the corn mixture back to a boil. In a bowl, whisk the egg yolks and sugar together until smooth, then whisk in the cornflour. Whisk a small amount of the boiling corn mixture into this, then return this to the pot and whisk to combine. Cook over a medium heat, whisking constantly, until the custard boils. Remove from the heat and whisk in the gelatine. Allow to cool for 15–20 minutes, whisking occasionally, before pouring over the frozen caramel crémeux and returning to the freezer. Freeze overnight, or until solid.

Portioning

(page 22)

Portion the gâteau into 16 pieces that are 6 x 3.5cm rectangles. Store in the freezer and defrost fully before finishing.

Caramel popcorn

50g brown sugar
40g butter
30g golden syrup
20g popcorn (already popped)
¼ tsp flaky salt

Preheat the oven to 150°C and line a tray of any size with baking paper. Bring the sugar, butter and golden syrup to a boil in a large pot. Boil for 30 seconds. Remove from the heat and stir in the popcorn until well coated. Pour onto the baking tray and spread the popcorn out into an even layer. Sprinkle with the salt and bake for 30 minutes, stirring every 10 minutes. Leave to cool before storing in an airtight container at room temperature.

To finish

caramel popcorn
20g salted popcorn
gold leaf

Cover the tops of each gâteau with a mix of caramel popcorn and salted popcorn. Finish with a touch of gold leaf and serve immediately.

Mango and sake

Sake was not an ingredient that I was very familiar with until I was introduced to it by Valrhona pastry chef Guillaume Lopvet. While it can be quite a strong alcohol, I find that in this gâteau, it adds more of a background flavour, which enhances the natural sweetness of the mango. Finding a sake with tart and fruity notes will make an even better pairing.

Makes 20

Yuzu cake

45g melted butter
75g sugar
1 egg
1 egg yolk
30g canola or other flavourless oil
30g yuzu juice
75g flour (gluten free, if desired)
¾ tsp baking powder

Preheat the oven to 160°C and line the tin. Whisk the butter and sugar together, then whisk in the egg and egg yolk. Whisk in the oil and yuzu juice until well combined then whisk in the flour and baking powder until smooth. Pour into the lined tin, level off with a palette knife and bake for 10–12 minutes, until the cake is just set to the touch. Allow to cool completely while you make the mango curd.

Mango curd

10g sugar
¾ tsp pectin
½ tsp cornflour
120g mango purée (page 12)
10g yuzu juice
20g soft butter

Whisk the sugar, pectin and cornflour together. Bring the mango purée and yuzu juice to a boil in a pot, then whisk in the sugar mixture. Boil for 30 seconds or until thickened, then remove from the heat. Cool to 45°C and blend the butter in with a stick blender until well combined. Pour over the cooled yuzu cake and spread evenly with a palette knife. Freeze for at least half an hour before making the mango mousse.

Mango mousse

mango mousse (recipe page 240)
2 tbsp sake

Make the mango mousse recipe, adding the sake in with the mango purée. Pour over the mango curd, level off with a palette knife and freeze overnight, or until solid.

Mango sake gel

2 sheets gelatine
100g sake
40g yuzu juice
60g mango purée (page 12)
30g sugar
2 tsp pectin

Soak the gelatine sheets in cold water until soft. Drain and set aside. Bring the sake, yuzu juice and mango purée to a boil in a small pot. Whisk the sugar and pectin together in a small bowl, then whisk this into the boiling mango mixture. Boil for 1 minute, whisking constantly. Remove from the heat and whisk in the gelatine. Allow to cool to room temperature before pouring over the frozen mousse. Return to the freezer until solid.

Portioning

(page 22)

Portion the gâteau into 20 pieces that are 2.5 x 7cm rectangles. Store in the freezer and defrost before finishing.

To finish

2 mangoes
edible flowers

Slice the cheeks off the mangoes and cut 2 x 2cm squares out of them, ensuring you have at least 20. Reserve the scraps to eat, or blend them with a stick blender to create more mango purée. Place a square of mango on each gâteau and finish with some edible flowers. Serve immediately.

Hazelnut chocolate

This gâteau was created for one of my regular customers, who wanted to make something using two of her favourite ingredients from France, smooth hazelnut praline paste, and feuilletine (flakes of crispy crêpes). Both pastry ingredients can be hard to find, but they are so incredibly delicious that its worth the effort.

Makes 28

Chocolate cake

chocolate cake (recipe page 239)

Once baked, allow the cake to cool completely while you make the feuilletine crunch.

Feuilletine crunch

55g milk chocolate
75g smooth hazelnut praline
45g feuilletine

Melt the milk chocolate and hazelnut praline together either in the microwave in 10-second bursts, or in a bain-marie, until smooth. Stir in the feuilletine and pour over the cooled cake. Spread out evenly with a palette knife and allow to set at room temperature while you make the praline crémeux.

Praline crémeux

¾ sheet gelatine
110g smooth hazelnut praline
20g milk
70g cream

Soak the gelatine sheet in cold water until soft. Drain and put in a bowl with the hazelnut praline. Bring the milk and cream to a rolling boil. Pour over the hazelnut and gelatine and whisk to combine. Allow to cool for 5–10 minutes before pouring over the feuilletine crunch layer. Level off with a palette knife and freeze for at least 30 minutes before making the chocolate mousse.

Milk chocolate mousse

milk chocolate mousse (recipe page 240)

Pour over the frozen praline crémeux and smooth off with a palette knife. Return to the freezer and freeze overnight, or until solid.

Milk chocolate glaze

milk chocolate glaze (recipe page 240)

Follow the instructions on page 21 for glazing the gâteau. Allow to set for a few minutes in the freezer before portioning.

Portioning

(page 22)

Portion the gâteau into 28 pieces that are 3.5 x 3.5cm squares. Store in the freezer until ready to finish.

To finish

50g dark chocolate
50g caramelised white chocolate

Melt both chocolates separately and pour each into a small piping bag. Follow the instructions on page 29 for piped chocolate decorations, and pipe a flower in the centre of each gâteau, using the dark chocolate for the petals and the caramelised white chocolate for the centre. Pipe dots of caramelised white chocolate around the flowers on each gâteau. Defrost fully before serving.

Strawberry shortcake

I love fresh strawberries; they are my favourite fruit to bake with. So here I wanted to create a gâteau that allows the flavour of strawberries to shine! Macerating the strawberries in a touch of balsamic vinegar not only gives them a great colour, but really enhances their natural sweetness. This shortcake sponge is inspired by a Japanese strawberry shortcake, which is a light airy cake, rather than an American shortcake, which is more similar to a sweet scone.

Makes 16

Shortcake sponge

shortcake sponge (recipe page 241)

Once baked, trim the sponge and place in the freezer while you make the pâte de fruit.

Strawberry pâte de fruit

20g sugar
1½ tsp pectin
½ tsp citric acid
170g seedless strawberry purée (page 12)
10g lemon juice
100g sugar
40g liquid glucose

Whisk the first measure of sugar, pectin and citric acid together. Bring the strawberry purée and lemon juice to a boil in a small pot. Whisk the pectin mix into the purée and bring back to the boil. Whisk in the second measure of sugar and glucose. Once the mixture reaches 106°C, use a spoon to drip a small amount of the pâte de fruit mix on a plate to check if it's starting to set. Once you get a drip that sets fully — like a more solid jelly — then the pâte de fruit is done. Immediately pour over the sponge, quickly level it out and leave to cool completely before starting the mousse. You want to cool this at room temperature only, as condensation on top of the pâte de fruit will stop the mousse from sticking properly.

Strawberry mousse

strawberry mousse (recipe page 241)

Pour the strawberry mousse mixture on top of the pâte de fruit and level out with a palette knife. Freeze overnight, or until solid.

Portioning

(page 22)

Portion the gâteau into 16 pieces that are 7 x 3cm rectangles. Store in the freezer and defrost fully before finishing.

Chocolate plaques

300g white chocolate, coloured red (page 24)

Temper the chocolate following the instructions on page 24. Follow the guide on page 27 for creating flat chocolate decorations. Spread half the chocolate over an A4 sheet of acetate and cut the chocolate into 7 x 3.5cm rectangles. Repeat with the remaining chocolate, so that you have at least 32 rectangles. Allow to set before removing from the acetate and storing in an airtight container in the pantry for up to 1 month.

To finish

250g fresh strawberries
2 tbsp balsamic vinegar
chocolate plaques
fresh or dried edible flowers

Remove the tops from the strawberries and cut them into 6-8 pieces lengthways. Toss in the balsamic vinegar and leave to macerate for 5-10 minutes. Press two chocolate plaques into each gâteau; one into each of the long sides. Top with the strawberries and finish with the flowers. Serve immediately.

The symphony

This gâteau was inspired by a visit to the symphony orchestra. A friend had invited me and I didn't think I was anywhere near cultured enough to enjoy a classical music concert, but it was truly inspiring. This gâteau aims to incorporate all the aspects of the concert into a pastry. It's smooth, with bursts of acid and excitement from the lemon, and layers of flavour with the lavender and chocolate.

Makes 28

Lavender cake

1 tsp dried lavender buds
100g sugar
60g melted butter
2 eggs
50g canola or other flavourless oil
50g milk
100g flour (gluten free, if desired)
1 tsp baking powder

Preheat the oven to 160°C and line the tin. Use a food processor to blend the lavender and sugar together until the lavender is finely ground in with the sugar. Whisk the butter and lavender sugar together in a bowl until well combined, then whisk in the eggs one at a time. Whisk in the oil and milk, followed by the flour and baking powder. Pour into the lined tin and bake for 12–15 minutes, until the cake is just set to the touch. Remove from the oven and allow to cool completely. If the cake has domed, use a large knife to level it off so that it's flat.

Lemon crémeux

¾ sheet gelatine
75g lemon juice
75g sugar
1 egg
1 egg yolk
75g butter

Soak the gelatine sheet in cold water until soft. Drain and set aside. Whisk the lemon juice, sugar, egg and egg yolk together in a small pot. Cook over a medium heat, while whisking constantly, until the mixture boils. Remove from the heat and whisk in the gelatine. Allow to cool to 45°C, then use a stick blender to blend in the butter. Once the butter has blended in, pour the crémeux over the cooled cake and level off with a palette knife. Freeze for at least 1 hour before making the chocolate mousse.

Milk chocolate mousse

1 sheet gelatine
150g milk chocolate
75g milk
165g cream

Soak the gelatine sheet in cold water until soft. Drain and set aside in a bowl with the chocolate. Bring the milk to a boil in a pot, then pour over the chocolate and gelatine. Whisk to combine. Set aside to cool while you whip the cream to medium peaks. Once the chocolate base has reached about 30°C, or body temperature, fold in the cream until just combined. Pour over the lemon crémeux and smooth with a palette knife. Freeze overnight or until solid.

Black glaze

Black glaze (recipe page 238)

Follow the instructions on page 21 to glaze the top of the gâteau. Allow the glaze to set before portioning the gâteau.

Portioning

(page 22)

Portion the gâteau into 28 pieces that are 3.5 x 3.5cm squares. Store in the freezer and defrost before finishing.

Chocolate curls

100g dark chocolate

Temper the chocolate, following the instructions on page 24. Use the guide for curved chocolate decorations on page 27 to make chocolate curls, using an A5 sheet of acetate to spread the chocolate over and ensuring you have at least 28 curls.

To finish

dried edible flowers
chocolate curls

Finish each gâteau with dried flowers and a chocolate curl.

Peach and sweet wine

I love a glass of dessert wine to end a meal. My favourite is a noble Riesling; deliciously sweet while still being light and fresh, it also pairs perfectly with the peaches in this gâteau. You can substitute the wine for elderflower cordial or something similar if you want to make this alcohol free.

Makes 24

Shortcake sponge

shortcake sponge (recipe page 241)

Once baked, place the sponge in the freezer for at least 30 minutes before you start making the sweet wine mousse.

Sweet wine mousse

1½ sheets gelatine
50g yellow peach purée or juice (page 12)
50g noble Riesling
100g cream
1 egg white
20g sugar

Soak the gelatine sheets in cold water until soft. Drain and put in a pot with the peach purée or juice. Cook over a low heat, stirring constantly, until the gelatine has fully melted. Remove from the heat and stir in the Riesling. Set aside to cool. Whip the cream to medium peaks and set aside. Make the Swiss meringue (page 18) by whisking the egg white and sugar together in a bain-marie using a metal bowl. Whisk constantly until the mixture reaches 75°C or is hot to the touch. Remove from the heat and whisk with an electric whisk or a stand mixer until you have a stiff-peaked meringue. Fold the Riesling mixture into the meringue, then fold in the cream until just combined. Pour over the frozen sponge, level off with a palette knife and return to the freezer. Freeze overnight, or until solid.

Peach compote

2 sheets gelatine
250g roughly diced peaches
100g noble Riesling
¼ tsp vanilla bean paste
25g sugar

Soak the gelatine sheets in cold water until soft. Drain and set aside. Put the peaches, Riesling, vanilla and sugar together in a small pot. Cook over a low heat, stirring occasionally, until the peaches have completely broken down. If the peaches are unripe this will take much longer, and you may need to use a stick blender to help break them down. If you find the mixture is becoming dry and at risk of burning, add a splash of water and continue cooking. Once the compote is the correct consistency, stir in the gelatine and allow to cool to room temperature before spreading over the frozen mousse. Freeze for 1 hour, or until solid.

Portioning

(page 22)

Portion the gâteau into 24 pieces that are 7 x 2cm rectangles. Store in the freezer and defrost fully before finishing.

To finish

2 fresh peaches
edible flowers

Slice the peaches into at least 24 thin wedges. Decorate each gâteau with one peach slice and some edible flowers just before serving.

Summer

114	S'mores
117	Anzac biscuit
121	Banoffee
122	Apple crumble
125	Gianduja gâteau Basque
129	Butternut and maple
132	Mille-feuille
135	Poire belle Hélène
139	Sesame and caramel
140	Apricot and goat's cheese
143	Afghan biscuit
145	Buckwheat and quince
148	Passionfruit chocolate
150	Marble cake
153	Pineapple and rum
154	Chai latte
156	Speculoos crunch
159	Bergamot and Earl Grey
160	Opera

Autumn

S'mores

These petits gâteaux blur the line between a petit gâteau and a candy bar, but they are too good not to include. The chewy cookie with the soft marshmallow and the dense ganache is a match made in heaven. If you don't have a blowtorch to brûlée the tops, don't worry; it looks cool, but these will taste just as good without it.

Makes 24

Cookie base

100g butter
60g brown sugar
50g sugar
½ tsp vanilla extract
1 egg
125g flour
⅛ tsp baking powder
⅛ tsp baking soda
½ tsp cornflour
100g roughly chopped milk chocolate

Preheat the oven to 170°C and line the tin. Cook the butter in a small pot over a medium heat. Whisk every few minutes, making sure to scrape the base of the pot as you whisk, as some of the milk solids in the butter will stick and will burn quite easily. Continue to cook until the butter is a deep, toasty brown. Pour into a bowl and leave to cool for 15 minutes. Be careful as the butter will be very hot. Whisk both sugars into the butter, followed by the vanilla and the egg. Use a spatula to stir in the flour, baking powder, baking soda and cornflour. When almost combined, add the chocolate and continue to stir until fully combined. Press the cookie dough into the tin. Bake for 10–12 minutes, until lightly golden and puffed at the edges. Allow to cool completely before making the ganache.

Milk chocolate ganache

75g cream
150g milk chocolate, roughly chopped
20g very soft butter

Bring the cream to a boil in a small pot. Once boiling, pour the cream over the chocolate and whisk until the chocolate is completely melted and the mixture is smooth. Add the butter and whisk until combined. Pour over the cooled cookie base and level off with a palette knife. Chill in the fridge while you make the marshmallow.

Vanilla marshmallow

100g cold water
5 sheets gelatine
1 tsp vanilla bean paste
260g sugar
20g liquid glucose
100g water

Put the first measure of water, the gelatine and the vanilla in a large bowl (use the bowl of a stand mixer if you have one). Stir to combine, making sure the gelatine sheets are fully submerged in the water, and set aside for the gelatine to soften. Put the sugar, glucose and second measure of water in a small pot. Stir just to combine then cook, without stirring, over a medium heat to 120°C (if you stir the syrup as it cooks, you risk it crystallising). Once it has reached the desired temperature, pour on top of the gelatine mixture. Whisk on a low speed in a stand mixer or with an electric whisk for 2–3 minutes, to help release some steam and heat, then turn the mixer up to a medium-high speed. Whisk until the mixture has at least doubled in size and is just cool to the touch. Pour on top of the ganache and spread with a palette knife to smooth off the top. Refrigerate for at least 2 hours or overnight to set the marshmallow.

Portioning

(page 22)

Portion the gâteau into 24 pieces that are 7 x 2cm rectangles. Store in the fridge until ready to serve.

To finish

gold leaf

If you have a blowtorch, lightly flame the tops of the marshmallow to get a toasted look. If you don't have a blowtorch, use a touch of gold leaf to decorate the tops.

Anzac biscuit

The Anzac biscuit is a true classic Kiwi treat. The chewy biscuit is characterised by its oaty texture and buttery golden syrup flavour. I've taken advantage of these signature qualities to create a fancy Anzac petit gâteau that's just as delicious and perfect for your next afternoon tea. This one is finished with a golden syrup whipped ganache, which needs to be chilled overnight before whipping, so make sure to schedule that into your bake time.

Makes 30

Anzac base

90g butter
35g golden syrup
150g brown sugar
1 egg yolk
100g flour
80g rolled oats
20g desiccated coconut
½ tsp baking soda

Preheat the oven to 160°C and line the tin, plus a baking tray. In a small pot, brown the butter by cooking it over a medium heat, whisking constantly, until it turns a deep nutty brown. Remove from the heat and pour into a metal bowl with the golden syrup and sugar. The butter is very hot at this stage and will sizzle slightly. Whisk together, then leave to cool for about 15 minutes, or until it is slightly warm to the touch or cooler, but not quite set. Whisk in the egg yolk, then use a spatula to fold in the flour, rolled oats, coconut and baking soda. Remove 40g of the Anzac mix and crumble on the prepared baking tray. Press the remaining mixture into the lined tin, using a palette knife to press it into an even layer. Bake both trays for 10 minutes, until lightly golden brown. Remove from the oven and leave to cool. Crumble the 40g of baked biscuit into a fine crumb and reserve in an airtight container for later.

Golden syrup whipped ganache

¼ sheet gelatine
50g caramelised white chocolate
50g cream
15g golden syrup
75g cream

Soak the gelatine sheet in cold water until soft. Drain and set aside in a bowl with the chocolate. Bring the first measure of cream and the golden syrup to a boil. Pour over the chocolate and whisk to combine until the chocolate is fully melted. Whisk in the second measure of cream. Place a layer of cling film over the ganache and press it onto the surface to prevent a skin from forming. Chill overnight before using.

Golden syrup bavarois

2 sheets gelatine
125g milk
⅛ tsp flaky salt
70g golden syrup
2 egg yolks
150g cream

Soak the gelatine sheets in cold water until soft. Drain and set aside. Begin by making the anglaise base. In a small pot bring the milk and salt to a boil. While you wait for it to boil, whisk the golden syrup and egg yolks together in a bowl. Whisk about a third of the boiling milk into the egg mix until fully combined, then return this to the pot with the remaining milk. Whisk to fully combine then return to a very low heat, stirring constantly until the anglaise has lightly thickened, or reaches 75°C — this shouldn't take more than 30 seconds. Make sure the anglaise doesn't boil, as you will end up with scrambled eggs (troubleshooting, page 35)! Pour the anglaise through a sieve into a bowl with your drained gelatine. Whisk together to melt the gelatine and set aside to cool, stirring every 5 minutes, until the anglaise has reached about 30°C, or body temperature. This will take longer than most mousse bases, so be patient. While you wait, whip the cream to stiff peaks. Once the anglaise has reached the desired temperature, fold in the cream until just combined. Pour the bavarois on top of the cooled biscuit base and freeze overnight or until solid.

Continued overleaf

Portioning	Portion into 15 pieces that are 5 x 5cm squares, and cut each square in half to make a triangle, resulting in 30 pieces. Return to the freezer and keep frozen until ready to finish.
(page 22)	

Anzac chablon	Melt the chocolate and oil, stirring until smooth. Stir in the Anzac crumb. Dip each gâteau in the chablon, following the instructions on page 30 for fully coating. When you put each triangle on the baking paper, place it so it's standing upright. Leave to set before decorating.
300g caramelised white chocolate	
25g canola or other flavourless oil	
crushed Anzac crumb	

To finish	Using a whisk, whip the ganache to stiff peaks. Use a piping bag with a 1cm Saint Honoré tip (page 33) to pipe a zigzag of whipped ganache on the upward facing edge of the triangle. Finish with a touch of gold leaf and allow to defrost fully before serving.
golden syrup whipped ganache	
gold leaf	

Banoffee

Banoffee pie is a traditional English dessert made of toffee sauce, chopped banana and whipped cream. The original combination, while delicious, can be very sweet. Here I have added some miso paste into the caramelised white chocolate mousse to add an umami undertone to the dessert. I know it sounds a bit weird, and you can definitely leave it out, but once you try it with the miso you'll never go back!

Makes 16

Banana cake

banana cake (recipe page 238)

Once baked, leave the cake to cool completely while you make the miso mousse.

Miso mousse

1½ sheets gelatine
100g caramelised white chocolate
30g water
30g sugar
25g miso paste
200g cream

Soak the gelatine sheets in cold water until soft. Drain and put in a bowl with the chocolate. In a pot, bring the water and sugar to a boil. Tip in the chocolate and gelatine and whisk until melted. Add the miso paste and whisk to combine. Return to the bowl. Leave to cool while you whip the cream to medium peaks. Check the temperature of the mousse base — once it reaches 30°C, or body temperature, fold in the cream until just combined. Pour over the cake and level off with a palette knife. Freeze overnight or until solid.

Portioning

(page 22)

Portion the gâteau into 16 pieces that are 7 x 3cm rectangles. Store in the freezer and defrost fully before finishing.

Mascarpone whip

150g cream
100g mascarpone
¼ tsp vanilla bean paste
30g icing sugar

Whisk all the ingredients together to form stiff peaks. Spoon into a piping bag with a 1cm round piping tip and use immediately to finish the gateaux.

To finish

2 bananas
100g sugar
mascarpone whip

Peel the bananas and slice into 1cm thick rounds. Dip the face of each round into the sugar and blowtorch the sugar side to caramelise. Alternatively, put a non-stick pan over a medium heat and place the banana slices sugar side down in the pan until the sugar is caramelised. Remove from the pan and place the bananas sugar side up to set. For both methods, allow the bananas to cool while you pipe the cream. Pipe three large kisses (page 32) of mascarpone whip on each defrosted gâteau. Just before serving, top each kiss with a caramelised banana slice.

Autumn

Apple crumble

When I was about 13 we had our first assessment in our food technology class. My mum gave me Delia Smith's apple crumble recipe and showed me how to make the outline of a spoon on the plate with a dusting of cinnamon. It was definitely the coolest dish in the class (or that's how I remember it at least!). That memory of learning how to make the crumble with my mum is what inspired this gâteau.

Makes 24

Brown sugar cake

30g soft butter
75g brown sugar
1 egg yolk
30g milk
30g canola or other flavourless oil
60g flour (gluten free, if desired)
¼ tsp baking powder

Preheat the oven to 170°C and line the tin. Whisk the butter and sugar together until smooth. Whisk in the egg yolk, followed by the milk and oil. Add the flour and baking powder and whisk until you have a smooth batter. Pour into the lined tin and spread out with a palette knife. Bake for 10–12 minutes, until lightly golden and the cake is just set to the touch. Allow to cool while you make the apple compote.

Apple compote

1 sheet gelatine
300g peeled Granny Smith apples, cut into large dice
½ tsp vanilla bean paste
50g water

Soak the gelatine sheet in cold water until soft. Drain and set aside. Put the apples in a pot with the vanilla and water. Cover with a lid and cook over a low heat, stirring every few minutes, until the apples have completely broken down into a compote. If needed, add more water to help finish cooking the apples so the compote doesn't burn. Remove from the heat and stir in the gelatine. Pour over the cake and level off with a palette knife. Freeze for at least 1 hour before making the cinnamon mousse.

Cinnamon mousse

1½ sheets gelatine
30g sugar
60g crème fraîche
¼ tsp vanilla bean paste
¼ tsp ground cinnamon
60g mascarpone
180g cream

Soak the gelatine sheets in cold water until soft. Drain and put in a small pot with the sugar, crème fraîche, vanilla and cinnamon. Cook over a low heat, stirring constantly, until the gelatine is fully melted. Remove from the heat and stir in the mascarpone, then set aside to cool to 30°C, or body temperature. Whip the cream to medium peaks and fold into the mousse base until just combined. Pour over the frozen apple compote and spread evenly with a palette knife. Freeze overnight, or until solid.

Portioning

(page 22)

Portion the gâteau into 24 pieces that are 4 x 6 x 6cm tall triangles. Store in the freezer and defrost fully before finishing.

Vanilla poached apples

100g sugar
100g water
½ tsp vanilla bean paste
2 Granny Smith apples, peeled and cut into 1cm dice

Bring the sugar, water and vanilla to a boil. Add the apples and turn the heat down to a simmer. Simmer for 1½ minutes, until just cooked but not mushy. Remove from the heat and allow to cool in the syrup before storing in the fridge for up to 3 days before using.

Brown sugar crumble

40g melted butter
50g brown sugar
80g flour (gluten free, if desired)

Preheat the oven to 170°C and line a baking tray with baking paper. Mix the butter, sugar and flour together until you have a well combined, fine crumble. Pour onto the prepared tray and bake for 10–15 minutes, until lightly golden and fragrant. Allow to cool before storing in an airtight container in the pantry for up to 1 week before using.

To finish

vanilla poached apples
brown sugar crumble
edible flowers

Pour the poached apples through a sieve to drain off the poaching liquid. Spoon a heaped tablespoon of poached apple on top of each gâteau. Sprinkle a spoonful of brown sugar crumble on top of each gâteau and decorate with edible flowers. Serve immediately.

Autumn

Gianduja gâteau Basque

This gâteau is inspired by Anthony, one of my mentors from my time in Paris. He once told me his guilty pleasure was Twix bars dipped in Nutella, and that his favourite thing to make was gâteau Basque. I decided to combine the two together to create a gianduja gâteau Basque (gianduja being the pastry chef's name for the combination of chocolate and hazelnut – the same flavours that create Nutella). Each slice is topped with caramelised hazelnuts, a technique that Anthony also taught me. Like other whipped ganache, this recipe needs to chill overnight before being whipped to prevent it from splitting, so make sure to include this in your prep schedule.

Makes 14

Gianduja whipped ganache

½ sheet gelatine
40g milk chocolate
40g chocolate hazelnut spread
220g cream

Soak the gelatine sheet in cold water until soft. Drain and set aside in a bowl with the chocolate and chocolate hazelnut spread. Bring the cream to a boil in a pot and pour over the chocolate and chocolate hazelnut spread. Whisk until the chocolate is melted and the mixture is fully combined. Pour through a sieve into a bowl and cover with cling film, pressing the cling film onto the surface to stop a skin from forming. Leave to chill overnight.

Gâteau Basque dough

100g very soft butter
100g sugar
1 egg
1 egg yolk
15g ground almonds
140g flour
10g Dutch cocoa powder
1¼ tsp baking powder

Whisk the butter and sugar together until well combined. Add the egg, followed by the egg yolk and whisk to combine thoroughly. Use a spatula to stir in the almonds, flour, cocoa and baking powder until you've got a soft dough. Wrap dough in cling film and chill for at least 1 hour, or up to 3 days.

Gâteau Basque custard

120g milk chocolate
210g cream
2 egg yolks
60g chocolate hazelnut spread

Put the chocolate in a bowl. Bring the cream to a boil in a small pot. Pour the cream over the chocolate and whisk until the chocolate is melted and fully combined. Whisk in the egg yolks, followed by the chocolate hazelnut spread. Cover with cling film pressed onto the surface to stop a skin from forming. Chill for at least 1 hour or overnight.

Gâteau Basque assembly

Preheat the oven to 175°C and line the tin. Split the dough into two equal pieces. Lightly knead each portion of dough until it's soft enough to roll out and is one consistent texture. Roll one piece to be a few centimetres larger than the tin, both lengthways and widthways, either in between two sheets of baking paper or using plenty of flour, as this dough will be super soft and a little sticky. Roll the other piece to be the same size as the tin. Use the larger piece of dough to line the tin as though it's a tart tin, pressing the dough into the base and up the sides. Pour the custard on top and spread it into an even layer. Top with the second piece of dough, and press the edges together to enclose the custard fully. Bake for 20 minutes, until the gâteau has risen in the centre slightly. Remove from the oven and leave to cool. Chill the gâteau overnight in the fridge before portioning.

Portioning

(page 22)

Portion the gâteau into 14 pieces that are 4 x 12 x 12cm triangles. Store in the fridge until ready to finish.

Continued overleaf

Caramelised hazelnuts

100g hazelnuts
100g sugar
20g water

Preheat the oven to 180°C. Roast the hazelnuts for 12–15 minutes, until fragrant and the skins have cracked. Remove from the oven and allow to cool before rolling the hazelnuts in your hands to remove the skins. Discard the skins and put the hazelnuts in a bowl. Lay out a sheet of baking paper on a heat-proof tray next to the stovetop. Put the sugar and water into a small pot and bring to a boil. Turn the heat down to low and add the hazelnuts. Stir constantly over a low heat until the sugar starts to become sandy and crystallise. Continue to cook as the sugar starts to caramelise, stirring rapidly until you have an amber caramel coating all the hazelnuts. Pour onto the baking paper and leave to cool completely before storing in an airtight container in the pantry.

To finish

gianduja whipped ganache
caramelised hazelnuts
flaky salt
gold leaf

Whip the ganache to stiff peaks and spoon into a piping bag. Cut a 1cm hole in the tip of the bag. Pipe a 1cm-thick layer of whipped ganache on the top of each slice, leaving a 3mm border around the edges. Roughly chop the caramelised hazelnuts and cover the ganache on each slice with the chopped nuts. Sprinkle a wee bit of flaky salt on top of each gâteau and finish with a touch of gold leaf.

Butternut and maple

Butternut squash has a beautiful sweetness to it that lends itself perfectly to desserts. The snickerdoodle base of this pastry has a delightful cookie-like chew to it, and the maple cream adds an extra dimension to the flavour. Finished with crystallised salted pumpkin seeds, this gâteau is one that delivers on both texture and flavour.

Makes 20

Butternut purée

½ butternut squash

Preheat the oven to 180°C and line a tray with baking paper. Remove the seeds from the butternut and place it cut side down on the prepared tray. Bake for 30–40 minutes, until the skin is wrinkled and the squash is super soft when pierced with a fork. Allow to cool before peeling off the skin and blending the flesh to make a smooth purée. Reserve two portions of the purée — 75g and 140g — for the recipes below. Freeze the remaining purée for later use, or use it to make a butternut soup for dinner.

Butternut snickerdoodle base

80g butter
75g butternut purée
90g brown sugar
110g flour (gluten free, if desired)
½ tsp cream of tartar
½ tsp baking soda
1 tsp ground cinnamon

Preheat the oven to 180°C and line the tin. Put the butter in a small pot and cook over a high heat, stirring constantly, until it is a deep nutty brown. Pour into a bowl with the butternut purée and the sugar and mix with a spatula until everything is well combined. Stir in the flour, cream of tartar, baking soda and cinnamon until you have a smooth dough. Press into the tin in an even layer and bake for 8 minutes. Allow to cool at room temperature while you make the mousse.

Butternut mousse

2½ sheets gelatine
140g butternut purée
3 egg yolks
100g sugar
160g cream

Soak the gelatine sheets in cold water until soft. Drain and put into a small pot with 40g of the butternut purée. Cook over a very low heat, stirring constantly, until the gelatine has melted. Remove from the heat and stir in the remaining purée. Set aside while you make a pâte à bombe (page 18). Whisk the egg yolks and sugar together in a metal bowl over a pot of simmering water, until the mixture is hot to the touch, or reaches 75°C. Transfer to a stand mixer, or use an electric whisk, to whip to ribbon stage (page 18), before gently whisking in the butternut base. Whip the cream to medium peaks. Check the temperature of the butternut base. Once it reaches about 30°C, or body temperature, fold in the whipped cream until just combined. Pour on top of the snickerdoodle base, level out with a palette knife and freeze overnight or until solid.

Portioning

(page 22)

Portion the gâteau into 20 pieces that are 7 x 2.5cm rectangles. Store in the freezer until ready to finish.

Chocolate chablon

caramelised white chocolate chablon (recipe page 239)

Follow the instructions on page 30 for dipping the gâteaux in chablon, leaving the top exposed. Return to the freezer, and defrost before finishing.

Continued overleaf

Crystallised pumpkin seeds

100g pumpkin seeds
50g sugar
20g water
¼ tsp salt

Preheat the oven to 180°C. Roast the pumpkin seeds for 10 minutes or until fragrant. Remove from the oven and allow to cool. Bring the sugar, water and salt to a boil in a pot over a medium heat. Add the pumpkin seeds and turn the heat down to low. Stir constantly until the sugar crystallises around the seeds and the mixture looks powdery and white. Pour onto a baking tray lined with baking paper and leave to cool. Store in an airtight container in the pantry for up to 1 month.

Maple cream

100g mascarpone
100g cream
50g maple syrup

Whisk all ingredients together until the cream forms stiff peaks. Use immediately to finish the gâteaux.

To finish

maple cream
crystallised pumpkin seeds

Use a teaspoon to make a small quenelle of cream (page 30) and place on top of each mousse. Top with some crystallised pumpkin seeds and serve.

Mille-feuille

A true classic, a mille-feuille is a real test of a pastry chef's skill. You want your puff pastry to be crisp, and your custard to be set enough that it holds up, but not so firm that it's like a piece of rubber. The glaze has to be done in one or two swift motions to prevent the pastry from breaking up, and the feathering has to happen quickly before the glaze starts to set. It sounds stressful, but this gâteau is definitely worth it. And even an ugly mille-feuille will still be delicious.

Makes 12

Puff pastry layers

750g puff pastry, either homemade (recipe page 33) or store-bought
icing sugar

Preheat the oven to 200°C. Split the puff pastry into three 250g pieces. Roll each piece into a 20 x 30cm rectangle that's 1–2mm thick. Freeze each piece for 5–10 minutes, or chill for 10–20 minutes. Place each sheet of pastry on a separate tray of any size lined with baking paper, put another piece of baking paper on top, then another tray to weigh it down — you may need to bake the pastry sheets one at a time depending on how many trays you have. Bake for 15–20 minutes, checking the pastry after 15 minutes. It should be a light golden brown all over. Remove the top tray and baking paper and sift 1–2 tablespoons of icing sugar over the top of the pastry. Return to the oven for about 5 minutes, until the icing sugar has melted and lightly caramelised. This will prevent the pastry from becoming too soggy. Allow the pastry to cool fully before trimming all three pieces to fit inside the tin. Set aside.

Vanilla pastry cream

750g milk
1 vanilla pod or 1 tsp vanilla bean paste
200g sugar
9 egg yolks
55g custard powder
75g butter

Put the milk in a large pot, scrape the seeds from the vanilla pod and put them in the milk along with the pod, or add the vanilla bean paste. Bring to a boil. Whisk the sugar and egg yolks together in a bowl until smooth, then whisk in the custard powder. Add an eighth of the hot milk to the eggs and whisk to combine, then pour this back into the pot. Cook over a medium heat, whisking constantly, until the mixture boils. Boil for at least 30 seconds, making sure to whisk and scrape the bottom of the pot to stop the pastry cream scorching. Remove from the heat and whisk in the butter. Allow to cool to room temperature, either on the bench or in the fridge, stirring every 5–10 minutes. Once the pastry cream is cool, use it immediately to build the mille-feuille.

Assembly

puff pastry layers
vanilla pastry cream

Line the tin with baking paper. Place the first pastry layer on the base, icing sugar side up. Pour 600g of pastry cream on top and level off with a palette knife. Place the second layer of pastry on top, once again icing sugar side up, and press down slightly to stick. Repeat with the remaining pastry cream and the final layer of pastry. Chill for a few hours or preferably overnight.

Glaze and decoration

30g butter
10g liquid glucose
45g milk
320g icing sugar
50g dark chocolate

Melt the butter and glucose together. Whisk in the milk and then whisk this into the icing sugar until you have a thick but smooth glaze. Melt the chocolate and pour into a piping bag. Cut a small tip just big enough for the chocolate to easily flow out when squeezed and set aside. Follow the instructions on page 22 for glazing and decorating the mille-feuille.

Portioning and finishing

(page 22)

Portion the mille-feuille into 12 pieces that are 4 x 7cm rectangles. Use a large serrated knife to portion it, using a sawing motion to gently cut through the top layer of pastry, and then slice down through the remaining layers. Store in the fridge and serve within 12 hours.

Poire belle Hélène

Poire belle Hélène is a classic dessert of poached pear, vanilla ice cream and chocolate sauce. Here I've reimagined it as a petit gâteau, keeping the flavours true to the original. The technique of using a melon baller for the pears is one I learnt while working at The Fat Duck. It's incredibly simple but so effective. Blend what's left of the pear after making your balls to use in the pâte de fruit.

Makes 21

Chocolate cake

chocolate cake (recipe page 239)

Once baked, leave to cool completely while you make the vanilla and pear pâte de fruit.

Vanilla and pear pâte de fruit

70g lemon juice
120g pear purée (page 12) or pure pear juice
½ tsp vanilla bean paste
20g sugar
1½ tsp pectin
½ tsp citric acid
100g sugar
40g liquid glucose

In a medium-sized pot, bring the lemon juice, pear purée or juice and vanilla to a boil. In a small bowl, whisk the first measure of sugar, pectin and citric acid together. Stream the pectin mixture into the pot and bring back to the boil. Whisk in the second measure of sugar and the glucose and bring the mix back to the boil. Continue to boil while whisking until the mixture reaches 108°C, or it sets firmly within 30 seconds of being dripped onto a plate. Pour over the chocolate cake and leave to cool completely at room temperature before making the mousse.

Pear mousse

2¼ sheets gelatine
180g pear purée or pure pear juice
30g sugar
¼ tsp vanilla bean paste
180g cream

Soak the gelatine sheets in cold water until soft. Drain and place in a pot with 20g of pear purée or juice and the sugar. Cook over a low heat until the gelatine has completely melted. Pour into a bowl and mix with the remaining purée or juice and vanilla. Leave to cool while you whip the cream to medium peaks. Once the pear mixture has reached 30°C, or body temperature, fold in the cream until just combined. Pour over the cooled pâte de fruit and freeze overnight, or until solid.

Portioning

(page 22)

Portion the gâteau into 21 pieces that are 8 x 2cm rectangles. Store in the freezer until ready to finish.

Poached pear balls

6–7 large Packham pears
150g sugar
50g lemon juice
200g water
½ tsp vanilla bean paste

Peel the pears and use a melon baller to take scoops out to create nice round balls; you should get 10–11 balls per pear and you will need at least 63 of them. Keep the balled pears in a bowl of cold water as you make them to stop them going brown. Use the remainder of the pears to create purée or juice for the recipes above (or eat them!). In a medium-sized pot, bring the sugar, lemon juice, water and vanilla to a boil. Turn the heat down to a simmer and add the pear balls. Make a cartouche by cutting a piece of baking paper into a circle the same size as the pot, and cutting a small hole in the centre the size of a one-dollar coin. Press this down on top of the pears and simmer gently for 15 minutes. Remove from the heat and allow to cool to room temperature before storing in the fridge. The pears will last up to 1 week in the fridge covered in the poaching syrup.

Continued overleaf

Chocolate sauce

75g water
60g cream
15g liquid glucose
1½ tbsp cocoa powder
35g sugar
35g dark chocolate

In a small pot, bring the water, cream and glucose to a boil. Whisk the cocoa and sugar together in a small bowl and then stream this into the boiling cream. Boil for 30 seconds, then remove from the heat and whisk in the chocolate. Once the chocolate has fully melted, return to the heat and simmer, scraping the base of the pot continuously with a spatula, for another 20 seconds. Leave to cool and store in the fridge until ready to use.

Chablon

dark chocolate chablon
 (recipe page 239)

Follow the instructions on page 30 for dipping the gâteaux in chablon, leaving the top exposed. Store in the freezer and defrost fully before finishing.

To finish

poached pear balls
chocolate sauce

Drain off the poached pears, laying them on a paper towel for a minute or so to remove any excess moisture that may cause them to slip off the gâteaux. Place three balled pears on top of each gâteau. Serve the gâteaux and pour the chocolate sauce over, tableside, and enjoy!

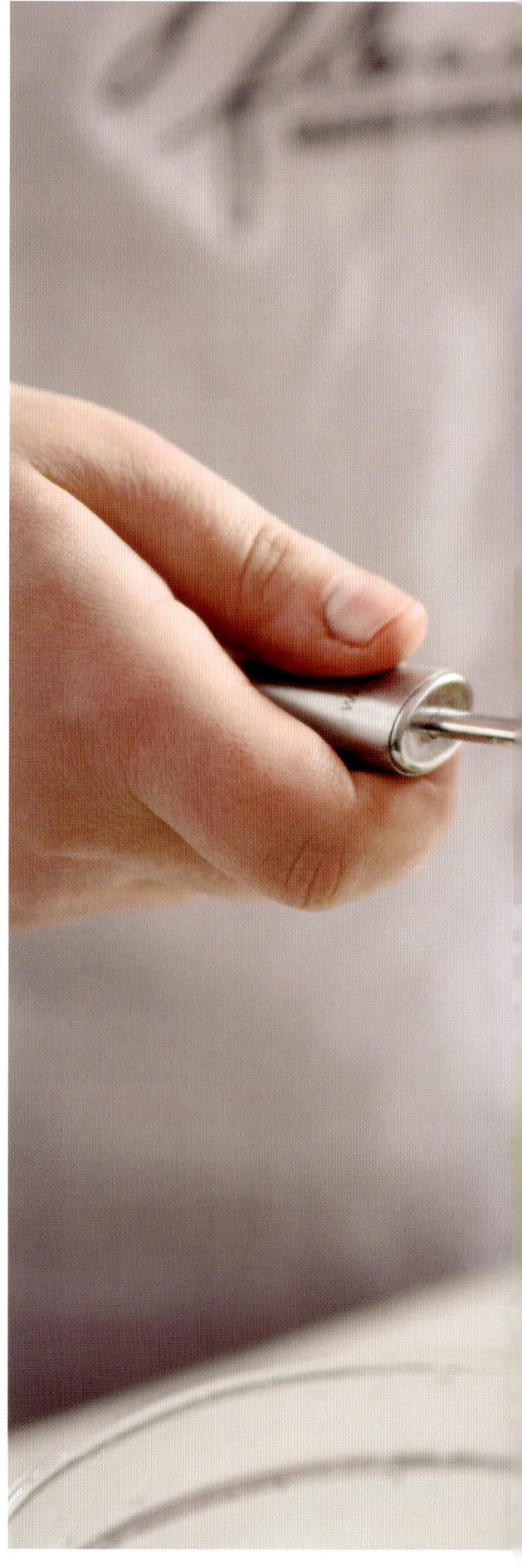

Sesame and caramel

Sesame isn't a super conventional flavour in Western desserts, but it has a great nutty, savoury flavour that works perfectly with caramelised white chocolate. The cookie base not only has tahini (sesame paste) but also halva, which is a fudge-like sesame treat that melts into the cookie dough. If you can't get any halva you can leave it out, but it's definitely worth trying to track some down.

Makes 24

Cookie base

90g butter
60g brown sugar
50g sugar
50g tahini
1 tsp vanilla extract
1 egg
125g flour
¼ tsp baking powder
¼ tsp baking soda
100g chopped milk chocolate
100g halva, chopped into rough 2cm cubes
1 tsp flaky salt

Preheat the oven to 170°C and line the tin. Melt the butter in a small pot and cook over a medium heat, whisking constantly, until you get a nutty brown butter. Pour into a bowl and whisk in both sugars, tahini and vanilla, stirring together until smooth. Whisk in the egg until well combined. Fold in the flour, baking powder and baking soda, then stir in the chocolate and halva. Press into the tin and sprinkle with the salt. Bake for 10 minutes, until lightly puffed and slightly golden. Set aside to cool completely while you make the sesame praline.

Sesame praline

150g sugar
30g water
150g tahini

Make a wet caramel (page 19) by cooking the sugar and water together in a small pot, without stirring until it starts to caramelise. Once the mixture is a light golden brown, remove from the heat and pour the caramel onto a sheet of baking paper. Leave to cool for 15 minutes, or until cool to the touch. Blend the caramel in a food processor until it's turned into a fine crumb. Add the tahini and blend to combine. Pour over the cookie base and freeze while you make the sesame mousse.

Sesame mousse

¾ sheet gelatine
60g caramelised white chocolate
20g water
15g sugar
60g tahini
110g cream

Soak the gelatine sheet in cold water until soft. Drain and put in a bowl with the chocolate. Bring the water and sugar to a boil in a small pot. Remove from the heat and add the chocolate and gelatine. Stir until fully melted, then whisk in the tahini. Set aside to cool while you whip the cream to soft peaks. Once the base has reached 30°C, or body temperature, fold in the cream until just combined. Pour over the frozen sesame praline and level off with a palette knife. Freeze overnight, or until solid.

Portioning

(page 22)

Portion the gâteau into 24 pieces that are 4 x 4cm squares. Store in the freezer until ready to finish.

Sesame tuile

50g butter
30g liquid glucose
70g icing sugar
30g flour
30g white sesame seeds
30g black sesame seeds

Preheat the oven to 180°C and line a baking tray with baking paper. Melt the butter and glucose together, either in a small pot or in a microwave. Whisk in the icing sugar and flour together until smooth. Stir in the sesame seeds. Spread the tuile over the prepared baking tray to about 1mm thick. Bake for 10–12 minutes, until golden brown. Remove from the oven and allow to cool ever so slightly (for at most 1 minute) before using a 3cm cutter to cut circles of tuile out. If the tuile begins to harden, return to the oven to soften slightly before cutting out more circles. Leave to cool completely. Store in an airtight container in the pantry.

Caramelised white chocolate chablon

caramelised white chocolate chablon (recipe page 239)

Dip each gâteau in the chablon, following the instructions for fully coating on page 30. Press a tuile circle on top of each gâteau before the chablon sets. Store in the freezer and defrost fully before serving.

Apricot and goat's cheese

One of my biggest gripes about cheese plates at restaurants is that they never seem to display as much effort or technique as the other desserts. I wanted to include something that works perfectly as a dessert for those who always order the cheese plate, and is just as special as everything else in the book. You can swap out the apricot for another fruit of a similar texture, and if you aren't a fan of goat's cheese you can replace it with equal quantities of cream cheese for a delicious cheesecake.

Makes 16

Honey cake

120g melted butter
60g sugar
20g honey
30g milk
1 egg yolk
1 egg
110g flour (gluten free, if desired)
½ tsp baking powder

Preheat the oven to 190°C and line the tin. Whisk the butter, sugar, honey and milk together until combined. Add the egg yolk and the egg, and whisk to combine. Whisk in the flour and baking powder until fully combined. Pour into the lined tin and level off with a palette knife. Bake for 10–12 minutes, until the cake is just set to the touch. Leave to cool completely.

Apricot compote

200g dried apricots
50g sugar
150g water
¼ tsp vanilla bean paste

Put all the ingredients together in a small pot and bring to the boil. Turn the heat down and simmer for 1 minute. Allow to cool slightly, then blend with a stick blender to create a smooth compote, adding more water if needed, a tablespoon at a time. You want the compote to be very thick as there is no gelling agent in it, so add water sparingly. Taste the compote and add more sugar if desired. Spread the compote over the cooled sponge and store in the freezer while you make the goat's cheese cheesecake.

Goat's cheese cheesecake

200g soft goat's cheese (chèvre)
150g cream cheese
40g icing sugar
20g honey
¼ tsp vanilla bean paste
180g cream

Using a spatula, mix the goat's cheese until it's softened slightly. Add the cream cheese and stir again until smooth. Whisk in the icing sugar until combined, followed by the honey and vanilla. Gradually add the cream, whisking well in between each addition until all the cream is fully mixed in. Whisk, either by hand or with an electric whisk, until the mixture has reached stiff peaks. Spread evenly over the apricot compote and freeze overnight, or until solid.

Glaze

coloured glaze (recipe page 239), coloured yellow (page 24)

Glaze the top of the gâteau, following the guide on page 21. Allow to set for a few minutes before portioning.

Portioning

(page 22)

Portion the gâteau into 16 pieces that are 7 x 3cm rectangles. Store in the freezer and defrost before finishing.

Chocolate 'cheese' slices

200g white chocolate, melted and coloured cheese yellow (page 24)

Temper and colour the chocolate following the instructions on page 24. Follow the instructions on page 27 for making flat chocolate decorations. Spread the chocolate over an A4 sheet of acetate. Use various sized circle cutters and round piping tips to cut different sized circles randomly out of the chocolate to create the holey cheese effect, then use a knife to cut the chocolate into 8 x 3cm rectangles, ensuring you have at least 16. Allow to set before removing from the acetate. They will keep in an airtight container in the pantry for up to 1 month.

To finish

Place a chocolate 'cheese' slice on top of each glazed gâteau before serving.

Autumn

Afghan biscuit

Afghan biscuits were one of the first recipes I learnt to bake, and they were always a hit. Here I've taken inspiration from the original biscuit to create a petit gâteau that will feel like the fanciest afghan you could ever eat. The walnut praline will make much more than you need, but it is easier to make a larger batch, and it tastes great on toast!

Makes 28

Cocoa brownie

70g melted butter
125g sugar
1 egg
30g flour (gluten free, if desired)
30g Dutch cocoa powder

Preheat the oven to 180°C and line the tin. Whisk the butter and sugar together, followed by the egg. Once thoroughly combined, whisk in the flour and cocoa, until you have a smooth, runny batter. Pour into the lined tin and bake for 10 minutes. Leave to cool at room temperature.

Walnut praline

200g walnuts
200g sugar
50g water

Roast the walnuts at 180°C for 12 minutes, until lightly brown and fragrant. Set aside to cool. Make a wet caramel (page 19) by bringing the sugar and water to a boil. Cook over a high heat until you have a light amber-coloured caramel. Pour onto a sheet of baking paper and leave to cool. The caramel will take about 10–15 minutes to cool at room temperature. It will get quite sticky if left longer than that, as it attracts moisture from the air, so only make it just before you need it. Break the caramel up into pieces and place in a blender or food processor. Blend the caramel until it turns into a powder. Add the walnuts and blend until you have a liquid praline, that has a slightly sandy texture. Store in an airtight container in the pantry for up to 3 months.

Walnut cornflake crunch

150g walnut praline
100g milk chocolate
60g cornflakes, lightly crushed
¼ tsp flaky salt

Melt the walnut praline and chocolate together in a bain-marie until smooth. Remove from the heat and stir in the cornflakes and flaky salt. Pour on top of the brownie base and level off with a palette knife. Set aside at room temperature while you make the mousse.

Milk chocolate mousse

milk chocolate mousse (recipe page 240)

Pour the mousse on top of the walnut cornflake crunch layer and level off with a palette knife. Freeze overnight, or until solid.

Portioning

(page 22)

Portion the gâteau into 28 pieces that are 3.5 x 3.5cm squares. Store in the freezer until ready to finish.

Afghan chablon

300g milk chocolate
25g canola or other flavourless oil
20g cornflakes, lightly crushed

Melt the chocolate and oil together in a bain-marie until smooth and runny. Stir in the cornflakes. Follow the instructions on page 30 for dipping the gâteau in chablon, leaving the base exposed. Store frozen and defrost fully before finishing.

Milk chocolate whipped ganache

milk chocolate whipped ganache (recipe page 240)

Spoon the whipped ganache into a piping bag with a 1cm round piping tip and use immediately.

To finish

milk chocolate whipped ganache
100g roasted salted walnuts, roughly chopped

Pipe a kiss (page 32) of ganache in the centre of each gâteau. Finish with pieces of walnut and serve.

Buckwheat and quince

Both buckwheat and quince are slightly more unusual flavours, but they pair so well together. Buckwheat is very earthy, and quince is fresh and acidic. The floral orange blossom helps tie the flavours together. You'll notice when you peel the quince that they're off-white inside, rather than the apricot-toned pink you may have seen before. Once you poach the quince it will start to develop the beautiful pink hue, which will become even darker if you rest it in the poaching liquid overnight before turning it into the jelly layer. If you can't get hold of quince, you can replace them with apples.

Makes 14

Poached quince

150g lemon juice
150g sugar
¼ tsp vanilla bean paste
1–2 large quince, peeled, cored and chopped into large chunks to weigh 150g

Bring the lemon juice, sugar and vanilla to a boil. Reduce to a simmer and add the quince chunks. Simmer for about 20 minutes, until the quince is super soft and can be easily pierced with a fork. Allow to cool in the syrup and either chill overnight (to develop more of the rose colour) or proceed immediately to making the compote.

Quince compote

1½ sheets gelatine
poached quince
30g sugar

Soak the gelatine sheets in cold water until soft. Drain and set aside. Strain the liquid off the poached quince and blend the quince with a stick blender to form a smooth purée. Push through a sieve to help get the purée extra smooth. Mix a tablespoon or so of the quince in a small pot with the sugar and gelatine. Cook over a low heat, stirring constantly, until the gelatine is fully melted. Whisk this into the remaining quince purée. Pour over the buckwheat dacquoise and level off with a palette knife. Freeze for at least an hour before making the bavarois.

Buckwheat dacquoise

110g butter
55g buckwheat flour
20g ground almonds
45g icing sugar
3 egg whites
30g sugar

Preheat the oven to 170°C and line the tin. Cook the butter over a medium heat in a small pot, whisking constantly, until it turns a light nutty brown. Whisk the flour, almonds, icing sugar and butter together in a bowl. In a stand mixer or with an electric whisk, whip the egg whites and sugar together until stiff peaks form. Whisk an eighth of the meringue into the buckwheat base to loosen it, then fold the remaining meringue gently into the base until just combined. Pour into the lined tin and level off with a palette knife. Bake for 10–12 minutes, until the dacquoise is just set to the touch. Leave to cool at room temperature.

Orange blossom bavarois

2 sheets gelatine
60g milk
¼ tsp vanilla bean paste
2 egg yolks
30g sugar
140g cream
60g mascarpone
1 tbsp orange blossom water

Soak the gelatine sheets in cold water until soft. Drain and set aside. Begin by making an anglaise. Boil the milk and vanilla together in a small pot. In a bowl, whisk the egg yolks and sugar together until well combined. Whisk a small amount of the boiled milk into the egg yolk mixture, then pour this back into the pot of milk. Whisk to combine, then swap to a spatula. Over a low heat, cook, stirring constantly, until the anglaise has thickened slightly or reaches 75°C. Remove from the heat and stir in the gelatine until melted. Leave to cool to 30°C, or body temperature, stirring every few minutes. Whip the cream, mascarpone and orange blossom water to medium peaks. Fold this into the cooled base until just combined. Pour over the quince compote and level off with a palette knife. Freeze overnight, or until solid.

Continued overleaf

Glaze

coloured glaze (recipe page 239), coloured white (page 24) (if desired)

Glaze the top of the gâteau following the guide on page 21 and allow to set for 1–2 minutes before portioning.

Portioning

(page 22)

Portion the gâteau into 14 triangles that are 4 x 12 x 12cm long. Store in the freezer and defrost fully before finishing.

Crystallised buckwheat

50g sugar
20g water
50g roasted buckwheat (kasha)

Line a tray with baking paper. Bring the sugar and water to a boil over a medium-high heat and boil for 30 seconds. Add the buckwheat, turn the heat down to low and stir constantly until the sugar starts to crystallise. Remove from the heat and tip onto the prepared tray. Leave to cool and then store in an airtight container in the pantry for up to 1 month.

To finish

crystallised buckwheat
gold leaf

Sprinkle crystallised buckwheat over each triangle. Finish with a few touches of gold leaf.

Passionfruit chocolate

Passionfruit and milk chocolate may sound like an unlikely match, but the acidity of the passionfruit really helps cut through the richness of this gâteau. The chocolate curls are one of the harder decorations to make, but they look incredibly effective.

Makes 21

Chocolate sponge

2 eggs
30g melted butter
30g flour
10g cocoa powder
60g sugar

Preheat the oven to 180°C and line the tin. If you have two tins, line the second one with baking paper also. Separate the eggs, putting the egg whites in a stand mixer bowl or a large bowl. Put the egg yolks in a bowl with the butter and whisk to combine. Whisk in the flour and cocoa until smooth. Whisk the egg whites in the stand mixer or with an electric whisk until they've doubled in size. Add the sugar and continue to whisk until you have a stiff-peaked meringue. Whisk a large scoop, about an eighth, of the meringue into the egg yolk base to loosen it, then fold in the remaining meringue until just combined. Pour 110g of the sponge mix into the prepared tin and level off with a palette knife. Spread the remaining sponge mixture into a rectangle the same size as the tin on a sheet of baking paper at the same time you spread the first sponge mix in the tin. You don't want to leave the second half in the bowl and spread it after the first half is baked, as you'll end up with a more deflated sponge. Bake the first half for 8–10 minutes or until just set to the touch. Remove from the tin, insert the baking paper with the other half of the mixture on it into the tin, and bake the second half the same way. Allow to cool before removing the sponges from the baking paper. Of course, if you do happen to have two tins then you can bake them both at the same time.

Passionfruit crémeux

passionfruit crémeux (recipe page 240)

Line the tin with baking paper and place the first cooled sponge in the base. Pour the crémeux on top, level it off with a palette knife and then freeze for at least an hour before placing the second sponge on top and making the mousse.

Milk chocolate mousse

¾ sheet gelatine
100g milk chocolate
50g milk
110g cream

Soak the gelatine sheet in cold water until soft. Drain and put in a bowl with the chocolate. Bring the milk to a boil and pour over the chocolate and gelatine. Whisk to combine until completely smooth. Whip the cream to stiff peaks. Once the milk chocolate base is about 30°C, or body temperature, fold in the cream until just combined. Pour over the second sponge layer and level off with a palette knife. Freeze overnight, or until solid.

Black glaze

black glaze (recipe page 238)

Use the instructions on page 21 to glaze the top of the gâteau. Allow to set in the fridge or freezer for 5 minutes before portioning.

Portioning

(page 22)

Portion the gâteau into 21 pieces that are 2 x 8cm rectangles. Store frozen and defrost before finishing.

Chocolate curls

100g white chocolate, coloured yellow (page 24)
100g dark chocolate

Temper the chocolate, following the instructions on page 24. Spread it over an A5 sheet of acetate, following the guide to make chocolate curls on page 27. Repeat with another acetate sheet and the dark chocolate. They will keep in an airtight container in the pantry for up to 1 month.

To finish

Decorate each gâteau with a yellow chocolate curl and a dark chocolate curl and serve.

Marble cake

Marble cake is always a beautiful showstopper, but turning it into a petit gâteau takes it to the next level. Using a high-quality chocolate and vanilla is really important in this gâteau, as these will make it truly special.

Makes 28

Marble cake

100g melted butter
150g sugar
2 eggs
50g canola or other flavourless oil
120g milk
1 tsp white vinegar
¼ tsp vanilla bean paste
1 tsp vanilla extract
200g flour (gluten free, if desired)
1½ tsp baking powder
15g cocoa powder
30g milk

Preheat the oven to 170°C and line the tin. Whisk the butter and sugar together until smooth, then whisk in the eggs one at a time, followed by the oil, first measure of milk, vinegar, vanilla paste and extract. Once smooth, whisk in the flour and baking powder. In a separate bowl, whisk the cocoa and second measure of milk together until smooth. Mix half of the cake mix into this until well combined. Spoon alternating scoops of the vanilla and chocolate cake mix into the cake tin, using all of the cake mix. Use a small knife to slightly swirl the two batters together. Bake for 15–20 minutes, until the cake is just set to the touch in the centre. Remove from the oven and leave to cool completely. If the cake has domed on top, use a large knife to level off the top of the cake (and eat the scraps!).

White chocolate mousse

1¼ sheets gelatine
75g white chocolate
30g water
30g sugar
¼ tsp vanilla bean paste
150g cream

Soak the gelatine sheets in cold water until soft. Drain and put in a bowl with the white chocolate. Bring the water, sugar and vanilla to a boil in a small pot. Remove from the heat and pour in the white chocolate and gelatine and stir until melted. Whip the cream to medium peaks. Once the white chocolate base has cooled to about 30°C, or body temperature, fold in the cream until just combined. Set aside while you make the milk chocolate mousse.

Milk chocolate mousse

¾ sheet gelatine
100g milk chocolate
50g milk
110g cream

Soak the gelatine sheet in cold water until soft. Drain and put in a bowl with the milk chocolate. Bring the milk to a boil in a small pot and pour over the chocolate and gelatine. Stir to combine until the chocolate has melted. Whisk the cream to medium peaks. Once the chocolate base has cooled to about 30°C, or body temperature, fold in the cream until just combined. Spoon alternating scoops of white and milk chocolate mousse on top of the cooled cake. Use a small knife to swirl the two mousses together, then level off with a palette knife. Freeze overnight, or until solid.

Portioning

(page 22)

Portion the gâteau into 28 pieces that are 3.5 x 3.5cm squares. Store in the freezer until ready to dip in the chablon.

Chablon

white chocolate chablon (recipe page 239)
dark chocolate chablon (recipe page 239)

Pour the white chocolate chablon into a deep container, and pour the dark chocolate chablon into a piping bag with a 1mm hole, or into a jug. Pipe or pour lines of dark chocolate chablon onto the surface of the white chocolate chablon, using only a tablespoon or so of the dark chocolate chablon to start with. Dip each gâteau in the chablon, following the instructions on page 30 for fully coating. Twist the gâteaux as you pull them out of the chablon to help create a swirl effect, adding more lines of dark chocolate as needed. Store in the freezer and defrost before serving.

To finish

gold leaf

Decorate each gâteau with gold leaf and serve.

Pineapple and rum

I have never been a big rum fan, but my brother introduced me to pineapple rum, which has the right amount of sweetness and fruit flavour to make it a firm favourite of mine. When used in these petits gâteaux, it helps to enhance the pineapple flavour without overpowering it. If you can't get pineapple rum, feel free to use whatever rum you like; rum that pairs well with ginger will have the right notes to work well in this gâteau.

Makes 16

Dark sugar sponge

1 egg
100g water
100g dark cane or muscovado sugar
80g golden syrup
60g canola or other flavourless oil
¼ tsp baking soda
110g flour (gluten free, if desired)

Preheat the oven to 170°C and line the tin. Whisk the egg, water, sugar, golden syrup and oil together until well combined. Whisk in the baking soda and flour until well combined and no lumps remain. The mix will be very runny. Pour into the tin and bake for 15–20 minutes, until the sponge is just set to the touch. Remove from the oven and leave to cool completely.

Coconut rum mousse

1½ sheets gelatine
20g sugar
110g coconut cream
10g pineapple rum
120g cream
¼ tsp vanilla bean paste

Soak the gelatine sheets in cold water until soft. Drain and put in a small pot with the sugar and 20g of the coconut cream. Cook over a very low heat, stirring constantly until the gelatine has completely melted. Remove from the heat and stir in the remaining coconut cream and the pineapple rum. Pour into a bowl and set aside while you whip the cream and vanilla to medium peaks. Check the temperature of the coconut cream mixture. Once it has reached 30°C, or body temperature, fold in the cream until just combined. Pour on top of the cooled sponge, level off with a palette knife, and freeze for at least an hour, or until set on the surface.

Pineapple rum gel

2 sheets gelatine
200g pineapple juice
15g pineapple rum
2 tsp pectin
30g sugar
⅛ tsp citric acid

Soak the gelatine sheets in cold water until soft. Drain and set aside. In a small pot, bring the pineapple juice and rum to a boil. Whisk the pectin, sugar and citric acid together in a small bowl, and stream this into the boiling pineapple juice. Boil while whisking for 1 minute. Remove from the heat and stir in the gelatine. Leave to cool to room temperature before pouring on top of your frozen mousse. Freeze overnight, or until the gâteau is solid.

Portioning

(page 22)

Portion the gâteau into 16 pieces that are 7 x 3cm rectangles. Store in the freezer and defrost fully before finishing.

Caramel poached pineapple

100g sugar
1 pineapple, peeled and cut into 1cm dice
50g pineapple rum
½ tsp vanilla bean paste

In a large pot or pan, make a dry caramel (page 19) with the sugar by cooking it over a high heat, stirring constantly, until you have a deep amber colour. Add the pineapple and stir to combine. The caramel will seize up and make big clumps. Add the pineapple rum and vanilla and turn the heat down to low, stirring every minute or so. Cook until the caramel has melted and the pineapple has turned translucent on the edges. Remove from the heat and allow to cool. Refrigerate until ready to use.

To finish

1 lime
micro coriander

Drain any excess syrup off the poached pineapple and spoon the dice on top of the gâteaux. Zest the lime over the top and finish with a few leaves of micro coriander.

Chai latte

Chai lattes are my go-to cold weather drink. They're the perfect warm, comforting, spicy treat. Finished with a whipped milk jelly that emulates the foam on a chai latte, this pastry is a delicious take on the equally delicious drink.

Makes 21

Chai spice

6 tsp ground ginger
4 tsp ground cinnamon
2 tsp ground cardamom
2 tsp ground allspice
2 tsp ground nutmeg
2 tsp ground cloves

Mix all the spices together. Store in an airtight container in the pantry.

Chai spiced cake

spice cake (recipe page 241), using chai spice

Once baked, allow the cake to cool while you make the chai mousse.

Chai mousse

1 sheet gelatine
70g white chocolate
40g water
20g sugar
1 tsp loose-leaf black tea
140g cream
1 tsp chai spice

Soak the gelatine sheet in cold water until soft. Drain and set aside in a bowl with the white chocolate. Put the water, sugar and tea in a pot and bring to a boil. Allow to infuse for 5 minutes. Boil again, then strain over the chocolate and gelatine. Whisk to combine until smooth. Whisk the cream and spice together until medium peaks form. Once the white chocolate base has reached about 30°C, or body temperature, fold in the cream until just combined. Pour over the cooled cake, level off with a palette knife and freeze overnight, or until solid.

Milk jelly

2 sheets gelatine
180g milk
20g sugar
¼ tsp vanilla bean paste

Soak the gelatine sheets in cold water until soft. Drain and set aside. Bring the milk, sugar and vanilla to a boil. Remove from the heat and whisk in the gelatine. Chill for 1–2 hours, until the jelly has started to set around the outside but is still runny in the middle. You can leave it for longer, but will need to melt half of it in the microwave before proceeding to the next step. Use an electric whisk or a stand mixer to whip the jelly until it's turned into a thick foam that has almost doubled in size. Pour over the frozen mousse and level off with a palette knife. Freeze for at least 2 hours before portioning.

Portioning

(page 22)

Portion the gâteau into 21 pieces that are 2 x 8cm rectangles. Store frozen and defrost fully before finishing.

Chocolate squares

200g caramelised white chocolate

Temper the chocolate following the instructions on page 24. Follow the guide for making curved decorations on page 27, spreading the chocolate on an A4 acetate sheet and cutting into 2 x 2cm squares, before rolling around a rolling pin to create the curve. You need at least 42 squares. Allow to set before removing from the acetate and storing in an airtight container.

To finish

chai spice
chocolate squares

Use a sieve to dust the gâteaux with chai spice and decorate with two chocolate squares on each gâteau. Serve immediately.

Speculoos crunch

Speculoos cookies are an incredible mix of cinnamon and brown sugar. A genius somewhere decided to make them into a spread, and it is possibly the best invention on this planet. This gâteau will seem incredibly thin while you're making it, but don't stress — once it has the whipped caramel on top and the chocolate coating it will look, and taste, perfect!

Makes 20

Speculoos spiced sponge

75g brown sugar
75g water
60g golden syrup
1 egg yolk
45g canola or other flavourless oil
80g flour
⅛ tsp baking soda
1 tsp ground cinnamon
100g smooth speculoos spread

Preheat the oven to 180°C and line the tin. Whisk the sugar, water, golden syrup, egg yolk and oil together until well combined. Whisk in the flour, baking soda and cinnamon. Pour into the lined tin and bake for 10–12 minutes, until the sponge is just set to the touch. Melt the speculoos spread in the microwave or over a pot of simmering water until liquid. Spread over the cake while the cake is still warm and leave to cool completely while you make the whipped crème fraîche.

Speculoos chablon

300g caramelised white chocolate
30g canola or other flavourless oil
20g speculoos cookies, crushed to a fine crumb

Melt the chocolate and oil in a bain-marie, or in the microwave. Once melted, stir in the speculoos cookies. Leave to cool to 35°C before using. Dip each gâteau in the chablon, following the instructions on page 30 for fully coating. Store in the freezer, and defrost before finishing.

Whipped crème fraîche

100g crème fraîche
15g icing sugar
¼ tsp vanilla bean paste
100g cream

Whisk everything together either by hand or in a stand mixer until the mixture reaches stiff peaks. Spread on top of the cooled sponge with an offset palette knife until smooth. Freeze overnight or until solid.

Whipped caramel

whipped caramel (recipe page 242)

Whip to stiff peaks just before using.

Portioning

(page 22)

Portion the gâteau into 20 pieces that are 4 x 7 x 7cm triangles. Store in the freezer until ready to finish.

To finish

whipped caramel
20g speculoos cookies, crushed to a fine crumb
gold leaf

Using a 1cm Saint Honoré tip (page 33), pipe the whipped caramel on the gâteaux in a zigzag pattern, starting from the wide base up to the tip of the triangle. Sprinkle some speculoos crumbs over the top and decorate with gold leaf as desired.

Bergamot and Earl Grey

Bergamot is such a beautiful, floral citrus flavour, and is one of the defining features in Earl Grey tea. Here I've swapped it round so the bergamot is the main flavour, and the Earl Grey is more of an accent. You can buy bergamot purée and juice online, or replace it with another citrus fruit. The cream for the Earl Grey mousse needs to be chilled overnight to infuse properly, and so does the bergamot whipped ganache, so make sure you start this gâteau with plenty of time.

Makes 21

Bergamot cake

45g melted butter
75g sugar
1 egg
1 egg yolk
30g canola or other flavourless oil
30g bergamot purée
75g flour (gluten free, if desired)
¾ tsp baking powder

Preheat the oven to 170°C and line the tin. Whisk the butter and sugar together in a bowl, then whisk in the egg and egg yolk. Once well combined, whisk in the oil and bergamot purée. Whisk in the flour and baking powder until smooth. Pour into the lined tin and bake for 12–15 minutes, until the cake is just set to the touch. Leave to cool while you make the bergamot gel.

Bergamot gel

150g bergamot purée
¼ tsp vanilla bean paste
100g sugar
1 tsp pectin

Bring the bergamot purée and vanilla to a boil in a small pot. Whisk the sugar and pectin together, then whisk this into the boiling purée. Cook to 105°C, whisking constantly. Pour over the cake and spread evenly with a palette knife. Leave to cool at room temperature while you make the mousse.

Earl Grey mousse

250g cream
3 tbsp loose leaf Earl Grey tea
1½ sheets gelatine
100g white chocolate
30g water
30g sugar

The day before you intend to make the mousse, bring the cream and the tea to a boil in a small pot. Cover and chill overnight to infuse. The next day strain through a sieve, pushing down on the tea leaves to extract as much flavour as possible. Weigh out 200g of cream, discarding any leftovers. If you don't have enough cream, top it up slightly with fresh cream. Whip to soft peaks and reserve in the fridge while you make the mousse base. Soak the gelatine sheets in cold water until soft. Drain and set aside in a bowl with the chocolate. Bring the water and sugar to a boil and pour over the chocolate and gelatine. Allow to sit for a minute or two before stirring to create a smooth base. If the chocolate doesn't all melt you can heat the base up slightly until everything is just melted together. Allow to cool to about 30°C, or body temperature. Stir a large tablespoon of the infused whipped cream into the base to loosen it, then fold in the remaining whipped cream. Pour over the bergamot gel and level off with a palette knife. Freeze for at least 2 hours before piping the whipped ganache on top.

Bergamot whipped ganache

¾ sheet gelatine
70g white chocolate
100g cream
160g cream
60g bergamot juice

Soak the gelatine sheet in cold water until soft. Drain and set aside in a bowl with the chocolate. Bring the first measure of cream to a boil in a small pot and pour over the chocolate and gelatine. Whisk to combine before whisking in the second measure of cream and bergamot juice. Blend with a stick blender to help emulsify, then cover with cling film on the surface to stop a skim forming and chill overnight. The next day whip to stiff peaks and spoon into a piping bag with a 1cm round tip. Follow the guide on page 32 for the squished kiss effect. Freeze overnight as instructed before removing the acetate sheet.

Portioning

(page 22)

Portion the gâteau into 21 pieces that are 2 x 8cm rectangles. Store in the freezer, or defrost before finishing.

To finish

zest of 1 lemon
micro sorrel
dried cornflowers

Defrost the gâteaux completely then decorate with lemon zest, micro sorrel and dried cornflowers (or whatever flowers and greens you want!).

Opera

An opera is one of the most traditional French pastries around, but it can be very rich and dense. Here I've tried to modernise and lighten it by replacing the buttercream with a coffee milk chocolate whipped ganache. If you have two baking tins it's easier to spread the joconde mix over them both and bake them together, but if you only have one tin you can bake them one after the other. Note that you want to make the whipped ganache a day before everything else, as it needs to chill overnight before whipping.

Makes 21

Coffee chocolate whipped ganache

¼ sheet gelatine
125g milk chocolate
150g cream
2 tsp instant coffee powder

Soak the gelatine sheet in cold water until soft. Drain and put in a bowl with the chocolate. Bring the cream and coffee powder to a boil. Pour over the chocolate and whisk until the mix is smooth and all the chocolate has melted. Strain through a sieve and press a layer of cling film onto the surface of the ganache to prevent a skin forming. Refrigerate overnight.

Cocoa joconde

2 eggs
60g ground almonds
60g icing sugar
40g flour
10g cocoa powder
2 egg whites
20g sugar

Preheat the oven to 190°C and line the tin (or two tins if you have a second one). Whisk the eggs, almonds and icing sugar together until combined. Whisk in the flour and cocoa until smooth. Make a French meringue (page 18) by whisking the egg whites in a stand mixer or with an electric whisk until the egg whites have doubled in size. Add the sugar and continue to whisk until the meringue reaches stiff peaks. Gently fold the meringue into the joconde base until just combined. Spread half the joconde mix in the lined tin, and the other half on a sheet of baking paper to the same size as the tin. If you leave the mix in the bowl while the other half bakes, the egg whites will start to coagulate and when you go to spread it later on you'll lose a lot of the air in the mix trying to get it smooth. If you do have two tins you can spread the mix over both tins and bake at the same time. Bake for 6–8 minutes, until the joconde is just set to the touch. Leave to cool for a few minutes before removing from the tin and putting the second joconde in the tin and then into the oven. Cook as above and leave to cool in the tin.

Coffee syrup

50g water
50g sugar
1 tsp instant coffee powder

Bring the water and sugar to a boil. Once boiling, remove from the heat and whisk in the coffee powder until dissolved. Set aside at room temperature until ready to use.

First layer

Brush half the coffee syrup over the joconde sponge that is still in the tin. Whip half of the coffee ganache (135g) until it reaches stiff peaks. Spread this evenly over the soaked joconde and freeze for at least half an hour or until firm to the touch.

Milk chocolate ganache 1

40g cream
60g milk chocolate

In a small pot, bring the cream to a boil. Remove from the heat and add the chocolate. Stir until the chocolate is completely melted. Pour over the firmed whipped ganache and spread evenly with a palette knife. Return to the freezer for 5–10 minutes to firm up.

Continued overleaf

Autumn

Second layer

Lay the second joconde over the set ganache and press down lightly to adhere them together. Brush the joconde with the remaining coffee syrup. Whip the remaining half of the coffee ganache until it forms stiff peaks and spread evenly over the joconde. Return to the freezer again for another 30 minutes, or until firm to the touch.

Milk chocolate ganache 2

40g cream
60g milk chocolate

In a small pot, bring the cream to a boil. Remove from the heat and add the chocolate into the pot. Stir until the chocolate is completely melted. Pour over the whipped ganache and spread evenly with a palette knife. Freeze overnight, or until solid.

Portioning

(page 22)

Portion the opera into 21 pieces that are 8 x 2cm rectangles. Store in the freezer and defrost fully before finishing.

To finish

100g milk chocolate
gold leaf

Melt the chocolate and then allow to cool to about 35°C. Use a piping bag with a 0.5mm hole to pipe varying-sized dots on top of the ganache for decoration. Finish with gold leaf and allow to defrost fully before serving.

166	Sticky toffee pudding
169	Five textures of chocolate
172	A piece of toast
175	Mandarin and cardamom
177	Mont Blanc
178	Caramel, chocolate and peanut
181	Peppermint slice
182	Cookie caramel chip
184	Tonka chocolate
187	Yuzu and basil
190	Pistachio and yuzu
193	Mulled wine and pear
197	Tiramisu
198	Truffle and white chocolate
200	Ben's Belgian biscuit
203	Bread and butter pudding
205	Kūmara pie
206	Chocolate orange

Winter

Sticky toffee pudding

I fell in love with sticky toffee pudding while working in England. As a classic pub dish, it's hard to escape, and it very quickly became a true comfort food for me. While I think even a bad sticky toffee pudding is still better than no sticky toffee pudding, this one is pretty great. It's soft, moist, flavourful and makes everyone smile.

Makes 24

Sticky toffee cake

100g boiling water
100g pitted dates
½ tsp baking soda
30g soft butter
20g golden syrup
30g brown sugar
2 eggs
80g flour (gluten free, if desired)
1 tsp baking powder

Preheat the oven to 160°C and line the tin. Pour the boiling water over the dates and baking soda. Leave to sit for 15 minutes before blending into a paste with a stick blender (my preferred method) or crushing the dates with the water using a fork or a potato masher. Set aside. Mix the butter, golden syrup and sugar together in a bowl until smooth. Whisk in the eggs one at a time, followed by the date paste. It may be watery and look split at this point, but don't worry. Whisk in the flour and baking powder until well combined. Pour into the lined tin and level out with a palette knife. Bake for 20–25 minutes, until the cake is just set to the touch in the centre. Remove from the oven and allow to cool before using a large bread knife to level off the top of the cake if needed (and eat the scraps!).

Sticky toffee sauce

60g butter
120g brown sugar
30g golden syrup
75g cream
¼ tsp vanilla bean paste
¼ tsp salt

Mix all the ingredients together in a pot. Bring to the boil, whisking constantly, and cook to 105°C. Pour 80g of sauce on top of the trimmed, cooled cake and spread over the surface. Refrigerate the cake while you make the bavarois, and store the remaining sauce in the fridge.

Brown butter bavarois

brown butter bavarois (recipe page 238)

Pour the bavarois over the cooled cake and level off with a palette knife. Freeze overnight or until solid.

Milk chocolate glaze

milk chocolate glaze (recipe page 240)

Glaze the top of the gâteau following the guide on page 21. Allow to set before portioning.

Portioning

(page 22)

Portion the gâteau into 24 pieces that are 4 x 4cm squares. Store in the freezer and defrost before finishing.

To finish

sticky toffee sauce
gold leaf

Spoon the remaining toffee sauce into a piping bag and cut a small 1mm hole. Pipe a zigzag shaped squiggle over the top of each gâteau and finish with a touch of gold leaf.

Five textures of chocolate

This gâteau was created for a restaurant that wanted a chocolate dessert for their menu. One of the hardest things about creating chocolate desserts is trying to make sure they aren't too rich and overwhelming after a large meal, and I think this one fits that brief perfectly. It has been over four years since I developed this gâteau and it still remains one of my favourite chocolate creations.

Makes 21

Chocolate cake

90g water
150g sugar
40g canola or other flavourless oil
90g milk
1 tsp white vinegar
1 egg
80g flour (gluten free, if desired)
35g cocoa powder
½ tsp baking powder
¼ tsp baking soda

Preheat the oven to 160°C and line the tin. In a bowl, whisk the water, sugar, oil, milk, vinegar and egg together until well combined. Whisk in the flour, cocoa, baking powder and baking soda until you have a smooth, runny batter. Pour into the lined tin and bake for 15–20 minutes, until the cake is just set to the touch. Remove from the oven and allow to cool completely.

Hazelnut praline

125g sugar
50g water
250g hazelnuts
canola oil, if needed

Preheat the oven to 180°C and line a baking tray with baking paper. Make a wet caramel (page 19) by cooking the sugar and water together in a small pot over a high heat, without stirring, until you have a light amber-coloured caramel. Pour onto the prepared tray, and leave to cool at room temperature. Roast the hazelnuts for 12 minutes. Break up the caramel into chunks and put in a blender or food processor. Blend until you have a caramel powder. Add the hazelnuts and blend until the hazelnuts and caramel powder turn into a runny paste. This will take a bit of time, and may require you to add one or two tablespoons of canola oil to help the blender loosen the paste. Reserve 20g for the praline and store the rest in an airtight container in the pantry for up to 3 months. It is easier to make a large quantity like this, and it's delicious so you'll use it up quickly! If you can't be bothered making the hazelnut praline, you can use a store-bought chocolate hazelnut spread or hazelnut butter.

Chocolate praline

80g milk chocolate
20g hazelnut praline

Melt the chocolate and praline together in a microwave in 10-second bursts or in a bain-marie until smooth. Pour over the cooled cake and level off with a palette knife. Leave to set at room temperature while you make the milk chocolate mousse.

Milk chocolate mousse

milk chocolate mousse (recipe page 240)

Pour the mousse over the praline and level off with a palette knife. Freeze overnight or until solid.

Continued overleaf

Caramel ganache

30g sugar
60g cream
20g butter
60g milk chocolate
5g cocoa butter

Make a dry caramel (page 19) by cooking the sugar in a pot over a high heat, stirring constantly, until you have a light amber-coloured caramel. Remove from the heat and immediately add the cream, allowing it to bubble up before stirring. Add the butter and whisk to combine. Pour over the chocolate and cocoa butter and whisk until smooth. Remove the gâteau from the tin. Pour the ganache on the top of the left-hand side of the gâteau, and immediately spread the ganache over to the right-hand side using a large palette knife. You want to do this in one go as the ganache will set very quickly. Return to the freezer until ready to portion.

Portioning

(page 22)

Portion the gâteau into 21 pieces that are 8 x 2cm rectangles. Store in the freezer and defrost fully before finishing.

Cocoa tuile

20g butter
15g liquid glucose
15g cocoa powder
30g water
55g sugar
¼ tsp pectin

Preheat the oven to 160°C and line a large baking tray with baking paper. In a small pot, melt the butter, glucose, cocoa and water together. Whisk the sugar and pectin together in a bowl, then whisk this into the pot. Bring to a boil, and boil for 1 minute, whisking constantly. Pour onto the prepared tray and spread into a thin 0.5mm layer. Bake for 15 minutes. Remove from the oven and allow to cool before breaking into shards and storing at room temperature in an airtight container. If the tuile is completely cold but is bendy rather than snapping, put it back in the oven for another 5 minutes.

To finish

cocoa tuile

Plate each gâteau on its side, so you can see all the beautiful layers. Finish with a piece of tuile and serve immediately.

A piece of toast

This gâteau is inspired by all the delicious toasty flavours that come from brown butter. As well as using brown butter in the cake and in the bavarois, we are also using dulce de leche and caramelised white chocolate. These are both created by caramelising the milk solids in their respective mixtures – the same thing that happens when butter is browned, giving us a mouthful of toasty goodness.

Makes 30

Brown butter cake

50g butter
80g brown sugar
1 egg
35g milk
20g canola or other flavourless oil
¼ tsp vanilla bean paste
80g flour (gluten free, if desired)
½ tsp baking powder

Preheat the oven to 180°C and line the tin. Melt the butter in a small pot and cook over a medium heat, whisking constantly, until you get a nutty brown butter. Pour into a bowl, being careful as the butter will be very hot, and leave to cool for 10 minutes before continuing. Whisk the sugar into the butter, followed by the egg, then the milk, oil and vanilla. Once well combined, whisk in the flour and baking powder. Pour into the lined tin and bake for 8–10 minutes, until lightly golden and the cake is just set to the touch. Remove from the oven and allow to cool completely before making the bavarois.

Brown butter bavarois

brown butter bavarois (recipe page 238)

Pour the bavarois over the cooled cake and level off with a palette knife. Freeze overnight, or until solid.

Portioning

(page 22)

Portion the gâteau into 15 pieces that are 5 x 5cm squares, then cut each in half diagonally to create 30 triangles. Store in the freezer until ready to finish.

Caramelised white chocolate chablon

caramelised white chocolate chablon (recipe page 239)

Follow the instructions on page 30 for dipping the gâteaux in chablon, leaving the top exposed, so that the chablon looks like the crust on toast. Return to freezer and store until ready to finish.

Sourdough crumb

100g sourdough bread, crusts removed
40g melted butter
15g sugar

Preheat the oven to 180°C and line a tray of any size with baking paper. Rip the sourdough into small pieces about the size of your fingernail. Toss the bread in a bowl with the butter and sugar until well combined. Spread on the tray and bake for 10–15 minutes, until golden brown, stirring every few minutes. Allow to cool and store in an airtight container at room temperature for up to 1 month.

To finish

250g dulce de leche, or caramelised condensed milk
sourdough crumb
flaky sea salt
gold leaf

Spoon the dulce de leche into a piping bag. Cut a 0.5cm hole in the bag and pipe a thin layer of dulce de leche on top of each toast, swirling it as you go to try to make it seem like it's been spread with a knife. It's very important the toast triangles are still frozen at this point otherwise the bavarois will smush around everywhere when you try to pipe the dulce de leche on top. Place a few sourdough crumbs on top. Sprinkle some salt on top of each piece of toast and decorate with some gold leaf. Allow to defrost fully before serving.

Mandarin and cardamom

Mandarins are so deliciously sweet, and they pair so well with the light cardamom fragrance. Cleaning the pith off the mandarin segments can be a little bit of a pain, but it makes them look so fancy! If you can't be bothered you can either skip it, or use tinned mandarin segments.

Makes 16

Mandarin cardamom syrup

50g mandarin juice
50g sugar
¼ tsp vanilla bean paste
⅛ tsp citric acid
1 cardamom pod, lightly crushed

Mix everything together in a small pot and bring to the boil. Remove from the heat as soon as the mixture boils and leave at room temperature while you make the sponge.

Citrus sponge

30g melted butter
20g canola or other flavourless oil
20g milk
20g orange or lemon juice
1 egg
50g sugar
50g flour (gluten free, if desired)
½ tsp baking powder

Preheat the oven to 180°C and line the tin. In a bowl, whisk the butter, oil, milk, orange or lemon juice, egg and sugar together until well combined. Whisk in the flour and baking powder until smooth. Pour into the lined tin and bake for 12–15 minutes, until lightly golden and the sponge is just set to the touch. Remove from the oven and brush with the mandarin cardamom syrup while still warm. Leave to cool completely before making the cardamom mousse.

Mandarin cardamom mousse

3 sheets gelatine
200g mandarin juice
8 cardamom pods, lightly crushed
200g cream
2 egg whites
90g sugar

Soak the gelatine sheets in cold water until soft. Drain and set aside. Bring the mandarin juice to a boil with the cardamom pods. Remove from the heat and leave to infuse for 5 minutes. Strain off the cardamom pods and stir in the drained gelatine. Whip the cream to medium peaks and set aside while you make the Swiss meringue (page 18). Whisk the egg whites together with the sugar in a bain-marie using a metal bowl. Whisk constantly until the mixture is hot to the touch, or reaches 75°C. Transfer to a stand mixer, or use an electric whisk, to whip the meringue to stiff peaks. Remove from the stand mixer and begin to gently whisk in the mandarin gelatine mix. Once completely combined, fold in the whipped cream. Pour on top of the cooled sponge and freeze for at least 1 hour, or until set to the touch.

Orange jelly

1½ sheets gelatine
2 tsp pectin
1 tbsp sugar
⅛ tsp citric acid
200g orange juice

Soak the gelatine sheets in cold water until soft. Drain and set aside. Whisk the pectin, sugar and citric acid together in a bowl. Bring the orange juice to a boil and whisk in the pectin mix. Boil for 1 minute, whisking constantly. Remove from the heat and whisk in the gelatine. Leave to cool to room temperature before pouring on top of the frozen mousse and spreading evenly with a palette knife. Freeze overnight, or until solid.

Portioning

(page 22)

Portion the gâteau into 16 pieces that are 7 x 3cm rectangles. Store in the freezer and defrost fully before finishing.

To finish

8 mandarins
zest of 1 lime
¼ tsp vanilla bean paste
micro coriander

Peel the mandarins and separate into segments. Use a small paring knife to clean any stringy bits of pith off the mandarins and cut off the straight edge. Cut each segment in half widthways to create little triangles of mandarin. Put the mandarins in a bowl with the lime zest and vanilla and stir to combine. Spoon the mandarins evenly on top of the defrosted petits gâteaux and finish with the micro coriander.

Mont Blanc

The Mont Blanc is a traditional French dessert that consists of chestnut cream, meringue and whipped cream. Its signature is the vermicelli of chestnut cream, which is normally piped tall to represent a mountain. The piping tip for this is the same one that many cake makers use to pipe grass on their cakes, making it super easy to find in any cake decorating store.

Makes 21

Chestnut cake

50g sugar
60g canola or other flavourless oil
50g water
50g chestnut cream
¼ tsp vanilla bean paste
1 egg yolk
55g flour
⅛ tsp baking powder
⅛ tsp baking soda

Preheat the oven to 160°C and line the tin. In a bowl, whisk the sugar, oil, water, chestnut cream, vanilla and egg yolk together until well combined. Whisk in the flour, baking powder and baking soda until smooth. Pour into the lined tin and bake for 12–15 minutes, until the cake is just set to the touch. Allow to cool while you make the blackcurrant gel.

Blackcurrant purée

150g fresh or frozen blackcurrants
100g water

Using a blender, or stick blender, blend the blackcurrants and water together for 1 minute. Pass through a sieve and weigh out 150g of strained purée. Discard the solids, and save the remaining purée for later on (or use it in a soda or G&T!).

Blackcurrant gel

1 sheet gelatine
150g blackcurrant purée
1½ tsp pectin
¼ tsp citric acid
75g sugar

Soak the gelatine sheet in cold water until soft. Drain and set aside. Put the blackcurrant purée into a pot and bring to a boil. Whisk the pectin, citric acid and sugar together in a small bowl and then whisk this into the boiling blackcurrant. Cook for 3 minutes, whisking constantly. Remove from the heat and stir in the gelatine. Pour over the cooled sponge and level off with a palette knife. Freeze for at least 1 hour before making the chestnut mousse.

Chestnut mousse

1½ sheets gelatine
200g chestnut cream
200g cream

Soak the gelatine sheets in cold water until soft. Drain and put into a pot with 20g of the chestnut cream. Cook over a low heat, stirring constantly, until the gelatine is fully melted. Remove from the heat and whisk in the remaining chestnut cream. Set aside to cool while you whip the cream to soft peaks. Once the base has reached about 30°C, or body temperature, fold in the cream until just combined. This mousse will split very easily, so mix it incredibly carefully, stopping as soon as it is fully combined. Pour the mousse over the blackcurrant gel and level off with a palette knife. Freeze overnight, or until solid.

Chestnut vermicelli

350g chestnut cream

Put the chestnut cream in a piping bag with a grass/vermicelli piping tip. Pipe lengths of vermicelli along the width of the chestnut mousse, completely covering the top of the gâteau. Return to the freezer for at least 1 hour, or until the vermicelli is solid.

Portioning

(page 22)

Portion the gâteau into 21 pieces that are 8 x 2cm rectangles. Store in the freezer and defrost fully before finishing.

Mini meringues

1 egg white
60g sugar

Preheat the oven to 90°C and turn the fan off if you can. Whisk the egg white in a stand mixer or with an electric whisk until it is foamy and doubled in size. Add the sugar and continue to whisk until you have a stiff-peaked meringue. Use a piping bag with a small 0.5cm round tip to pipe little kisses (page 32) of meringue on a baking tray. Bake for 2–3 hours, until the meringues are dry to the touch. Allow to cool and store in an airtight container at room temperature.

To finish

mini meringues

Place three mini meringues on top of each gâteau and serve immediately.

Caramel, chocolate and peanut

There is nothing quite as special as the combination of salty peanuts, sweet caramel and delicious dark chocolate. This petit gâteau plays on these classic flavours to create a decadent treat that is sure to please a crowd. You can change it up using different nuts to create different flavours; this pastry would work particularly well with pecans, hazelnuts or macadamias.

Makes 28

Chocolate cake

chocolate cake (recipe page 239)

Once baked, leave to cool completely while you make the peanut chocolate mousse.

Peanut chocolate mousse

1¼ sheets gelatine
150g milk chocolate
75g milk
50g smooth peanut butter
160g cream

Soak the gelatine sheets in cold water until soft. Drain and place in a bowl with the chocolate. Bring the milk to a boil and pour over the chocolate and gelatine. Stir until the chocolate is melted and the mixture is smooth. Whisk in the peanut butter. Whisk the cream to medium peaks and set aside. Check the temperature of the peanut butter base. Once it reaches 30°C, or body temperature, fold in the cream until just combined. Pour over the cooled cake and level off with a palette knife. Freeze overnight, or until solid.

Portioning

(page 22)

Portion the gâteau into 28 pieces that are 3.5 x 3.5cm squares. Store in the freezer until ready to finish.

Soft caramel

90g sugar
45g cream
75g butter

Make a dry caramel (page 19) by cooking the sugar over a high heat, stirring constantly, until you have a deep amber-coloured caramel. Remove from the heat and immediately deglaze with the cream, allowing it to bubble up before stirring so as not to burn yourself on the steam, and scraping the bottom of the pot. Return to the heat and bring to the boil. Remove from the heat and whisk in the butter. Allow to cool for a minute or two before blending with a stick blender to emulsify the butter. Pour into a piping bag and store in the fridge for up to 1 month.

Caramelised peanuts

120g sugar
60g water
150g roasted peanuts

Line a baking tray with baking paper. In a small pot, bring the sugar and water to a boil. Add the peanuts and stir vigorously over a medium heat. The sugar may go all white and crystallised, which is fine, but don't stress if it doesn't. Continue to cook until the crystallised sugar starts to melt and turn into an amber caramel, stirring constantly as the nuts will burn easily once desired colour is reached. Pour onto the prepared tray and leave to cool. Store in an airtight container in the pantry for up to 1 month.

To assemble and finish

soft caramel
caramelised peanuts
flaky salt
dark chocolate chablon (recipe page 239)
gold paint (recipe page 239)

Pipe about a teaspoon of caramel on top of each gâteau square. Stud the caramel with a few pieces of caramelised peanuts and a sprinkle of salt. Dip each gâteau in the chablon, following the instructions on page 30 for fully coating. Allow the chablon to set before flicking gold paint over the gâteaux. Defrost fully before serving.

Peppermint slice

Inspired by the classic After Eight mint chocolates, these are the perfect way to end a meal. The use of cocoa rice puffs may seem odd, but it gives a great crunch to the gâteaux. The technique of cutting circles out of the mint leaves is one I learnt while working in Paris, and really takes the decoration of this pastry to the next level. I always use the mint leaf scraps in my dinners, so they don't go to waste. The egg white coating on the mint leaves is unpasteurised, so if you're serving this to pregnant women or young children either leave the mint uncrystallised, or use pasteurised egg whites, which you can purchase at the supermarket.

Makes 21

Fondant base

100g butter
100g dark chocolate
3 eggs
60g sugar
50g flour
2 tsp peppermint essence

Preheat the oven to 180°C and line the tin. Melt the butter in a small pot. Remove from the heat and whisk in the chocolate until it is fully melted. Transfer to a bowl and whisk in the eggs one at a time until fully combined. Whisk in the sugar, followed by the flour, until the mix is completely smooth. Whisk in the peppermint essence until combined. Pour into the lined tin and bake for 10 minutes, until the base is just set to the touch. Leave to cool completely while you make the cocoa rice crunch.

Cocoa rice crunch

75g dark chocolate
15g coconut oil
1 tsp peppermint essence
50g cocoa rice puffs

Melt the chocolate and coconut oil, stirring until smooth. Stir in the peppermint essence, followed by the rice puffs, mixing until they're completely coated in chocolate. Pour this over the cooled fondant base. Spread with a palette knife to an even layer and set aside at room temperature while you make the mousse.

Peppermint mousse

1 sheet gelatine
100g dark chocolate
80g milk
150g cream
1½ tsp peppermint essence

Soak the gelatine sheet in cold water until soft. Drain and put into a bowl with the chocolate. Bring the milk to a boil in a small pot and pour over the chocolate and gelatine. Whisk to combine until the chocolate is melted. Set aside to cool to 30°C, or body temperature. Whip the cream and peppermint essence to stiff peaks. Once the chocolate mix has cooled down, fold in the whipped cream until just combined. Pour over the cocoa rice crunch and level off with a palette knife. Freeze for at least 2 hours before making the peppermint crème.

Peppermint crème

200g icing sugar
1 tbsp peppermint essence
30g water

Whisk all ingredients together until smooth. Pour over the frozen mousse and spread out to an even layer. Freeze for at least 1 hour or overnight.

Portioning

(page 22)

Portion the gâteau into 21 pieces that are 8 x 2cm rectangles. Store in the freezer until ready to finish.

Crystallised mint leaves

1 egg white
21 large fresh mint leaves
100g sugar

Line a baking tray of any size with baking paper. Whisk the egg white to loosen it slightly. Use a 2cm circle cutter to cut circles out of the mint leaves. Dunk each mint round in egg white, then toss in the sugar. Place on the prepared tray and repeat with the remaining mint rounds. Leave at room temperature for at least 2 hours, but preferably overnight, to allow the sugar to crystallise. Store for up to 3 days in an airtight container.

Dark chocolate chablon

dark chocolate chablon (recipe page 239)

Dip each gâteau in the chablon, following the instructions on page 30 for fully coating. Finish the gâteaux as below before the chablon sets.

To finish

crystallised mint leaves

Place a crystallised mint round on the corner of each gâteau before the chablon sets. Defrost fully before serving.

Winter

Cookie caramel chip

This gâteau is inspired by the sweet-salty combination that works so well with milk chocolate and salted caramel. The potato chips add a great texture, as well as making this gâteau fun and playful. The whipped caramel needs to chill overnight before whipping, so make sure to include that in your prep time.

Makes 24

Whipped caramel

whipped caramel (recipe page 242)

Chill the whipped caramel overnight before using as instructed below.

Cookie base

100g butter
60g brown sugar
50g caster sugar
½ tsp vanilla extract
1 egg
125g flour (gluten free, if desired)
⅛ tsp baking powder
⅛ tsp baking soda
½ tsp cornflour
100g roughly chopped milk chocolate

Preheat the oven to 170°C and line the tin. Cook the butter in a small pot over a medium heat, whisking constantly, making sure to scrape the base of the pot as you whisk, as some of the milk solids in the butter will stick and burn quite easily. Continue to cook until the butter is a deep, toasty brown. Pour into a bowl and leave to cool for 15 minutes. Be careful as the butter will be very hot. Whisk both sugars into the butter, followed by the vanilla and the egg. Use a spatula to stir in the flour, baking powder, baking soda and cornflour. When almost combined, add the chocolate and continue to stir until fully combined. Press the cookie dough into the lined tin. Bake for 10–12 minutes, until lightly golden and puffed at the edges. Allow to cool completely before starting the milk chocolate mousse.

Milk chocolate mousse

milk chocolate mousse (recipe page 240)

Spread the mousse over the cooled cookie base and freeze overnight, or until solid.

Portioning

(page 22)

Portion the gâteau into 24 pieces that are 7 x 2cm rectangles. Store in the freezer until ready to finish.

Chablon

20g ready salted potato chips, lightly crushed
milk chocolate chablon (recipe page 239)

Stir the crushed chips into the chablon. Follow the instructions on page 30 for dipping the gâteaux in chablon, leaving the top exposed. Store in the freezer and defrost fully before finishing.

Caramel sauce

75g sugar
75g cream, boiled and set aside
15g butter

Make a dry caramel (page 19) by cooking the sugar over a high heat, stirring constantly, until you have a smooth amber-coloured caramel. Remove the pot from the heat and immediately add the cream. Allow the cream to bubble before stirring to avoid burning yourself on the steam. Whisk in the butter, return to the heat and boil for 30 seconds to help thicken the caramel. Chill until ready to use.

To finish

whipped caramel
caramel sauce
20g ready salted potato chips

Whip the whipped caramel to stiff peaks using an electric whisk or stand mixer. Spoon into a piping bag with a 1cm round nozzle. Pipe three kisses of whipped caramel on top of each gâteau. Follow the instructions on page 32 for creating an indent in the kisses. Using a piping bag, fill each cavity with the caramel sauce. Finish with a salted chip standing up between each caramel kiss just before serving, so that the potato chip stays fresh and crisp.

Winter

Tonka chocolate

This recipe is inspired by the toasty flavours of a campfire. The torched meringue, mixed with the scent of the tonka bean, creates a rich, almost smoky flavour. If you can't find tonka beans, don't stress, this gâteau will still be incredibly delicious. It really is one of my favourite chocolate desserts.

Makes 28

Cocoa base

80g melted butter
100g sugar
100g flour (gluten free, if desired)
60g cocoa powder

Preheat the oven to 150°C and line the tin. Mix all the ingredients together until you have a crumbly mixture. Press into the base of the lined tin and bake for 10 minutes. Leave to cool completely while you make the cheesecake filling.

Cheesecake filling

250g cream cheese
120g mascarpone
30g sugar
1 egg
60g dark chocolate
1 tbsp cocoa powder

Preheat the oven to 125°C. In the bowl of a stand mixer with the paddle attachment, or in a bowl with a spatula, stir the cream cheese until soft and smooth. Add the mascarpone and mix until well combined, followed by the sugar. Whisk in the egg. Melt the chocolate, and gently whisk this into the cheesecake filling. Finally, whisk in the cocoa. Pour the cheesecake mix over the cooled cocoa base and level off with a palette knife. Bake for 30–45 minutes, until the cheesecake is just set in the centre and lightly puffed at the edges. Remove from the oven and allow to cool to room temperature before freezing overnight, or until solid.

Portioning

(page 22)

Portion the cheesecake into 28 pieces that are 3.5 x 3.5cm squares. Store in the freezer until ready to finish.

Chocolate chablon

milk chocolate chablon (recipe page 239)

Follow the instructions on page 30 for dipping the gâteaux in chablon, leaving the top exposed. Store in the freezer and defrost fully before finishing.

Chocolate squiggles

150g milk chocolate

Lay a sheet of baking paper on the bench. Temper the chocolate following the instructions on page 24. Spoon the chocolate into a piping bag and cut a small 1mm hole. Follow the instructions on page 29 for piping squiggle decorations, making them about the same size as the gâteaux.

To finish

Swiss meringue (recipe page 241)
chocolate squiggles
1 tonka bean

Spoon the Swiss meringue into a piping bag fitted with a 1cm round tip. Pipe a round kiss (page 32) of meringue on top of each gâteau. Lightly torch the meringue with a blowtorch if you have one, or leave it as is if you don't. Press a chocolate squiggle into each meringue kiss and finish with a light grating of tonka bean.

Yuzu and basil

Yuzu is such a special flavour to me. I don't remember where I first tasted it, but I know the first pastry I ever made with it. It was also the first pastry of mine that my now parents-in-law tasted. It was before they'd even met me, and it secured my place in the family pretty early on! Since then yuzu has become somewhat of a signature flavour of mine, and I think this pastry showcases it perfectly.

Makes 28

Yuzu cake

30g melted butter
50g sugar
1 egg
20g canola or other flavourless oil
20g yuzu juice
50g flour (gluten free, if desired)
½ tsp baking powder

Preheat the oven to 170°C and line the tin. Whisk the butter and sugar together in a bowl until well combined, then whisk in the egg, followed by the oil and yuzu juice, and then the flour and baking powder. Pour into the lined tin and bake for 10–12 minutes, until lightly golden and the cake is just set to the touch. Leave to cool completely while you make the yuzu marmalade.

Yuzu marmalade

150g yuzu juice
¼ tsp vanilla bean paste
fine zest of 2 lemons (or yuzu if you're lucky enough to have a fresh one)
100g sugar
1 tsp pectin

Put the yuzu juice and vanilla in a small pot. Add the lemon zest and bring to a boil. Whisk the sugar and pectin together and whisk this into the boiling yuzu juice. Cook to 105°C and pour over the cooled cake. Spread with a palette knife and leave to cool at room temperature.

Yuzu basil crémeux

15g basil
50g sugar
70g yuzu juice
½ sheet gelatine
1 egg
50g butter

Put the basil, sugar and yuzu juice in a pot. Bring to a boil, remove from the heat and cover with a lid or cling film. Leave to infuse for 30 minutes then pour through a sieve into a small pot. Discard the basil. Soak the gelatine sheet in cold water until soft, then drain and set aside. Whisk the egg into the infused yuzu and bring to a boil, whisking constantly. Once boiled, remove from the heat and whisk in the gelatine. Cool to 45°C then blend the butter in with a stick blender. Pour on top of the marmalade and level off with a palette knife. Freeze for at least 1 hour before making the yuzu basil mousse.

Continued overleaf

Yuzu basil mousse

25g basil
120g yuzu juice
1½ sheets gelatine
100g cream
1 egg white
45g sugar

Bring the basil and yuzu juice to a boil in a small pot. Remove from the heat, cover with a lid or cling film and leave to infuse for 30 minutes. Soak the gelatine sheets in cold water until soft then place in a pot. Strain the yuzu juice into the pot with the gelatine. Heat gently, stirring constantly, until the gelatine is fully melted. Remove from the heat and set aside. Whip the cream to medium peaks and set aside. Make a Swiss meringue (page 18) by whisking the egg white and sugar together in a bain-marie using a metal bowl, whisking constantly until the mixture reaches 75°C or is hot to the touch. Remove from the heat and whisk with an electric whisk or stand mixer until the meringue is doubled in size. Gently whisk in the yuzu juice, then fold in the cream until just combined. Pour over the frozen crémeux and level off with a palette knife. Freeze overnight, or until solid.

Yellow glaze

coloured glaze (recipe page 239), coloured yellow

Glaze the top of the gâteaux, following the instructions on page 21, and allow the glaze to set for a few minutes before portioning.

Portioning

(page 22)

Portion the gâteau into 28 pieces that are 3.5 x 3.5cm squares. Store frozen and defrost before finishing.

To finish

baby basil
store-bought candied citrus peel

Just before serving, decorate the top of each gâteau with sprigs of baby basil and a few pieces of candied citrus peel.

Pistachio and yuzu

Everyone who knows me well has been shocked by my recent conversion to pistachio! For years it has been a flavour that I just couldn't bring myself to like, but after trying pistachio and yuzu together, I was converted. The sharp yuzu helps to brighten the earthy pistachio flavour, and mixed with the sweetness of the white chocolate it becomes a winning flavour combination.

Makes 16

Yuzu cake

30g melted butter
50g sugar
1 egg
20g canola or other flavourless oil
20g yuzu juice
½ tsp baking powder
50g flour (gluten free, if desired)

Preheat the oven to 170°C and line the tin. Whisk the butter and sugar together in a bowl, then whisk in the egg. Add the oil and yuzu juice and whisk to combine, followed by the baking powder and flour. Once you have a smooth batter, pour into the lined tin and bake for 10–12 minutes, until the cake is just set to the touch. Allow to cool completely while you make the yuzu crémeux.

Yuzu crémeux

yuzu crémeux (recipe page 242)

Pour the yuzu crémeux over the cooled sponge, level off with a palette knife and freeze while you make the pistachio mousse.

Pistachio mousse

1¼ sheets gelatine
110g white chocolate
90g milk
50g pistachio paste
120g cream

Soak the gelatine sheets in cold water until soft. Drain and put in a bowl with the white chocolate. Bring the milk to a boil in a small pot and pour over the gelatine and chocolate. Whisk until smooth, then whisk in the pistachio paste. Blend with a stick blender to fully emulsify the pistachio. Set aside and whip the cream to medium peaks. Check the temperature of the mousse base, once it's around 30°C, or body temperature, fold the cream in until just combined. Pour this over the frozen crémeux and level off with a palette knife. Freeze overnight, or until solid.

Portioning

(page 22)

Portion the gâteau into 16 pieces that are 7 x 3cm rectangles. Store in the freezer and defrost before finishing.

Pistachio-green chocolate curls

200g white chocolate, coloured pistachio green (page 24)

Temper and colour the chocolate following the instructions on page 24. Follow the guide to making curved chocolate decorations on page 27, spreading the chocolate over an A4 sheet of acetate and wrapping around a rolling pin. Allow to set fully before unrolling, allowing the chocolate to break into organic shards approximately the same size as the gâteaux. Store in an airtight container in the pantry for up to 1 month.

To finish

pistachio-green chocolate curls
liquid glucose
50g pistachios, roughly chopped
edible flowers

Place a pistachio-green chocolate curl on top of each gâteau. Use glucose as small drops of glue to stick pieces of pistachio to the chocolate. Do the same with the flowers.

Mulled wine and pear

The smell of mulled wine takes me back to the Christmas markets in Paris. I'm not a red wine fan, and didn't think I'd like mulled wine, but I was so cold I thought I would give it a go, and I was in love! This pastry is inspired by that warm fuzzy feeling you get when the scent of spiced mulled wine appears on the coldest of days. The veil technique is one I learnt working at Sketch, in London, and is such a cool way to create a natural shape and texture while working with the rectangular tin.

Makes 28

Mulled wine

750g merlot
50g fresh orange juice
2 cinnamon sticks
4 cloves
3 lightly crushed cardamom pods
100g brown sugar

Bring all the ingredients to a boil in a large pot and simmer over a low heat for 15 minutes. Leave to cool before straining through a sieve. This recipe isn't cooked as much as it would be if we were making it just for drinking, as it will reduce down more in the recipes we use it in.

Mulled wine pâte de fruit

135g mulled wine
135g pear purée (page 12) or pure pear juice
30g sugar
2½ tsp pectin
¾ tsp citric acid
150g sugar
50g liquid glucose

Bring the mulled wine and pear purée or juice to a boil in a small pot. In a bowl, whisk the first measure of sugar, pectin and citric acid together and then whisk this into the boiling mulled wine mixture. Bring back to the boil, then add the second measure of sugar and glucose. Whisk constantly while boiling to cook to 108°C, or until the mixture sets within 30 seconds of being dripped onto a plate. Pour over the cooled cake and allow to set at room temperature. Once cool, begin to make the vanilla mousse.

Ginger cake

60g butter
115g golden syrup
125g milk
60g brown sugar
1 egg yolk
110g flour
1 tsp baking powder
½ tsp baking soda
½ tsp ground ginger
½ tsp ground cinnamon

Preheat the oven to 170°C and line the tin. Melt the butter and golden syrup together in a small pot over a low heat until liquid. Transfer to a bowl and whisk in the milk, sugar and egg yolk until well combined. Whisk in the flour, baking powder, baking soda, ginger and cinnamon until well combined. The mix will be very runny. Pour into the lined tin and bake for 15–20 minutes, until the cake is just set to the touch, especially in the centre. As the mixture is quite runny the cake can take longer to bake. Remove from the oven and leave to cool. If the cake has domed in the middle, level it off with a large serrated knife so you get a nice flat layer.

Vanilla mousse

1 sheet gelatine
80g mascarpone
20g brown sugar
¼ tsp vanilla bean paste
¼ tsp vanilla extract
120g cream

Soak the gelatine sheet in cold water until soft. Drain and put in a pot with 40g of the mascarpone, sugar, vanilla paste and extract. Cook over a very low heat, stirring constantly, until the mix is smooth and the gelatine has melted. Remove from the heat and allow to cool to 30°C, or body temperature. Whip the cream and remaining mascarpone to medium peaks while you wait for the base mixture to cool. Fold the cream into the cooled base until just combined. It can be hard to see if the mousse is properly combined because the base and the cream are such similar colours, so give it a small mix with a whisk to make sure everything is well incorporated. Pour over the pâte de fruit and level off with a palette knife. Freeze overnight, or until solid.

Portioning

(page 22)

Portion the gâteaux into 28 pieces that are 3.5 x 3.5cm squares. Store in the freezer and defrost fully before finishing.

Continued overleaf

Mulled wine veil

180g mulled wine
25g sugar
1 tsp pectin
½ tsp agar-agar

Spray a baking tray that's approximately 40 x 30cm with spray oil, or cut a sheet of baking paper the same size and lay it on a heat-proof surface (the kitchen counter should be fine), and spray with spray oil. Get a large palette knife ready if using the baking paper. Bring the mulled wine to a boil in a small pot. Whisk the sugar, pectin and agar-agar together in a small bowl. Whisk this into the boiling wine and reduce to a simmer. Simmer for 30 seconds, then begin to test the set by spooning a small drop onto a plate. It should set solid within 30 seconds. Continue to simmer and repeat this test until the set point is reached. Pour the mixture onto the oiled tray or baking paper. If you're using the tray, lift it up and rotate it to allow the mix to evenly coat the base in a thin layer. If you're using the baking paper, pour the mix onto the paper and immediately spread it out using a palette knife to cover the whole sheet as quickly as possible. The mixture will set incredibly quickly. Once it starts to set, stop moving it, even if it's not covering the baking paper fully. Once set, use a 5cm round cutter to cut 28 circles out of the veil. Use a palette knife to gently lift each round up and lay them over the defrosted gâteaux. If needed, you can melt the offcuts of the veil over a very low heat and repeat the spreading process to get more veils.

To finish

fresh or dried flowers
micro sorrel

Decorate the top of the veils with fresh or dried flowers and a few pieces of micro sorrel.

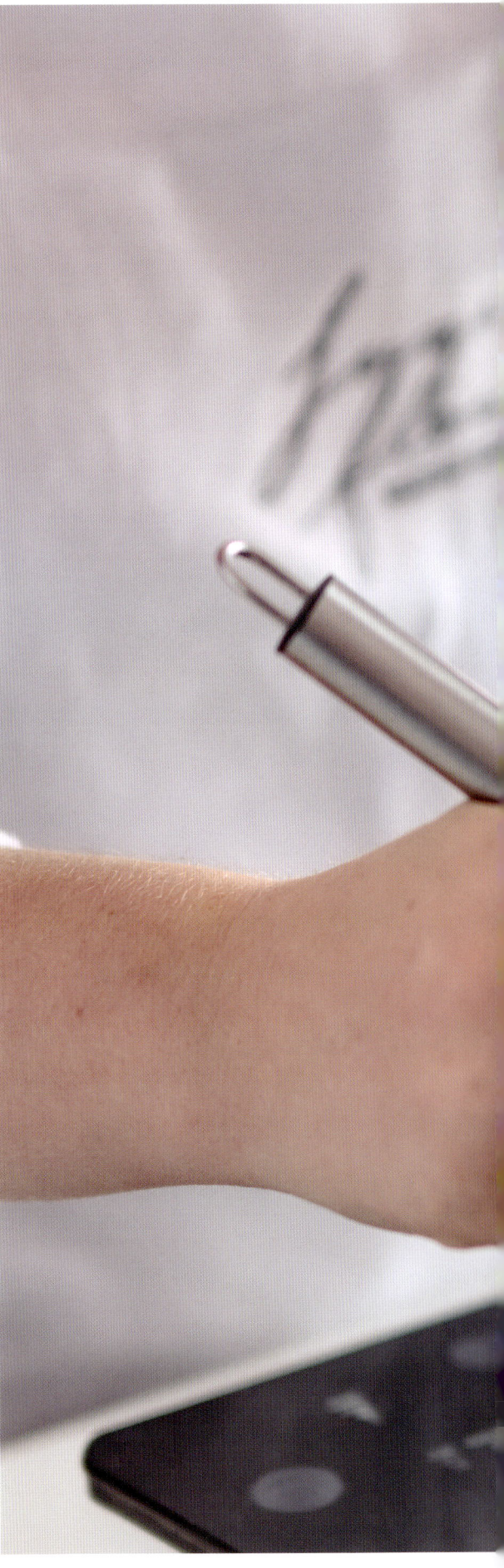

Tiramisu

I don't think there is a dessert that is more universally loved than tiramisu. It's hard to improve on a classic, so I haven't messed with it too much — I have merely adapted the traditional recipe to fit in the petit gâteau form. Store-bought savoiardi or ladyfinger biscuits are much drier than homemade ones, which means they can soak up more coffee, making the perfect tiramisu.

Makes 20

Coffee soak

400g fresh brewed coffee
50g sugar
20g marsala wine

Whisk all the ingredients together and store in the fridge while you make the sabayon cream.

Sabayon cream

4 egg yolks
100g sugar
350g mascarpone
100g cream
¼ tsp vanilla bean paste

To make the sabayon base, whisk the egg yolks and sugar together in a metal bowl over a pot of simmering water until it reaches 75°C. Remove from the heat and using a stand mixer or electric whisk, whisk the egg yolk until it's very light in colour and has reached ribbon stage (page 18). While this is whisking, whip the mascarpone, cream and vanilla to medium peaks. Fold the sabayon mix into the mascarpone cream until just combined. Use immediately to assemble the tiramisu as instructed.

To assemble

50g milk chocolate
40 savoiardi biscuits
coffee soak
sabayon cream
cocoa powder

Line the tin with baking paper. Melt the chocolate. Use a pastry brush to spread all of the chocolate over the base of the tin. Refrigerate for 5 minutes to set the chocolate slightly. Dunk 20 savoiardi biscuits in the coffee soak, placing each one in the tin on top of the chocolate until the base is completely covered, breaking some of the biscuits into smaller pieces if needed. Spread half the sabayon cream on top and level it off with a palette knife. Dust with an even layer of cocoa then repeat with the remaining biscuits and cream. Freeze overnight or until solid. You might not use all the biscuits, depending on the size of biscuits you've purchased.

Portioning

(page 22)

Portion the tiramisu into 20 pieces that are 2.5 x 7cm rectangles. Store in the freezer until ready to finish.

Milk chocolate chablon

milk chocolate chablon (recipe page 239)

Follow the instructions on page 30 for dipping the gâteaux in chablon, leaving the top exposed. Store in the freezer and defrost before finishing.

Mascarpone cream

150g cream
150g mascarpone
1 tbsp icing sugar
1 tbsp marsala wine

Whisk everything together to form stiff peaks. Spoon into a piping bag with a 1cm Saint Honoré tip (page 33) and use immediately to finish the gâteaux.

To finish

mascarpone cream
cocoa powder
gold leaf

Pipe lines of mascarpone cream lengthwise down the top of each gâteau. Dust with cocoa and finish with gold leaf.

Truffle and white chocolate

There is nothing quite as decadent as truffle. It can be a very polarising flavour, and there is a fine balance when using it in sweet preparations so that it is not overpowering. Paired with white chocolate and honey, the truffle in these petits gâteaux really shines. Using a high quality white truffle oil allows us to get a beautiful truffle flavour without breaking the bank, although I couldn't help but splurge on a fresh truffle for garnish when photographing this recipe! It will still look beautiful without the fresh truffle, and will taste just as delicious too.

Makes 28

Truffle sponge

60g melted butter
100g sugar
2 eggs
40g white truffle oil
40g milk
100g flour (gluten free, if desired)
1 tsp baking powder

Preheat the oven to 190°C and line the tin. Whisk the butter, sugar, eggs, truffle oil and milk together until well combined. Whisk flour and baking powder until smooth and pour into the lined tin. Bake for 10–12 minutes, until lightly golden and the sponge is just set to the touch. Leave to cool completely before you make the truffle white chocolate mousse.

Truffle white chocolate mousse

1½ sheets gelatine
100g white chocolate
30g water
30g honey
10g white truffle oil
200g cream

Soak the gelatine sheets in cold water until soft. Drain and put in a bowl with the chocolate. In a small pot, bring the water and honey to a boil. Once boiling, remove from the heat and tip in the chocolate and gelatine. Stir to combine until the chocolate is fully melted, then stir in the truffle oil. Pour into a bowl and leave to cool while you whip the cream to stiff peaks. Once the chocolate mix has cooled to at least 30°C, or body temperature, fold the cream in gently until just combined. Pour on top of the cooled sponge and freeze overnight, or until solid.

Portioning

(page 22)

Portion the gâteau into 28 pieces that are 3.5 x 3.5cm squares. Store in the freezer.

Black cocoa crumb

15g flour (gluten free, if desired)
15g sugar
10g black cocoa
15g melted butter

Preheat the oven to 150°C and line a baking tray or tin of any size with baking paper. Mix all the ingredients together in a bowl until you have large crumbs of dough. Pour onto the prepared tray or tin. Bake for 10 minutes, then leave to cool before pulsing in a blender to create a fine crumb.

Truffle chablon

300g white chocolate
10g white truffle oil
25g canola or other flavourless oil
black cocoa crumb

Melt the chocolate and both oils together, stirring until smooth. Stir in the black cocoa crumb. Dip each gâteau in the chablon, following the instructions on page 30 for fully coating. Store in the freezer and defrost before finishing.

Honey cream

100g cream
100g mascarpone
50g honey

Whisk all ingredients together until you have stiff peaks. Use a teaspoon to quenelle (page 30) the honey cream on top of each gâteau.

To finish

fresh black or white truffle (optional) or gold leaf

Use a very sharp vegetable peeler or a mandolin on a very thin setting to shave off rounds of fresh truffle. Place a truffle round on top of each quenelle. Alternatively, finish with some gold leaf.

Ben's Belgian biscuit

This gâteau is inspired by my husband Ben and his favourite lunchtime treat: the Belgian biscuit from a local bakery. These spiced biscuits are filled with raspberry jam and topped with icing sugar glaze. I've taken these elements and turned them into this gâteau, topped with a mini Belgian biscuit to finish. Using raspberry essence in the whipped ganache adds a hint of Kiwi nostalgia to the gâteaux. Like all whipped ganaches, it needs to chill overnight before being whipped.

Makes 20

Raspberry whipped ganache

¼ sheet gelatine
75g white chocolate
100g cream
¼ tsp vanilla bean paste
¼ tsp raspberry essence

Soak the gelatine sheet in cold water until soft. Drain and put into a bowl with the chocolate. Bring the cream and vanilla to a boil in a small pot and pour over the chocolate. Whisk until the chocolate is fully melted. Whisk in the raspberry essence and refrigerate overnight.

Spice cake

60g butter
115g golden syrup
125g milk
60g brown sugar
1 egg yolk
110g flour
1 tsp baking powder
½ tsp baking soda
1 tsp ground cinnamon
½ tsp ground ginger

Preheat the oven to 160°C and line two tins with baking paper (if you have two, otherwise you'll bake one cake after the other). Put the butter and golden syrup in a pot and cook over a low heat until the butter has fully melted. Remove from the heat and whisk in the milk and sugar. Whisk in the egg yolk until well combined, then whisk in the flour, baking powder, baking soda, cinnamon and ginger until you have a smooth mixture. Pour 240g of cake mixture into each tin and bake for 15–20 minutes, until the cake is set to the touch in the middle. Remove from the oven and allow to cool. Use a large serrated knife to level off the cakes so they have a flat top. Cool completely. Whip the chilled ganache to stiff peaks. Spread over one of the cakes, then top with the second cake. Press slightly to join them together. Freeze for at least 1 hour before making the raspberry compote.

Raspberry compote

raspberry compote (recipe page 240)

Pour on top of the frozen cake and level off with a palette knife. Return to the freezer and freeze overnight, or until solid.

Portioning

(page 22)

Portion the gâteau into 20 pieces that are 2.5 x 7cm rectangles. Store in the freezer and defrost fully before finishing.

Belgian biscuit

60g soft butter
50g brown sugar
1 egg yolk
125g flour
½ tsp baking powder
1 tsp ground cinnamon
½ tsp ground ginger
½ tsp mixed spice

Preheat the oven to 180°C and line a baking tray with baking paper. Use a spatula to mix the butter and sugar together until well combined. Stir in the egg yolk, then fold in the remaining ingredients. Mix until you have a smooth but soft dough. Roll the dough out between two sheets of baking paper to 1–2mm thick. Freeze the dough for a minimum of 10 minutes before cutting out 2.5cm circles. You will need at least 40. Place on the prepared tray and bake for 8–10 minutes, or until the biscuits are slightly golden on the edges. Remove from the oven and allow to cool.

Raspberry jam

100g seedless raspberry purée (page 12)
30g sugar
2½ tsp cornflour

Bring the raspberry purée to a boil in small pot. Whisk the sugar and cornflour together and whisk this into the boiling raspberry mixture. Continue to boil, whisking constantly, for about 1 minute, until you have a thick, jammy consistency. Allow to cool before spooning into a piping bag. Pipe about a quarter of a teaspoon of jam on half of the cooled biscuits, sandwiching each one with another biscuit. Use the icing recipe below to ice the biscuits.

Belgian biscuit icing

85g icing sugar
15g raspberry jam
1–2 tsp cold water
freeze-dried raspberries

Whisk the icing sugar and raspberry jam together. Whisk in cold water, a teaspoon at a time, until you have a smooth but thick, pipeable icing. Either pipe the icing on top of each biscuit, or spoon the icing on top. Sprinkle the top with some freeze-dried raspberry pieces. Store the biscuits in an airtight container and use them within 2 days to decorate the gâteaux.

To finish

iced Belgian biscuits

Place an iced Belgian biscuit on top of each defrosted gâteau. Serve immediately.

Bread and butter pudding

Traditional bread and butter pudding is delicious, but like almost anything else in the world, it's even better with the addition of chocolate. I've done many tests with this recipe using all different kinds of bread – brioche, challah, homemade and store-bought – and I have to say, my favourite version is with white sandwich bread from the supermarket. It absorbs the chocolate custard better than any of the other breads, resulting in the most delightful custardy texture. Don't forget to let your ganache chill overnight before whipping.

Makes 20

Chocolate custard

50g butter
220g milk
100g milk chocolate
2 tbsp cocoa powder
60g sugar
2 eggs

Put the butter and milk in a pot and bring to a boil. Remove from the heat and whisk in the chocolate. Once fully melted, whisk in the cocoa and sugar, followed by the eggs, whisking until you have a smooth custard. If you have any lumps, pour the custard through a sieve to get rid of them. Set aside at room temperature until cool enough to handle, about 5–10 minutes.

Pudding base

1 loaf white sandwich bread, crusts removed
chocolate custard

Preheat the oven to 125°C and line the tin. Dip each slice of bread in the custard, coating both sides, then place in the tin. Repeat with all the slices, shingling them so they slightly overlap. You should have at least two layers of bread. Pour any extra custard on top and press the bread down to help the custard soak in. Bake for 20–25 minutes, until the pudding appears set with a slight jiggle in the centre. Leave to cool before freezing for at least 2 hours.

Vanilla anglaise

¼ sheet gelatine
100g cream
200g milk
¼ tsp vanilla bean paste
2 egg yolks
50g sugar

Soak the gelatine sheet in cold water until soft. Drain and set aside in a bowl. Bring the cream, milk and vanilla to a boil. Whisk the egg yolks and sugar together in a bowl. Pour a small amount of the hot milk over the yolks and whisk to combine, then return all of the mixture to the pot. Whisk thoroughly, then return to a low heat, stirring constantly with a spatula, until the anglaise starts to thicken, or reaches 75°C. Remove from the heat and pour into the bowl with the gelatine, stirring until the gelatine has melted. Allow to cool to room temperature before pouring over the frozen pudding. Level off with a palette knife and freeze overnight, or until solid.

Portioning

(page 22)

Portion the gâteau into 20 pieces that are 7 x 2.5cm rectangles. Store frozen until ready to finish.

Milk chocolate chablon

milk chocolate chablon (recipe page 239)

Dip each gâteau in the chablon, following the instructions on page 30, for fully coating. Return to the freezer and defrost before finishing.

To finish

milk chocolate whipped ganache (recipe page 240)
cocoa nibs
gold leaf

Use a 1cm round piping tip to pipe three kisses (page 32) of whipped ganache on each gâteau. Sprinkle with cocoa nibs and gold leaf to finish.

Winter

Kūmara pie

I wanted to make a New Zealand version of the American pumpkin pie. Kūmara has a very similar flavour profile to pumpkin, making it an easy swap. Finished with speculoos to enhance the cinnamon flavour, you will never go back to pumpkin pie again!

Makes 22

Brown sugar base

100g melted butter
100g brown sugar
1 tsp ground cinnamon
150g flour (gluten free, if desired)

Preheat the oven to 160°C and line the tin. Put the butter, sugar, cinnamon and flour in a bowl. Mix together until you have a slightly crumbly dough. Press into the tin and bake for 10–12 minutes, until slightly puffed. Remove from the oven and leave to cool while you make the pie filling.

Kūmara purée

2 medium-sized orange kūmara (approximately 500g)

Preheat the oven to 180°C and line a baking tray with baking paper. Cut the kūmara in half lengthwise and place cut side down on the prepared tray. Bake for 30–40 minutes, until the kūmara are bubbling at the edges and are soft when pierced with a fork. Leave to cool before removing the skins. Blend the flesh until smooth and weigh out 300g of purée. Freeze the remaining purée for later use (or use it to make something fun for dinner!).

Kūmara pie filling

300g kumara purée
90g brown sugar
1 tsp ground cinnamon
⅛ tsp salt
225g cream
2 eggs

Preheat the oven to 125°C. Blend all the ingredients together until smooth. Pour over the brown sugar base. Bake for 45–60 minutes, turning halfway through. The filling is baked when it is slightly puffed on the edges and is just set in the middle. Remove from the oven and allow to cool to room temperature before storing in the fridge.

Speculoos topping

125g smooth speculoos spread

Melt the speculoos spread until it's runny, either in a bain-marie or in the microwave in 10-second bursts. Pour over the pie filling and spread over the top with an offset palette knife. Freeze overnight, or until solid.

Portioning

(page 22)

Allow the pie to sit at room temperature for 5 minutes before portioning. Portion into 22 pieces that are 4 x 7 x 7cm triangles. Store in the freezer and defrost before finishing.

Cinnamon cream

100g cream
100g mascarpone
30g icing sugar
1 tsp ground cinnamon

Whisk everything together until it forms stiff peaks. Spoon into a piping bag with a 1cm Saint Honoré tip (page 33). Use immediately to finish the gâteaux.

To finish

cinnamon cream
ground cinnamon

Pipe a small squiggle of cinnamon cream on top of each gâteau. Dust lightly with cinnamon. Defrost fully before serving.

Winter

Chocolate orange

Chocolate and orange is such a classic flavour combination, and I wanted to create a gâteau that spoke to the simplicity of this flavour pairing, using just a few simple elements. Finished with a slice of candied orange peel, the decoration is just as simple as the gâteau itself, but equally beautiful. You can make the candied orange yourself, but store-bought works just as well.

Makes 16

Chocolate cake

100g flour (gluten free, if desired)
100g sugar
20g cocoa powder
½ tsp baking soda
40g canola or other flavourless oil
½ tbsp white vinegar
110g water

Preheat the oven to 170°C and line the tin. Whisk the flour, sugar, cocoa and baking soda together in a bowl, then whisk in the oil, vinegar and water until smooth. Pour into the lined tin and bake for 15–20 minutes, until the cake is just set to the touch. Remove from the oven and allow to cool to room temperature before storing in the freezer while you make the orange gel.

Orange gel

1½ sheets gelatine
200g fresh orange juice
zest of 2 oranges
½ tsp vanilla bean paste
20g sugar
2 tsp pectin
¼ tsp citric acid

Soak the gelatine sheets in cold water until soft. Drain and set aside. In a pot, bring the orange juice, zest and vanilla to a boil. Whisk the sugar, pectin and citric acid together, then whisk this into the boiling orange mixture. Cook over a medium heat, whisking constantly, for 1 minute. Remove from the heat and stir in the gelatine. Allow to cool to room temperature before pouring over the cake. Level off with a palette knife and return to the freezer. Allow to freeze for at least 1 hour before making the dark chocolate mousse.

Dark chocolate mousse

dark chocolate mousse (recipe page 239)

Pour the mousse over the orange gel, level off with a palette knife and freeze overnight, or until frozen solid.

Portioning

(page 22)

Portion the gâteau into 16 pieces that are 7 x 3cm rectangles. Store in the freezer until ready to finish.

To finish

dark chocolate chablon (recipe page 239)
candied orange peel

Dip each gâteau in the chablon, following the instructions on page 30 for fully coating. Before the chocolate sets, decorate with a piece of candied orange peel and allow to defrost fully before serving.

Winter

210 Easter egg nest
212 Tropical egg
215 Hot cross buns
216 Speculoos bûche de Noël
219 Boysenberry bûche de Noël
223 White forest
225 Pfeffernüsse Christmas tree
226 Berry pavlova
228 Russian honey cake
231 Tarte tatin
234 Birthday cake

Celebrations

Easter egg nest

Being Jewish, we never celebrated Easter growing up, but my mum would always buy us a Crunchie Easter egg, which is what inspired this gâteau. The hokey pokey crushed in the chablon is what transports me back to those Easter egg treats.

Makes 28

Chocolate cake

chocolate cake (recipe page 239)

Once baked, allow the cake to cool completely before making the caramel crémeux.

Caramel crémeux

caramel crémeux (recipe page 238)

Spread the caramel crémeux over the cooled chocolate cake and store in the freezer while you make the milk chocolate mousse.

Milk chocolate mousse

½ sheet gelatine
150g milk chocolate
75g milk
160g cream

Soak the gelatine sheet in cold water until soft. Drain and put in a bowl with the chocolate. Bring the milk to a boil in a small pot and pour over the gelatine and chocolate. Whisk until the chocolate is melted. Leave to cool to 30°C, or body temperature, while you whip the cream to medium peaks. Fold the cream into the chocolate base until just combined. Pour over the caramel crémeux and freeze overnight, or until solid.

Portioning

(page 22)

Portion the gâteau into 28 pieces that are 3.5 x 3.5cm squares. Store in the freezer until ready to finish.

Hokey pokey chablon

hokey pokey (recipe page 239)
caramelised white chocolate chablon (recipe page 239)

Crush 40g of the hokey pokey into crumbs (and eat the rest!). Mix the hokey pokey crumbs into the chablon and use immediately. Dip each gâteau in the chablon, following the instructions on page 30 for fully coating. Store in the freezer and defrost before finishing.

Kataifi nests

40g melted butter
100g kataifi pastry

Preheat the oven to 180°C and line a baking tray with baking paper. Toss the butter and kataifi together until the kataifi is well coated. Portion the kataifi into tablespoon-sized piles on the prepared baking tray. Bake for 15–20 minutes, until the kataifi is a nice golden brown. Allow to cool and use the same day to finish the gâteaux.

To finish

kataifi nests
84 mini chocolate Easter eggs

Place a kataifi nest on top of each defrosted gâteau. Sometimes the kataifi can flatten out as it bakes, so you can squash it back into a neat nest if needed. Place three mini eggs on top of each gâteau and serve immediately.

Celebrations

Tropical egg

Is there anything more symbolic of Easter than an egg? I thought it would be even more fun if we cracked that egg open and turned it into a fried egg petit gâteau. Flavoured with mango, coconut and yuzu, this tropical treat is sure to delight.

Makes 28

Coconut cake

60g very soft butter
120g sugar
3 egg whites
100g flour
¾ tsp baking powder
90g coconut cream
30g desiccated coconut

Preheat the oven to 170°C and line the tin. Whisk the butter and sugar together until smooth. Add the egg whites, one at a time, whisking in between each addition, until well combined. Whisk in the flour and baking powder, followed by the coconut cream, and finally the desiccated coconut. Pour into the lined tin and level off with a palette knife. Bake for 10–12 minutes, until the cake is just set to the touch. Remove from the oven and allow to cool completely before you make the yuzu crémeux.

Yuzu crémeux

yuzu crémeux (recipe page 242)

Pour the yuzu crémeux over the cooled cake, level off with a palette knife and store in the freezer while you make the mango mousse.

Mango mousse

mango mousse (recipe page 240)

Pour the mango mousse over the frozen crémeux, level off with a palette knife and freeze overnight, or until solid.

Portioning

(page 22)

Portion the gâteau into 28 pieces that are 3.5 x 3.5cm squares. Store in the freezer and defrost fully before finishing.

Coconut veil

¾ sheet gelatine
200g coconut cream
50g yuzu juice
20g liquid glucose
30g sugar
½ tsp agar-agar

Soak the gelatine sheet in cold water until soft. Drain and set aside. Spray a baking tray of approximately 40 x 30cm with spray oil, or cut a sheet of baking paper the same size and lay it on a heat-proof surface (the kitchen counter should be fine), then spray with spray oil. Get a large palette knife ready, if you're using the baking paper. Bring the coconut cream, yuzu juice and glucose to a boil. Whisk the sugar and agar-agar together. Whisk this into the boiling coconut mixture and reduce to a simmer. Simmer for 90 seconds. Remove from the heat and whisk in the gelatine. Pour the mixture onto the oiled tray or baking paper. If you're using the tray, lift it up and rotate it to allow the mix to evenly coat the base in a thin layer. If you're using the baking paper, pour the mix onto the paper and immediately spread it out to cover the whole sheet as quickly as possible. The mixture will set incredibly quickly. Once it starts to set, stop moving it, even if it's not covering the baking paper fully. Once set, use a 4cm round cutter to cut 28 circles out of the veil. Use a palette knife to gently lift each round up and lay them over the defrosted gâteaux. If needed you can melt the offcuts of the veil over a very low heat and repeat the spreading process to get more veils. Keep the gateaux chilled in the fridge while you make the mango gel.

Mango gel

250g mango purée (page 12)
½ tsp agar-agar

Bring the mango purée to a boil and whisk in the agar-agar. Boil for 1 minute and pour into a container. Leave for at least 1 hour to set fully. Use a stick blender to blend into a smooth gel. Spoon into a piping bag and store in the fridge for up to 1 week.

To finish

mango gel

Use a piping bag with a 1mm hole to pipe a round blob of mango gel on top of each coconut veil to mimic an egg yolk. Serve immediately.

Celebrations

Hot cross buns

It's not Easter without a hot cross bun, but sometimes it's fun to change it up a bit. These petits gâteaux are inspired by the flavours and spices of a fruit hot cross bun, in a delicious chocolate shell. Allowing the raisins to soak overnight before blending them helps get a much smoother jam, so make sure you allow the extra time into your bake schedule.

Makes 24

Hot cross bun spice

2 tsp ground cinnamon
1 tsp mixed spice
½ tsp ground nutmeg
½ tsp ground ginger

Mix all the spices together and store in an airtight container in the pantry.

Spice cake

spice cake (recipe page 241), using hot cross bun spice

Once baked, leave the cake to cool completely while you make the raisin jam.

Raisin jam

250g water
200g golden raisins

Bring the water to a boil. Pour over the raisins. Cover and leave overnight to soak at room temperature. The next day, blend the raisins and water together to form a paste. Push through a sieve to get a smooth paste. Cook over a medium heat, stirring constantly, for 5 minutes or until the paste has reduced by a third. It will splutter a lot as it cooks, so be careful not to burn yourself. Pour over the cake and freeze for 1 hour before making the spiced mousse.

Spiced mousse

1½ sheets gelatine
100g caramelised white chocolate
30g water
30g sugar
200g cream
2 tsp hot cross bun spice

Soak the gelatine sheets in cold water until soft. Drain and put in a bowl with the chocolate. Bring the water and sugar to a boil and pour over the gelatine and chocolate. Whisk until all the chocolate is melted and you have a smooth base. Whip the cream and spice together to medium peaks. Once the base has reached about 30°C, or body temperature, fold in the cream until just combined. Spread over the frozen jam and level off with a palette knife. Freeze overnight, or until solid.

Portioning

(page 22)

Portion the gâteau into 24 pieces that are 4 x 4cm squares. Store in the freezer until ready to finish.

Chablon

milk chocolate chablon (recipe page 239)

Dip each gâteau in the chablon, following the instructions on page 30 for fully coating. Store in the freezer until ready to finish.

To finish

100g caramelised white chocolate

Melt the chocolate, stirring until smooth, then allow it to cool to 30°C, or body temperature. Pour into a piping bag and cut a small 1mm hole. Pipe a cross of caramelised white chocolate on each gâteau. Allow to defrost fully before serving.

Speculoos bûche de Noël

Bûche de Noël, or Christmas logs, are a classical Christmas cake served in Europe. Traditionally they're made of a Swiss roll covered in buttercream to look like a log, but over the years, pastry chefs have adapted the bûche to become more modern. In this iteration I have made chocolate bark using caramelised white chocolate to create a bûche that really looks like a log.

Makes 16

Cinnamon cake

1 egg
100g water
100g brown sugar
60g canola or other flavourless oil
80g golden syrup
110g flour
1 tsp ground cinnamon
¼ tsp baking soda
50g crunchy speculoos spread

Preheat the oven to 160°C and line the tin. Whisk the egg, water, sugar, oil and golden syrup together until smooth. Whisk in the flour, cinnamon and baking soda until well combined. Pour into the lined tin and bake for 10–12 minutes, until the cake is just set to the touch. Remove from the oven and spoon the speculoos spread on top. Leave to sit for a few minutes before starting to spread with a palette knife. As the speculoos melts from the heat of the cake you can spread it into a smooth, even layer. Set aside at room temperature while you make the mousse.

Caramelised white chocolate mousse

1 sheet gelatine
30g water
15g sugar
75g caramelised white chocolate
150g cream

Soak the gelatine sheet in cold water until soft. Drain and set aside. Bring the water and sugar to a boil in a small pot, then add the gelatine and caramelised white chocolate. Stir until fully melted, then set aside to cool to about 30°C, or body temperature. Whip the cream to medium peaks. Stir a heaped tablespoonful of cream into the mousse base to loosen it up, then gently fold the remaining cream in. Pour over the cake base and level off with a palette knife. Freeze overnight, or until solid.

Portioning

(page 22)

Portion the gâteau into 16 pieces that are 7 x 3cm rectangles and store in the freezer until ready to finish.

Chocolate bark

300g caramelised white chocolate

Temper the chocolate following the instructions on page 24. Following the instructions on page 27 for making curved decorations, spread the chocolate over two A4 sheets of baking paper, and roll up around a rolling pin. Allow to set before removing from the rolling pin. As you unfurl the chocolate, it should break into large, uneven flakes. Store in an airtight container at room temperature for up to 1 month.

To finish

whipped crème fraîche (recipe page 242)
chocolate bark
cocoa powder
gold leaf

Spoon the whipped crème fraîche into a piping bag with a 1cm round piping tip. Pipe a line of crème fraîche down the centre of each gâteau. Using the crème fraîche as the glue, press the chocolate bark flakes on top of the portioned gâteaux pieces to create a flaky wood effect. Gently dust the gâteaux with cocoa and a few sprinkles of gold leaf. Allow to fully defrost before serving.

Celebrations

217

Boysenberry bûche de Noël

This is the most popular bûche de Noël I have made so far at Sugar Flour. Not only is it adorable, the flavour is also incredible. The fresh and tart boysenberry balances out the rich cheesecake and the slightly earthy cocoa crumb. The meringue mushroom lids can be a little fiddly but are well worth the effort. As with most things, the flavour will still be delicious, even if you can't be bothered with the faff.

Makes 20

Boysenberry cake

boysenberry cake (recipe page 238)

Once baked, allow the cake to cool completely before making the boysenberry gel.

Boysenberry gel

1 sheet gelatine
100g seedless boysenberry purée (page 12)
20g sugar
1 tsp pectin
⅛ tsp citric acid

Soak the gelatine sheet in cold water until soft. Drain and set aside. Put the boysenberry purée in a small pot and bring to a boil. Whisk the sugar, pectin and citric acid together in a bowl to combine and whisk this into the boiling purée. Continue to cook for 1 minute, whisking constantly. Remove from the heat and whisk in the gelatine. Pour over the cake and spread out with a palette knife. Freeze for at least 1 hour before starting the whipped cheesecake. You can make the boysenberry compote during this time.

Boysenberry compote

100g fresh or frozen boysenberries
30g sugar

Mix the boysenberries and sugar together in a small pot. Cook over a low heat, stirring constantly, until the mixture boils. Boil for 1 minute, while stirring, until the juices of the boysenberries have thickened slightly. Pour into a container and refrigerate until cool to touch before making the whipped cheesecake.

Whipped cheesecake

whipped cheesecake (recipe page 242)

Spread the whipped cheesecake over the frozen boysenberry gel. Before you have made the cheesecake layer completely smooth, spoon teaspoon-sized dollops of boysenberry compote over the top, until you've used it all. Use a knife to swirl them into the cheesecake and then level the top off with a palette knife. Freeze overnight, or until solid.

Portioning

(page 22)

Portion the gâteau into 20 pieces that are 6 x 3cm rectangles. Store in the freezer until ready to finish.

Cocoa crumb

40g melted butter
50g sugar
50g flour (gluten free, if desired)
30g cocoa powder

Preheat the oven to 170°C and line a baking tray with baking paper. In a bowl, stir all the ingredients together until you have a well-combined crumb. Pour onto the baking tray, spreading the mixture out, and bake for 12 minutes. Remove from the oven and allow to cool before pulsing in a food processor to create a fine crumb. Store in an airtight container in the pantry for up to 1 month.

Continued overleaf

Mushroom meringues

1 egg white
60g sugar
¼ tsp red colouring (adding more, if desired)

Preheat the oven to 90°C and turn the fan off if possible. Line a baking tray with baking paper. Using an electric whisk or a stand mixer (an electric whisk is better for this small amount of meringue), whisk the egg white until it is foamy and doubled in size. Add the sugar and whisk until you have a stiff-peaked meringue. Use a handheld whisk to whisk in red colouring until you have a glossy, medium-peaked red meringue. Spoon the meringue into a piping bag with a 0.5cm round tip, and pipe 2cm rounds onto the prepared tray, ensuring you have at least 20. Rather than making kisses like in other recipes, for the mushroom meringues you want to try to keep them flat, more like a disc than a kiss. Bake for 2 hours, or until the meringues are dry and crisp to the touch. Allow to cool before storing in an airtight container at room temperature for up to 1 week.

To finish

cocoa crumb
mushroom meringues
50g white chocolate
baby basil leaves

Take the portioned gâteaux out of the freezer and allow them to defrost for 5 minutes on the bench. Transfer the cocoa crumb to a wide, shallow container. Press the slightly softened tops of each gâteau into the crumb, using a little bit of pressure so the tops are completely coated in the crumb (they will still be quite frozen after 5 minutes at room temperature, so finger marks shouldn't be a concern). Place a meringue mushroom on top of each gâteau. Melt the chocolate to about 30–35°C, or body temperature, and spoon into a piping bag with a small 1mm opening. Pipe little dots of chocolate on top of each meringue, to create fairy tale-style mushrooms. Decorate the gâteaux with baby basil leaves and allow to defrost fully before serving.

Celebrations

White forest

Inspired by the same flavours you'll find in a Black Forest gâteau, this white forest gâteau is a little lighter, and makes the perfect mini bûche de Noël. While the white piping on top is reminiscent of a proper white snowy Christmas, the cherries are a homage to the summer Christmas that we have in New Zealand.

Makes 16

Shortcake sponge

shortcake sponge (recipe page 241)

Once baked, trimmed and in the freezer, begin to make the cherry gel.

Cherry gel

2 sheets gelatine
200g cherry juice or purée
30g sugar
½ tsp citric acid
2 tsp pectin

Soak the gelatine sheets in cold water until soft. Drain and set aside. In a small pot, bring the cherry juice to a boil. Whisk the sugar, citric acid and pectin together then whisk into the boiling cherry juice. Boil for 1 minute, whisking constantly. Remove from the heat and whisk in the gelatine. Leave to cool to room temperature before pouring over the sponge and spreading out with a palette knife. Return to the freezer for 1 hour before making the vanilla mousse.

Vanilla mousse

1½ sheets gelatine
30g sugar
¼ tsp vanilla bean paste
120g mascarpone
180g cream

Soak the gelatine sheets in cold water until soft. Drain and put into a pot with the sugar, vanilla and 20g of the mascarpone. Cook over a low heat, stirring constantly, until the gelatine and mascarpone have melted together. Remove from the heat and stir in the remaining mascarpone. Set aside while you whip the cream to medium peaks. Once the mascarpone base is about 30°C, or body temperature, fold the whipped cream into the mascarpone base until just combined. Pour over the frozen cherry gel and level off with a palette knife. Freeze overnight, or until solid.

Portioning

(page 22)

Portion the gâteau into 16 pieces that are 7 x 3cm rectangles. Store in the freezer until ready to finish.

Kirsch crème fraîche

75g crème fraîche
75g cream
15g icing sugar
1 tsp Kirsch

Line a tray with baking paper. Whisk everything together to form a very soft-peaked cream. Spoon into a piping bag with a small grass tip. Place the portioned gâteaux onto the prepared baking sheet, leaving at least 3cm in between each gâteau. Pipe the cream over each gâteau in a side to side motion, overlapping each stroke slightly to create a textured top. Either return to the freezer or allow to defrost before finishing.

To finish

16 fresh cherries

Trim the stalk of each cherry so they're nice and neat. Press one cherry into the end of each gâteau and serve immediately.

Pfeffernüsse Christmas tree

Every year for Christmas my mother-in-law makes the most delicious Pfeffernüsse biscuits. The spice mix in them tastes just like you think Christmas would, and mixed with a little bit of milk chocolate, they are a Christmas delight!

Makes 16

Pfeffernüsse spice

4 tsp ground cinnamon
2 tsp ground allspice
2 tsp ground nutmeg
1 tsp ground cloves
1 tsp ground black pepper
1 tsp ground cardamom

Mix all the spices together and store in an airtight container in the pantry.

Spice cake

spice cake (recipe page 241), using the Pfeffernüsse spice

Once baked, leave the cake to cool completely while you make the Pfeffernüsse crumb.

Pfeffernüsse crumb

15g melted butter
20g brown sugar
15g golden syrup
40g flour
¼ tsp Pfeffernüsse spice
⅛ tsp baking soda

Preheat the oven to 180°C and line a baking tray of any size with baking paper. Whisk the butter, sugar and golden syrup together until smooth. Stir in the flour, Pfeffernüsse spice and baking soda. Mix until you have a crumbly dough. Spread over the prepared tray and bake for 10–12 minutes, until fragrant and lightly golden. Allow to cool before blending into a fine crumb. Store in an airtight container in the pantry for up to 1 month.

Pfeffernüsse crunch

75g milk chocolate
30g coconut oil
50g Pfeffernüsse crumb

Melt the chocolate and coconut oil together, stirring until smooth. Stir in the Pfeffernüsse crumb and spread over the cooled spice cake. Leave to set at room temperature while you make the spiced milk chocolate mousse.

Spiced milk chocolate mousse

1¼ sheets gelatine
150g milk chocolate
1½ tsp Pfeffernüsse spice
75g milk
160g cream

Soak the gelatine sheets in cold water until soft. Drain and put in a bowl with the chocolate and spice. Bring the milk to a boil in a small pot and pour over the chocolate and gelatine, then whisk until combined. Leave to cool to about 30°C, or body temperature. Whip the cream to stiff peaks, then fold into the chocolate base, mixing only until just combined. Pour over the Pfeffernüsse crunch and level off with a palette knife. Freeze overnight, or until solid.

Glaze

milk chocolate glaze (recipe page 240)

Follow the instructions on page 21 for glazing the gâteau. Return to the freezer until ready to portion.

Portioning

(page 22)

Portion the gâteau into 16 pieces that are 3.5 x 6cm rectangles. Store in the freezer and defrost before finishing.

Christmas trees

200g white chocolate, coloured green (page 24)

Temper and colour the chocolate following the instructions on page 24. Spread the chocolate over an A4 acetate sheet, and follow the instructions on page 27 for flat chocolate decorations, using a Christmas-tree cutter, cutting at least 16. Allow to set before removing from the acetate and storing in an airtight container at room temperature for up to 1 month.

To finish

liquid glucose
Christmas-coloured nonpareils (sprinkles)

Pipe lines of the glucose on the chocolate trees where you would like the sprinkles to go. Cover the glucose lines with sprinkles to coat fully, then tip the chocolate trees to get rid of any excess sprinkles. Place one tree on each gâteau and serve.

Berry pavlova

Is there anything more Kiwi than a pavlova at Christmas? While it's hard to beat the classic, sometimes it's fun to change things up a bit. The crisp berry meringues on top of this gâteau bring the perfect pavlova crunch, while the berry mousse elevates it to a petit gâteau level.

Makes 20

Mini meringues

3 egg whites
150g sugar
¼ tsp vanilla bean paste
1 tbsp freeze-dried strawberry powder
1 tbsp freeze-dried raspberry powder
1 tbsp freeze-dried blackcurrant powder

Preheat the oven to 90°C, without the fan if possible, and line a baking tray with baking paper. Make a French meringue (page 18) by whisking the egg whites in a stand mixer, or with an electric whisk, until doubled in size. Add the sugar and continue to whip until the meringue forms stiff peaks. Split the meringue into four separate bowls. Whisk the vanilla into one bowl, the strawberry powder into another bowl, the raspberry powder into another and the blackcurrant powder into the last bowl. Use four piping bags with four different nozzle shapes to pipe out mini kisses (page 32) of meringue onto the prepared tray. Bake for 2 hours, or until the meringues are dry and crisp. Store for up to 1 week in an airtight container.

Shortcake sponge

shortcake sponge (recipe page 241)

Once baked, set aside to cool completely while you make the strawberry mousse.

Strawberry mousse

2 sheets gelatine
15g sugar
150g strawberry purée (page 12)
150g cream

Soak the gelatine sheets in cold water until soft. Drain and put in a pot with the sugar and 20g of the strawberry purée. Cook over a low heat, stirring constantly, until the gelatine is fully melted. Remove from the heat and stir in the remaining strawberry purée. Set aside to cool to 30°C, or body temperature. Whip the cream to medium peaks. Fold the cream into the cooled purée. Set aside at room temperature while you make the other two mousses.

Blueberry mousse

2 sheets gelatine
15g sugar
150g blueberry purée
150g cream

Follow the same method as for the strawberry mousse.

Blackcurrant mousse

2 sheets gelatine
15g sugar
150g seedless blackcurrant puree
150g cream

Follow the same method as for the strawberry mousse.

Once you have all three mousses ready, spoon them on top of the sponge in alternating blobs. Once you've used all of the mousses, use a toothpick to swirl them together, creating a marble effect. Level off with a palette knife and freeze overnight, or until solid.

Portioning

(page 22)

Portion the gâteau into 20 pieces that are 2.5 x 7cm rectangles. Store in the freezer.

Blackcurrant chablon

2 tbsp freeze-dried blackcurrant powder
white chocolate chablon (recipe page 239)

Use a stick blender to blend the blackcurrant powder into the chablon. Follow the instructions on page 30 for dipping the gâteaux in chablon, leaving the top exposed. Store in the freezer and defrost fully before finishing.

Vanilla mascarpone

80g mascarpone
80g cream
¼ tsp vanilla bean paste
15g icing sugar

Whisk everything together until it forms stiff peaks. Spoon into a piping bag and use immediately.

To finish

vanilla mascarpone
mini meringues

Pipe a 1cm wide line of vanilla mascarpone down the centre of each gâteau. Decorate each gâteau with a mixture of different mini meringues to completely coat the top. Serve immediately.

Celebrations

Russian honey cake

Medovik, also known as Russian honey cake, is a beautiful layered gâteau composed of a honey biscuit/cake and honey cream. A lot of recipes tend to be very complicated, with steps like burning the honey then stirring in the eggs while trying not to curdle them. After a lot of tinkering I've managed to make the recipe much less stressful but still equally delicious. The prominent honey flavour is what lands this recipe in the celebrations section, as it is perfect for Rosh Hashanah — Jewish New Year — where we celebrate by eating sweet, honey-flavoured treats. You can use whatever honey you like — keeping in mind that the flavour of the honey will determine the flavour of the gâteau. This recipe is much easier if you have multiple baking tins, but if you don't it will still work, you just need a bit of patience.

Makes 24

Honey cake

100g honey
100g brown sugar
85g butter
2 eggs
1 egg yolk
¾ tsp baking soda
1 tsp ground cinnamon
180g flour

Preheat the oven to 190°C. Cut four sheets of baking paper to fit the baking tin and line the tin with one sheet. If you have more tins line them with baking paper also. In a pot, heat the honey, sugar and butter together until fully melted. Remove from the heat and whisk in the eggs, one at a time, followed by the egg yolk. Whisk in the baking soda, cinnamon and flour until you have a thick batter. Weigh 110g of batter into the lined tin and spread into an even layer with a palette knife. It will be very thin. Bake for 4–6 minutes, until lightly golden, slightly puffed and just set to the touch. Remove from the oven and from the tin, and repeat with the remaining batter. You need four cakes in total, but you may have enough batter for a fifth, which means you get to eat the extra! The cake will feel very dry when you eat it, but when it absorbs the honey cream it'll be perfect. Set the cakes aside to cool completely before starting the honey cream.

Honey cream

125g sour cream
200g cream
50g honey
50g mascarpone
½ tsp vanilla bean paste

Line the tin with a fresh sheet of baking paper. Whip everything together until it forms soft peaks. Place a honey cake in the base of the prepared tin. Spread 140g of honey cream on top and level off with a palette knife. Top with another sheet of cake, followed by another layer of cream, repeating until you have four layers of cake and three layers of cream. Cover with cling film and refrigerate overnight. This step is super important as it will soften the cake and allow it to absorb moisture from the cream. You can refrigerate it for up to 3 days before portioning.

Portioning

(page 22)

Portion the gâteau into 24 pieces that are 4 x 4cm squares. Store in the fridge before finishing.

Honey cream topping

50g sour cream
100g mascarpone
100g cream
¼ tsp vanilla bean paste
25g honey

Whip everything together until stiff peaks form. Spoon into a piping bag with a 1cm round tip. Pipe one large kiss on top of each gâteau. Use a round tablespoon measure to create indents in the cream, following the guide on page 32.

To finish

runny honey
bee pollen, gold leaf or edible flowers

Pour some honey into a piping bag and fill the indents of the cream to just below the top with the honey. Decorate with bee pollen and serve. If you can't get bee pollen you can use a little gold leaf or some edible flowers instead.

Tarte tatin

One of my favourite memories from my time in Paris was when my parents came to visit me over the Christmas break. We happened to walk past one of the oldest and most famous pâtisseries, Ladurée, so of course we had to go in! There I had a tarte tatin that was one of the best things I have ever eaten. This simple gâteau is inspired by that memory. You need two tins for this gâteau in order to press the apples overnight – the caramelised apples will fall apart if you miss this important step.

Makes 22

Caramelised apples

150g sugar
70g butter
10 Braeburn apples

Preheat the oven to 150°C and line the tin. Make a dry caramel (page 19) by cooking the sugar in a pot over a high heat, stirring constantly, until you have a light amber-coloured caramel. Remove from the heat and add the butter, allowing it to sizzle for a few seconds before stirring. Once the butter is completely mixed into the caramel, pour it into the lined tin and set aside to cool while you work on the apples. Peel, core and halve the apples. Use a mandolin, or a knife, to cut the apples into half moon-shaped slices, about 0.5cm thick. Once all the apples have been cut, begin to layer them in a shingled pattern on the caramel, which should have set firmly by now. These bottom layers of apple will become the top of the tarte tatin, so try to take some care with the pattern of the first few layers, as this is what you'll see the most. The apples should be at the rim, if not coming above the rim of the tin. Cover the tin loosely with foil and place it on a baking tray or dish to catch any juices while baking, otherwise they will burn on the bottom of the oven. Bake for 2 hours, rotating the tin every 30 minutes. Remove from the oven and allow to cool to room temperature. Remove the foil and place a sheet of baking paper on top of the cooked apples. Take another baking tin and gently press it down on top of the apples to compress them and squeeze out any excess juice. Weigh the top tin down with a couple of cans or jars and refrigerate overnight, discarding any juice that comes out of the apples.

Portioning

(page 22)

Portion the caramelised apples into 22 pieces that are 4 x 7 x 7cm triangles. The butter that sets in the tin may stop the apples from coming out easily, so use a hot cloth held on the base of the tin to help heat it slightly if needed. Store the caramelised apple triangles in the fridge for up to 1 week or the freezer for up to 1 month.

Continued overleaf

Puff pastry

250g puff pastry, either homemade (recipe page 33), or store-bought
flour
1–2 tbsp icing sugar

Preheat the oven to 200°C and line a baking tray with baking paper. Roll the puff pastry into a 20 x 30cm rectangle about 1–2mm thick, using flour as needed to stop the pastry sticking. Freeze for 5–10 minutes, or refrigerate for 10–20 minutes. Place the pastry on the prepared tray, put another piece of baking paper on top, then another tray. Bake for 15–20 minutes, checking the pastry after 15 minutes. It should be a light golden brown all over, but not too dark. Remove the top tray and baking paper and sift icing sugar over the top of the pastry. Return to the oven for about 5 minutes, until the icing sugar has melted and lightly caramelised. This will prevent the pastry from becoming too soggy. Allow to cool before portioning into triangles the same size as the caramelised apples. The pastry is best used on the day it has been baked.

Vanilla crème fraîche

100g crème fraîche
100g cream
¼ tsp vanilla bean paste
30g icing sugar

Whisk everything together to form stiff peaks. Use immediately.

To assemble and finish

caramelised apple triangles
puff pastry triangles
vanilla crème fraîche

Place a caramelised apple triangle on top of each puff pastry triangle. Finish with a quenelle (page 30) of vanilla crème fraîche close to the wider end of the triangle. Allow the apples to warm up slightly or defrost if they were frozen before serving.

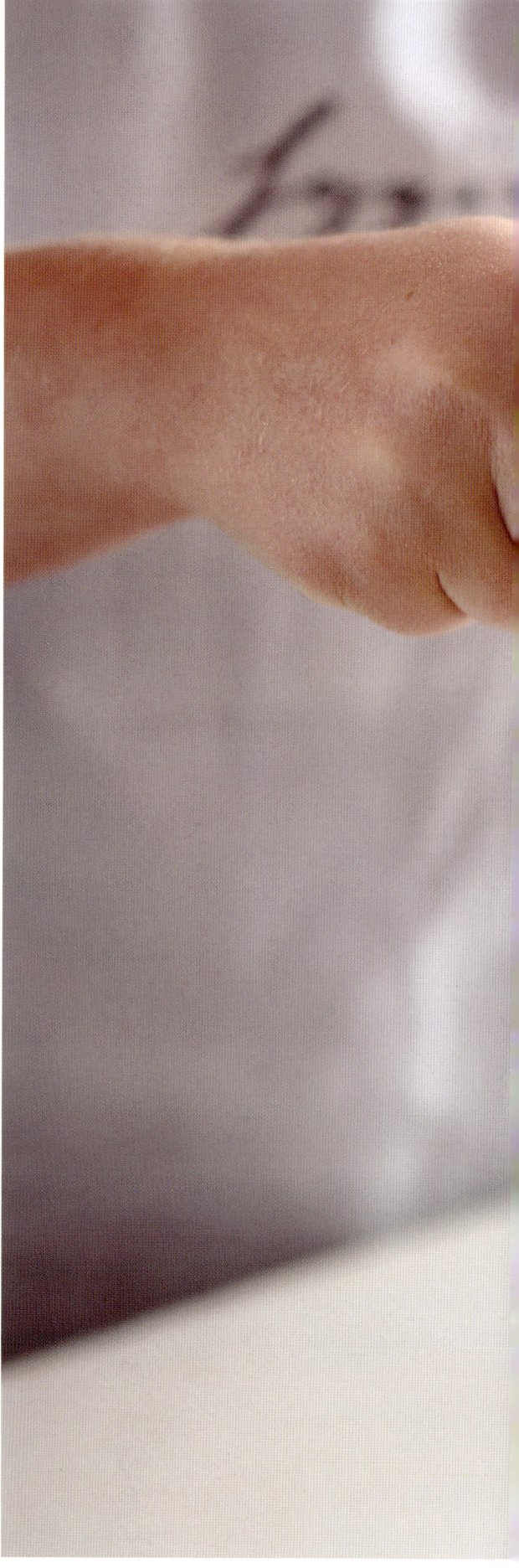

Celebrations

Birthday cake

It can't be a celebration chapter without a birthday cake! This gâteau is the perfect celebration dessert — made up of some classic flavours, finished with sprinkles and a maraschino cherry, it's sure to make anyone smile!

Makes 22

Sprinkle cake

40g melted butter
60g sugar
20g brown sugar
1 egg
35g milk
½ tsp white vinegar
20g canola or other flavourless oil
¼ tsp vanilla bean paste
80g flour (gluten free, if desired)
½ tsp baking powder
30g coloured sprinkles

Preheat the oven to 170°C and line the tin. Whisk the butter and both sugars together in a bowl until combined. Whisk in the egg followed by the milk, vinegar, oil and vanilla. Once well combined, add the flour and baking powder and whisk until smooth. Stir in the sprinkles. Pour into the lined tin. Bake for 10–12 minutes, until lightly golden and the cake is just set to the touch. Allow to cool completely while you make the raspberry compote.

Raspberry compote

raspberry compote (recipe page 240)

Pour the raspberry compote over the cooled sprinkle cake and level off with a palette knife. Freeze for at least 1 hour before making the whipped cheesecake.

Whipped cheesecake

350g cream cheese
60g icing sugar
1 tsp vanilla bean paste
180g cream

Using a spatula, stir the cream cheese until it's softened slightly. Whisk in the icing sugar until combined, followed by the vanilla. Gradually add the cream in four parts, whisking well in between each addition until all the cream is fully mixed in. Whisk, either by hand or with an electric whisk, until the cheesecake mix has reached stiff peaks. Pour over the frozen raspberry compote, then spread evenly with a palette knife. Freeze overnight, or until solid.

Glaze

coloured glaze (recipe page 239), coloured white, if desired

Follow the instructions on page 21 to glaze the top of the gâteau. Return to the freezer for at least 5 minutes, or store in the freezer until ready to portion.

Portioning

(page 22)

Portion the gâteau into 22 pieces that are 4 x 7 x 7cm triangles. Store in the freezer and defrost before finishing.

To finish

coloured sprinkles
maraschino cherries

Scatter the sprinkles on top of each gâteau. Finish with a maraschino cherry and serve.

Celebrations

238	Banana cake
238	Black glaze
238	Boysenberry cake
238	Brown butter bavarois
238	Caramel crémeux
239	Chocolate cake
239	Chocolate chablon
239	Coloured glaze
239	Dark chocolate mousse
239	Gold paint
239	Hokey pokey
240	Mango mousse
240	Milk chocolate glaze
240	Milk chocolate mousse
240	Milk chocolate whipped ganache
240	Passionfruit crémeux
240	Raspberry compote
241	Spice cake
241	Strawberry mousse
241	Shortcake sponge
241	Swiss meringue
242	Vanilla cake
242	Vanilla mascarpone
242	Whipped caramel
242	Whipped cheesecake
242	Whipped crème fraîche
242	Yuzu crémeux

Base recipes

Banana cake

60g melted butter
70g brown sugar
1 egg
120g mashed banana
90g flour (gluten free, if desired)
½ tsp baking soda
¼ tsp baking powder

Preheat the oven to 170°C and line the tin. In a bowl, whisk the butter and sugar together until combined. Whisk in the egg until well combined, followed by the banana. Whisk in the flour, baking soda and baking powder. Pour into the lined tin, level off with a palette knife, and bake for 12–15 minutes, until lightly golden and just set to the touch. Use as directed in the recipe.

Black glaze

3 sheets gelatine
90g sugar
70g water
50g cream
30g cocoa powder

Soak the gelatine sheets in cold water until soft. Drain and set aside. Whisk the sugar, water, cream and cocoa together in a small pot. Boil, while whisking constantly, for 3 minutes, being careful as this glaze will burn very easily. Remove from the heat and add the gelatine. Whisk until the gelatine has melted. Use at about 30°C, or body temperature, to glaze the gâteaux.

Boysenberry cake

30g melted butter
75g sugar
1 egg yolk
30g milk
30g canola or other flavourless oil
60g flour (gluten free, if desired)
¼ tsp baking powder
80g fresh or frozen boysenberries

Preheat the oven to 170°C and line the tin. Whisk the butter and sugar together until well combined. Whisk in the egg yolk, followed by the milk and oil, until smooth. Whisk in the flour and baking powder until you have a runny batter. Pour into the lined tin and level off with a palette knife. Slice or crumble the boysenberries into six pieces per berry and sprinkle over the cake batter. Bake for 12–15 minutes, until the cake is just set to the touch. Use as directed in the recipe.

Brown butter bavarois

25g butter
1½ sheets gelatine
125g milk
30g brown sugar
2 egg yolks
150g cream

Cook the butter in a small pot over a medium heat, whisking constantly until it is a fragrant, nutty brown. Set aside to cool to room temperature. Soak the gelatine sheets in cold water until soft. Drain and set aside. Begin by making an anglaise, bring the milk to a boil in a small pot while you whisk the sugar and egg yolks together in a bowl. Pour a small amount of the hot milk into the brown sugar mix. Whisk to combine then pour this back into the pot. Whisk, then return to a low heat. Stir constantly with a spatula until the anglaise thickens slightly, or reaches 75°C. Remove from the heat and pass through a sieve into a large bowl. Whisk in the brown butter and gelatine. Leave to cool either at room temperature or in the fridge, stirring every 5 minutes, until the anglaise has reached 30–35°C, or body temperature. Whip the cream to medium peaks and fold into the cooled anglaise until just combined. Use immediately, as directed in the recipe.

Caramel crémeux

½ sheet gelatine
35g cream
75g milk
35g sugar
1 egg yolk
1 tsp sugar
2 tsp cornflour
50g butter
25g caramelised white chocolate

Soak the gelatine sheet in cold water until soft. Drain and set aside. Bring the cream and milk to a boil in a small pot. In a separate pot, make a dry caramel (page 19) by cooking the first measure of sugar over a high heat, stirring constantly until you have a light amber caramel. Deglaze with the cream and milk, allowing the caramel to bubble up and steam before stirring, to avoid burning yourself. Return the mix to the heat and boil again. At this point it will look split and weird, but it will come back together later on. Whisk the egg yolk, second measure of sugar and cornflour together in a bowl, and whisk a quarter of the hot caramel mixture into this. Pour all of the egg yolk caramel mix back into the pot and whisk to combine. Cook over a low heat, whisking constantly until the mixture boils. Remove from the heat and let cool to 45°C. Whisk in the gelatine, butter and chocolate. Blend with a stick blender until smooth then use as directed in the recipe.

Chocolate cake

60g soft butter
100g sugar
1 egg
90g milk
20g canola or other flavourless oil
½ tsp white vinegar
80g flour (gluten free, if desired)
20g cocoa powder
¼ tsp baking powder

Preheat the oven to 170°C and line the tin. Whisk the butter and sugar together until well combined. Whisk in the egg, followed by the milk, oil and vinegar. Whisk in the flour, cocoa and baking powder until you have a smooth batter. Pour into the lined tin and level off with a palette knife. Bake for 10–12 minutes, until the cake is just set to the touch. Use as directed in the recipe.

Chocolate chablon

300g white, caramelised white, milk or dark chocolate
   (as specified in the recipe)
30g canola or other flavourless oil

Melt the chocolate and oil together, stirring until smooth. Use the chablon when its temperature is between 30 and 35°C, or as directed in the recipe. All chocolate brands contain differing amounts of cocoa butter, so sometimes the chablon can be too thick for dipping with only 30g of oil. Add more oil as needed to get the chocolate to a smooth, pouring consistency. If colouring the chablon, make sure to use fat-soluble colouring, just like you would with pure chocolate (page 24).

Coloured glaze

1¼ sheet gelatine
110g white chocolate
50g milk
15g liquid glucose
liquid or gel colouring, as desired or as directed in the recipe

Soak the gelatine sheet in cold water until soft. Drain and put in a bowl with the chocolate. Bring the milk and glucose to a boil in a small pot. Remove from the heat and whisk in the chocolate and gelatine. Stir in the colouring and allow to cool to between 30 and 35°C, or body temperature, before using as directed in the recipe.

Dark chocolate mousse

1 sheet gelatine
100g dark chocolate
80g milk
150g cream

Soak the gelatine sheet in cold water until soft. Drain and set aside in a bowl with the chocolate. Bring the milk to a boil in a small pot and pour over the chocolate and gelatine. Whisk to combine until the chocolate is melted. Set aside to cool to 30°C, or body temperature. Whip the cream to stiff peaks and fold into the cooled base until just combined. Use immediately, as directed in the recipe.

Gold paint

1 tsp edible gold lustre dust
½ tsp clear spirit such as gin or vodka

Mix together until you have a smooth liquid. Use immediately. Any leftovers can be stored at room temperature. The alcohol will evaporate over time and leave the powder behind, but you can top up with more alcohol as needed.

Hokey pokey

300g sugar
150g honey
150g water
3 tsp baking soda

Line a large baking tray with baking paper. In a very large pot, mix the sugar, honey and water together. Cook over a high heat until the mixture reaches 150°C. Remove from the heat and whisk in the baking soda. The mix will expand a huge amount, so be careful. Pour onto the prepared tray and leave to cool before breaking into pieces.

Mango mousse

1½ sheets gelatine
120g mango purée (page 12)
120g cream

Soak the gelatine sheets in cold water until soft. Drain and place in a small pot with 20g of the mango purée. Heat over a low heat, stirring constantly until the gelatine has melted. Pour into a bowl with the remaining purée and whisk to combine. Set aside while you whip the cream to medium peaks. Check the temperature of the mango base. Once it's reached 30°C, or body temperature, fold in the cream until just combined. Use immediately, as directed in the recipe.

Milk chocolate glaze

1¼ sheets gelatine
110g milk chocolate
50g milk
15g liquid glucose

Soak the gelatine sheets in cold water until soft. Drain and put in a bowl with the chocolate. Bring the milk and glucose to a boil in a small pot. Remove from the heat and whisk in the chocolate and gelatine. Allow to cool to between 30 and 35°C, or body temperature, before using as directed in the recipe.

Milk chocolate mousse

1¼ sheets gelatine
150g milk chocolate
75g milk
160g cream

Soak the gelatine sheets in cold water until soft. Drain and put in a bowl with the chocolate. Bring the milk to a boil in a small pot and pour over the chocolate and gelatine, then whisk until combined. Leave to cool to about 30°C, or body temperature. Whip the cream to stiff peaks, then fold into the chocolate base, mixing only until just combined. Use immediately, as directed in the recipe.

Milk chocolate whipped ganache

½ sheet gelatine
70g milk chocolate
140g cream

Soak the gelatine sheet in cold water until soft. Drain and put in a bowl with the chocolate. Bring the cream to a boil in a small pot and pour over the chocolate and gelatine. Whisk to combine, then blend with a stick blender to emulsify. Cover with cling film, pressing the cling film to the surface to stop a skin from forming. Refrigerate overnight. Whip to medium peaks before using. The ganache will split or overwhip very easily, so be cautious. If it does split, melt it down in a pot then chill overnight before whipping again.

Passionfruit crémeux

½ sheet gelatine
50g passionfruit purée or juice (page 12)
50g sugar
1 egg
50g butter

Soak the gelatine sheet in cold water until soft. Drain and set aside. Whisk the passionfruit purée, sugar and egg together in a small pot. Bring to a boil, whisking constantly. Remove from the heat and whisk in the gelatine. Allow to cool to 45°C and blend the butter in using a stick blender. Use as directed in the recipe.

Raspberry compote

1½ sheets gelatine
160g seedless raspberry purée (page 12)
¼ tsp vanilla bean paste
40g sugar
1½ tsp pectin
¼ tsp citric acid

Soak the gelatine sheet in cold water until soft. Drain and set aside. Bring the raspberry purée and vanilla to a boil. In a bowl, whisk the sugar, pectin and citric acid together. Whisk this into the boiling purée and continue to cook for 1 minute, whisking constantly. Remove from the heat and whisk in the gelatine. Use immediately as directed in the recipe.

Spice cake

75g brown sugar
75g water
60g golden syrup
45g canola or other flavourless oil
1 egg yolk
80g flour
⅛ tsp baking soda
2 tsp spice (specified in the recipe)

Preheat the oven to 160°C and line the tin. Whisk the sugar, water, golden syrup, oil and egg yolk together until well combined. Whisk in the flour, baking soda and spice until you have a smooth, runny batter. Pour into the lined tin and bake for 12–15 minutes, until set to the touch. Use as directed in the recipe.

Strawberry mousse

1½ sheets gelatine
120g strawberry purée (page 12)
20g sugar
120g cream

Soak the gelatine sheets in cold water until soft. Drain and place in a small pot with 20g of the strawberry purée and all of the sugar. Cook over a low heat, stirring constantly until the gelatine has melted. Pour this mixture into the remaining purée and stir to combine. Set aside to cool to room temperature while you whip the cream to medium peaks. Fold the cream into the strawberry base until just combined. Use immediately as directed in the recipe.

Shortcake sponge

3 eggs
60g sugar
30g canola or other flavourless oil
¼ tsp vanilla bean paste
40g sugar
65g flour
¼ tsp baking powder

Preheat the oven to 180°C and line the tin. Separate the egg whites and egg yolks into separate bowls. Using a stand mixer, or a very strong arm, whisk the egg yolks, first measure of sugar, oil and vanilla together until pale yellow and fluffy. In a separate stand mixer bowl, whisk the egg whites and the second measure of sugar together until you have a stiff-peaked meringue. Fold the whites into the yolks until half combined, then add the flour and baking powder. Use a whisk to finish folding until everything is just combined. Be careful not to over-mix, as the more air you knock out the denser the sponge will be. Pour into the lined tin and level off with a palette knife. Bake for 12–15 minutes, until lightly golden brown and the sponge feels just set to the touch. Leave to cool. As the sponge cools it will deflate and the edges will fold in on itself slightly. Remove the sponge from the tin and use a large serrated knife to level out the top of the sponge. Store in the freezer before using as directed in the recipe.

Swiss meringue

2 egg white
50g sugar

Whisk the egg white and sugar together in a bain-marie using a metal bowl. Whisk constantly until the mixture reaches 75°C, or is hot to the touch. Remove the bowl from the pot and whisk in a stand mixer or with a handheld electric whisk until the meringue has reached stiff peaks. Use immediately as directed in the recipe.

Vanilla cake

30g melted butter
50g sugar
1 egg
¼ tsp vanilla bean paste
20g canola or other flavourless oil
20g milk
1 tsp white vinegar
50g flour (gluten free, if desired)
½ tsp baking powder

Preheat the oven to 170°C and line the tin. In a bowl, whisk the butter and sugar together until well combined, followed by the egg, vanilla, oil, milk and vinegar. Whisk in the flour and baking powder until you have a smooth batter. Pour into the lined tin and level off with a palette knife. Bake for 10–12 minutes, until lightly golden and the cake is just set to the touch. Use as directed in the recipe.

Vanilla mascarpone

100g mascarpone
100g cream
¼ tsp vanilla bean paste
30g icing sugar

Whisk everything together to form stiff peaks. Use immediately, as directed in the recipe.

Whipped caramel

1 sheet gelatine
100g sugar
100g cream
¼ tsp vanilla bean paste
40g butter

Soak the gelatine sheet in cold water until soft. Drain and set aside. Make a dry caramel (page 19) by cooking the sugar over a high heat, stirring constantly until you have an amber-coloured caramel. Remove from the heat and immediately add the cream and vanilla. Allow the mix to bubble for a minute before you stir it, to avoid burning yourself on the steam. Once the cream is mixed in, stir in the gelatine. Blend the butter in using a stick blender. You want to blend it for at least 3 minutes to fully emulsify the butter and stop the mix from splitting when you whip it. Chill overnight before whipping to stiff peaks just before using. It's easiest to do this with a stand or electric mixer, but you can do it by hand if you're feeling strong!

Whipped cheesecake

100g cream cheese
20g icing sugar
¼ tsp vanilla bean paste
60g cream

Using a spatula, stir the cream cheese until it has softened slightly. Whisk in the icing sugar until combined, followed by the vanilla. Gradually add the cream in four parts, whisking well in between each addition until all the cream is fully mixed in. Whisk, either by hand or with an electric whisk, until the mixture has reached stiff peaks. Use immediately, as directed in the recipe.

Whipped crème fraîche

100g crème fraîche
100g cream
¼ tsp vanilla bean paste
30g icing sugar

Whisk all ingredients together until stiff peaks form. Use immediately, as directed in the recipe.

Yuzu crémeux

½ sheet gelatine
50g yuzu juice
50g sugar
1 egg
50g butter

Soak the gelatine sheet in cold water until soft. Drain and set aside. Whisk the yuzu juice, sugar and egg together in a small pot. Cook over a medium heat, whisking constantly, until the crémeux boils. Remove from the heat and whisk in the gelatine. Allow to cool to 45°C and then blend in the butter with a stick blender. Use immediately, as directed in the recipe.

Thank you

There are so many people to thank for helping me bring this book to life, words on a page don't feel enough to express how grateful I am, but I'll try anyway!

Ben, my incredible husband. This book is one of the hardest things I have ever done, and I couldn't have done it without you. Your consistent love, encouragement and support means so much to me, not to mention all the days you took off work to help with photoshoots and wash all my dishes. You really are the best.

Amber-Jayne, I feel like the universe really brought us together for this book and I am so happy it did. Not only are you the most talented photographer to walk this earth, you are the most incredible person and I'm so happy to have you as a friend.

Mum, Dad, Greg and Glynne, you guys are the best parents anyone could ever ask for. I'm so thankful to all of you for being on my team and supporting me through everything. Especially Glynne who washes and irons all my aprons, no mother-in-law could ever compare.

To those who have mentored me throughout my career, sharing their knowledge and giving me opportunities to learn and grow: Scott Campbell, Robert Bok, Shaun Clouston, Jacob Brown, Anthony Bertin, Ludovic Chaussard, Kevin Lopes, Jonny Lake, Michele Stanco, Anne Butcher and Rick Lowe. Thank you, I hope this book might inspire some future pastry chefs the way you all inspired me.

All my incredible friends who have helped me through this process, but especially Leila, Joshna and Lillian. To have such incredibly talented, smart, funny, strong and beautiful women by my side is something I will never take for granted.

Thomas Manch, Justus Smith, Leslie Craven, Harriet McFetridge, Dan Mercer and Brendan Austin. Thank you for all your help and for sharing your wisdom and expertise throughout this process.

Angela Francis from One of A Kind Ceramics, who so generously gave me so many of her beautiful plates, including those featured on the cover. As well as Shea Stackhouse and Felicity Donaldson, Tannaz and all the other makers, growers and artisans who crafted beautiful things for this book.

Louise, Hope, Sarah and the whole team at Bateman Books, for believing in me and giving this book a chance to exist, you have made a lifelong dream come true. Thank you doesn't even begin to cover it.

All my other friends and family who have supported and helped in so many different ways. My brother Thomas and friends Lena, Will, Abbey, Strawbridge, Erin, Nicola, Karl, Matt R, Stan, Yess, Matt K, Kim, Neave, Sarah and Latke.

Last, but absolutely not least, every single person who has supported Sugar Flour from day one. I started this business when I had what felt like no purpose in life, and it gave me a reason to be. I eat, sleep, drink and breathe Sugar Flour, but it would be absolutely nothing without my customers. It doesn't matter if you've been to one class or one hundred, your support is what made this happen. I wish I could name every single one of you, but that would probably take up the entire book.

Index

A
A piece of toast 172
Afghan biscuit 143
Afghan chablon 143
agar-agar 12
anglaise, Split 35
anglaise, vanilla 203
Anzac base 117
Anzac biscuit 117-8
Anzac chablon 118
apple
    Apple compote 122
    Apple crumble 122
    Caramelised apples 231
    Tarte tatin 231-2
    Vanilla poached apples 122
apricot
    Apricot and goat's cheese 140
    Apricot compote 140
avocado
    Avocado and lime 74
    Avocado cream 74

B
banana
    Banana cake 238
    Banana, passionfruit and coconut 69
    Banoffee 121
Banoffee 121
bark, Chocolate 216
basil
    Yuzu and basil 187-88
    Yuzu basil crémeux 187
    Yuzu basil mousse 188
bavarois
    Brown butter bavarois 238
    Golden syrup bavarois 117
    Hokey pokey bavarois 93
    Orange blossom bavarois 145
    Vanilla bavarois 44
beetroot
    Beetroot mousse 41
    Raspberry, Beetroot and Chocolate 41
Belgian biscuit, Ben's 200
Belgian biscuit icing 200
Ben's Belgian biscuit 200
Bergamot
    Bergamot and Early Grey 159
    Bergamot cake 159
    Bergamot gel 159
    Bergamot whipped ganache 159
Berry pavlova 226
Birthday cake 234
biscuit
    Afghan biscuit 143
    Anzac biscuit 117-8
    Ben's Belgian biscuit 200
    Belgian biscuit icing 200
    Tiramisu 197
    Black cocoa crumb 198
    Black Forest 94
    Black glaze 238
blackberry
    Blackberry mousse 96
    Lemon, poppy and blackberry 96
blackcurrant
    Blackcurrant and violet 46
    Blackcurrant chablon 46
    Blackcurrant compote 46
    Blackcurrant gel 177
    Blackcurrant mousse 46, 226
    Blackcurrant purée 177
    Mont Blanc 177
blueberry
    Blueberry compote 60, 81
    Blueberry mousse 226
    Blueberry pancake 81
    Blueberry yuzu cheesecake 60
boysenberry
    Boysenberry and elderflower 87
    Boysenberry bûche de Noël 219-20
    Boysenberry cake 238
    Boysenberry compote 219
    Boysenberry elderflower mousse 87
    Boysenberry gel 87, 219
Bread and butter pudding 203
brown butter
    A piece of toast 172
    Brown butter bavarois 238
    Brown butter cake 172
Brown sugar base 60, 205
Brown sugar cake 49, 122
Brown sugar crumble 122
brownie, Cocoa 143
bûche de Noël, boysenberry 219
bûche de Noël, speculoos 216
buckwheat
    Buckwheat and quince 145-46
    Buckwheat dacquoise 145
    Crystallised buckwheat 146
butter 12
butter pudding, bread and 203
butternut
    Butternut and maple 129-30
    Butternut mousse 129
    Butternut purée 129
    Butternut snickerdoodle base 129

C
cake (see also sponge)
    Banana cake 238
    Bergamot cake 159
    Birthday cake 234
    Boysenberry cake 238
    Brown butter cake 172
    Brown sugar cake 49, 122
    Carrot cake 55
    Chai spiced cake 154
    Chestnut cake 177
    Chocolate cake 169, 206, 239
    Cinnamon cake 216
    Coconut cake 53, 212
    Ginger cake 93, 193
    Grapefruit cake 78
    Honey cake 50, 140, 228
    Lavender cake 108
    Lemon cake 90
    Lemon poppy cake 96
    Lime cake 74
    Marble cake 150
    Pancake cake 81
    Pandan cake 59
    Passionfruit cake 73
    Russian honey cake 228
    Spice cake 200, 241
    Sprinkle cake 234
    Sticky toffee cake 166
    Strawberry shortcake 107
    Sweetcorn cake 101
    Vanilla cake 242
    Vanilla pound cake 70
    Yuzu cake 102, 187, 190
Candied rhubarb 43
caramel
    A piece of toast 172
    after caramelisation 20
    caramel 19
    Caramel, chocolate and peanut 178
    Caramel crémeux 238
    Caramel ganache 170
    Caramel glaze 49
    Caramel mousse 49
    Caramel poached pineapple 153
    Caramel popcorn 101
    Caramel sauce 182
    Cookie caramel chip 182
    dry caramel 19
    lumpy or seized caramel 34
    Macadamia and caramel 49
    Sesame and caramel 139
    Soft Caramel 178
    Sweetcorn and caramel 101
    wet caramel 19
    Whipped caramel 242
Caramelised apples 231
Caramelised hazelnuts 126
Caramelised peanuts 178
Caramelised white chocolate glaze 89
Caramelised white chocolate mousse 216
cardamom
    Mandarin and cardamom 175
    Mandarin cardamom mousse 175
    Mandarin cardamom syrup 175
Carrot cake 55
chablon
    Afghan chablon 143
    Anzac chablon 118
    Blackcurrant chablon 226
    chablon 29
    Chocolate chablon 239
    dipping in chablon 30
    Hokey pokey chablon 93, 210
    Speculoos chablon 156
    Truffle chablon 198
    ugly glaze or chablon 35
    Yellow chablon 84
chai
    Chai latte 154
    Chai mousse 154
    Chai spice 154
    Chai spiced cake 154
cheese
    Apricot and goat's cheese 140
    Goat's cheesecake 140
cheesecake
    Blueberry yuzu cheesecake 60
    Cheesecake filling 184
    Goat's cheesecake 140
    Soft cheesecake 55
    Whipped cheesecake 234, 242
cherry
    Black Forest 94
    Cherry compote 94
    Cherry gel 223
    White forest 223
chestnut
    Chestnut cake 177
    Chestnut mousse 177
    Chestnut vermicelli 177
    Mont Blanc 177
chip, cookie caramel 182
chocolate
    Afghan biscuit 143
    Black Forest 94
    Caramel, chocolate and peanut 178
    Caramelised white chocolate glaze 89
    Caramelised white chocolate mousse 216
    chocolate 12
    Chocolate bark 216
    Chocolate cake 169, 206, 239
    Chocolate chablon 239
    Chocolate 'cheese' slices 140
    Chocolate custard 203
    Chocolate curls 108, 148
    chocolate decorations 27
    Chocolate delice 67
    Chocolate disasters 35
    Chocolate discs 67
    Chocolate honeycomb 50
    Chocolate orange 206
    Chocolate plaques 73, 82, 107
    Chocolate praline 169
    Chocolate sauce 136
    Chocolate splats 74
    Chocolate sponge 148
    Chocolate squares 154
    Chocolate squiggles 184
    Coffee chocolate whipped ganache 160
    Cocoa base 184
    Cocoa brownie 143

Cocoa crumb 219
Cocoa joconde 160
Cocoa rice crunch 181
Cocoa tuile 170
colouring chocolate 24
Dark chocolate mousse 94, 239
Easter egg nest 210
Feuilletine crunch 105
Five textures of chocolate 169–70
Gianduja gâteau Basque 125–6
Hazelnut chocolate 105
Hot cross buns 215
Jelly tip 82
Marble cake 150
Matcha chocolate plaques 64
melting chocolate 23
Milk chocolate ganache 114, 160, 162
Milk chocolate glaze 240
Milk chocolate mousse 108, 148, 150, 210, 240
Milk chocolate whipped ganache 240
Miso mousse 121
Opera 160–2
Passionfruit chocolate 148
Peanut chocolate mousse 178
Peppermint Slice 181
Pistachio-green chocolate curls 190
Poire belle Hélène 135–6
Raspberry, beetroot and chocolate 41
Raspberry peanut chocolate discs 89
Rocky road 67
S'mores 114
Speculoos bûche de Noël 216
Spiced milk chocolate mousse 225
tempering chocolate 24, 27
The symphony 108
Tonka chocolate 184
Truffle and white chocolate 198
Truffle white chocolate mousse 198
White chocolate mousse 150
Choux pastry sponge 43
Christmas tree, Pfeffernüsse 225
Christmas trees 225
cinnamon
Cinnamon cake 216
Cinnamon cream 205
Cinnamon mousse 122
Speculoos bûche de Noël 216
Citrus sponge 175
coconut
Banana, passionfruit and coconut 69
Coconut cake 53, 210
Coconut mousse 59, 69
Coconut rum mousse 153
Coconut veil 212
Laming-not 53
Pandan, yuzu and coconut 59
Tropical egg 212
Whipped coconut cream 53
coffee
Coffee chocolate whipped ganache 160
Coffee soak 197
Coffee syrup 160
Opera 160–2
Tiramisu 197
collapsing gâteaux 35
Coloured glaze 239
colouring chocolate 24
compote
Apple compote 122
Apricot compote 140
Blackcurrant compote 46, 81
Blueberry compote 60, 81
Boysenberry compote 219
Cherry compote 94
Peach compote 110
Quince compote 145
Raspberry compote 240
Rhubarb elderflower compote 43
Rhubarb compote 70
cookie
Cookie base 114, 139
Cookie caramel chip 182
cornflake crunch, walnut 143

cream
Avocado cream 74
Cinnamon cream 205
cream 13
Honey cream 198, 228
Honey cream topping 228
Maple cream 130
Mascarpone cream 197
Sabayo cream 197
Vanilla pastry cream 132
Whipped coconut cream 53
whipping cream 17
crème fraiche, Kirsch 223
crème fraiche, vanilla 232
Crème fraiche, whipped 156, 242
crème, peppermint 181
crémeux
Caramel crémeux 238
Grapefruit gin crémeux 78
Lemon crémeux, 96, 108
Pandan yuzu crémeux 59
Passionfruit crémeux 63, 69, 240
Praline crémeux 105
Yuzu basil crémeux 187
Yuzu crémeux 190, 242
crumble, Apple 122
crumble, Brown sugar 122
curd, Mango 102
curls, Chocolate 108, 148
curls, Pistachio-green chocolate 190
custard
Chocolate custard 203
Gâteau Basque custard 125
Rhubarb and custard 43–4
Sweetcorn custard 101
Crystallised buckwheat 146
Crystallised mint leaves 181
Crystallised pumpkin seeds 130

D
dacquoise, buckwheat 145
Dark chocolate mousse 94, 239
Dark sugar sponge 153
delice, chocolate 67
discs, chocolate 67
discs, raspberry peanut chocolate 89
dough, Gâteau Basque 125

E
Earl Grey
Bergamot and Earl Grey 159
Earl Grey mousse 159
Easter egg nest 210
edible flowers 12
elderflower
Boysenberry and elderflower 87
Boysenberry elderflower mousse 87
Rhubarb elderflower compote 43
egg
Easter egg nest 210
eggs 12
Tropical egg 212

F
Feuilletine crunch 105
financier, peanut 89
Five textures of chocolate 169–70
flour 12
Fondant base 181
freeze-dried fruit 12
fruit purées 12

G
ganache
Bergamot whipped ganache 159
Caramel ganache 170
Coffee chocolate whipped ganache 160
Gianduja whipped ganache 125
Golden syrup whipped ganache 117
Matcha passionfruit ganache 63
Milk chocolate ganache 114, 160, 162
Raspberry whipped ganache 200
Gâteau Basque custard 125
Gâteau Basque dough 125

gâteau Basque, Gianduja 125–6
gâteau, cracking 34
gâteaux, collapsing 35
gel
Bergamot gel 159
Blackcurrant gel 177
Boysenberry gel 87, 219
Cherry gel 223
Lychee gel 56
Mango gel 212
Mango sake gel 102
Passionfruit gel 50
Peach gel 99
Pimm's gel 90
Pineapple rum gel 153
Yuzu gel 60
gelatine
gelatine 12
soaking gelatine 15
Gianduja gâteau Basque 125–6
Gianduja whipped ganache 125
gin
Grapefruit and gin 78
Grapefruit and gin mousse 78
Grapefruit gin crémeux 78
Ginger cake 93, 193
glaze
Black glaze 238
Caramel glaze 49
Caramelised white chocolate glaze 89
Coloured glaze 239
glazing 21
Milk chocolate glaze 240
Mille-feuille glaze 22
Ugly glaze or chablon 35
goat's cheese, apricot and 140
Goat's cheesecake 140
gold leaf 12
gold paint 239
golden syrup
Anzac biscuit 117–8
Golden syrup bavarois 117
Golden syrup whipped ganache 117
grapefruit
Grapefruit and gin 78
Grapefruit and gin mousse 78
Grapefruit cake 78
Grapefruit gin crémeux 78

H
hazelnut
Caramelised hazelnuts 126
Feuilletine crunch 105
Gianduja gâteau Basque 125–6
Hazelnut chocolate 105
Hazelnut praline 169
Praline crémeux 105
hokey pokey
Easter egg nest 210
Hokey pokey 93, 210, 239
Hokey pokey bavarois 93
Hokey pokey chablon 93, 210
honey
Hokey pokey 239
Honey bee 50
Honey cake 50, 140, 228
Honey cream 198, 228
Honey cream topping 228
Honey yoghurt mousse 50
Russian honey cake 228
honeycomb, chocolate 50
Hot cross bun spice 215
Hot cross buns 215

I
icing, Belgian biscuit 200
Isaphan 56
It's summer and it's hot and everything is melting! 35

J
jam
Raisin jam 215
Raspberry jam 200

jelly
   Jelly tip 82
   Milk jelly 154
   Orange jelly 175
   PB&J 89
   Raspberry jelly 82
joconde, cocoa 160
joconde, matcha 63

K
Kataifi nests 210
Kirsch crème fraîche 223
kisses, piping 32
kūmara
   Kūmara pie 205
   Kūmara pie filling 205
   Kūmara purée 205

L
Laming-not 53
latte, chai 154
lavender
   Lavender cake 108
   The symphony 108
layering 15
layers, Sliding 35
lemon
   Lemon cake 90
   Lemon crémeux 38, 96, 108
   Lemon meringue 38
   Lemon, poppy and blackberry 96
   Lemon poppy cake 96
   Pimm's 90
   The symphony 108
lime
   Avocado and lime 74
   Lime cake 74
   Lime mousse 74, 84
   Mango and lime 84
lining your tin 15
liquid glucose 13
lychee
   Isaphan 56
   Lychee gel 56

M
macadamia
   Macadamia and caramel 49
   Macadamia praline 49
mandarin
   Mandarin and cardamom 175
   Mandarin cardamom mousse 175
   Mandarin cardamom syrup 175
mango
   Mango and lime 84
   Mango and sake 102
   Mango curd 102
   Mango gel 212
   Mango mousse 84, 240
   Mango sake gel 102
   Tropical egg 212
maple
   Butternut and maple 129-30
   Maple cream 130
Marble cake 150
marmalade, yuzu 187
marshmallow, vanilla 114
mascarpone
   Mascarpone cream 197
   Mascarpone mousse 81
   Mascarpone whip 81, 121
   Vanilla mascarpone 226, 242
matcha
   Matcha chocolate plaques 64
   Matcha joconde 63
   Matcha mousse 63
   Matcha passionfruit ganache 63
   Matcha passionfruit opera 63-4
Melba, peach 99
melting chocolate 23
meringue
   Boysenberry bûche de Noël 219-20
   Lemon meringue 38
   meringue 18

   Mini meringues 177, 226
   Mont Blanc 177
   Mushroom meringues 220
   Swiss meringue 241
microgreens 13
milk 13
milk chocolate
   Milk chocolate ganache 114, 160, 162
   Milk chocolate glaze 240
   Milk chocolate mousse 108, 148, 150, 210, 240
   Milk chocolate whipped ganache 240
Milk jelly 154
Mille-feuille 132
Mille-feuille glaze 22
Mini meringues 177, 226
mint *see peppermint*
Miso mousse 121
Mont Blanc 177
mousse
   Beetroot mousse 41
   Blackberry mousse 96
   Blackcurrant mousse 46, 226
   Blueberry mousse 226
   Boysenberry elderflower mousse 87
   Butternut mousse 129
   Caramel mousse 49
   Caramelised white chocolate mousse 216
   Chai mousse 154
   Chestnut mousse 177
   Cinnamon mousse 122
   Coconut mousse 59, 69
   Coconut rum mousse 153
   Dark chocolate mousse 94, 239
   Early Grey mousse 159
   Grapefruit and gin mousse 78
   Honey yoghurt mousse 50
   Lime mousse 74, 84
   Mandarin cardamom mousse 175
   Mango mousse 84, 240
   Mascarpone mousse 81
   Matcha mousse 63
   Milk chocolate mousse 108, 148, 150, 210, 240
   Miso mousse 121
   mousse 16
   Peanut chocolate mousse 178
   Peanut mousse 89
   Pear mousse 135
   Peppermint mousse 181
   Pimm's mousse 90
   Pistachio mousse 190
   Raspberry mousse 53, 56, 67
   Sesame mousse 139
   Spiced milk chocolate mousse 225
   Spiced mousse 215
   Strawberry mousse 226, 241
   Sweet wine mousse 110
   Truffle white chocolate mousse 198
   Vanilla mousse 99, 193, 223
   Vanilla yoghurt mousse 82
   Yuzu basil mousse 188
   White chocolate mousse 150
mulled wine
   Mulled wine 193
   Mulled wine and pear 193-4
   Mulled wine pâte de fruit 193
   Mulled wine veil 194
Mushroom meringues 220

O
Opera 160-62
opera, matcha passionfruit 63
orange
   Chocolate orange 206
   Orange gel 206
   Orange jelly 175
orange blossom
   Orange blossom bavarois 145

P
paint, gold 239
pancake, blueberry 81
Pancake cake 81

pandan
   Pandan cake 59
   Pandan, yuzu and coconut 59
   Pandan yuzu crémeux 59
passionfruit
   Banana, passionfruit and coconut 69
   Matcha passionfruit ganache 63
   Matcha passionfruit opera 63-4
   Passionfruit cake 73
   Passionfruit chocolate 148
   Passionfruit crémeux 63, 69, 240
   Passionfruit gel 50
   Passionfruit strawberry 73
pastry
   Choux pastry sponge 43
   Mille-feuille 132
   puff pastry 33
   Puff pastry layers 132
   Tarte tatin 231-2
   Vanilla pastry cream 132
pâte à bombe 18
pâte de fruit
   Mulled wine pâte de fruit 193
   Strawberry pâte de fruit 107
   Vanilla and pear pâte de fruit 135
pavlova, Berry 226
PB&J 89
peach
   Peach and sweet wine 110
   Peach compote 110
   Peach gel 99
   Peach Melba 99
peanut
   Caramel, chocolate and peanut 178
   Caramelised peanuts 178
   PB&J 89
   Peanut chocolate mousse 178
   Peanut financier 89
   Peanut mousse 89
   Raspberry peanut chocolate discs 89
pear
   Mulled wine and pear 193-4
   Pear mousse 135
   Poached pear balls 135
   Poire belle Hélène 135-6
pectin 13
peppermint
   Crystallised mint leaves 181
   Peppermint crème 181
   Peppermint mousse 181
   Peppermint slice 181
petit gâteau?, What is a 10
Pfeffernüsse
   Pfeffernüsse Christmas tree 225
   Pfeffernüsse crumb 225
   Pfeffernüsse crunch 225
   Pfeffernüsse spice 225
pie filling, kūmara 205
pie, kūmara 205
Pimm's
   Pimm's 90
   Pimm's gel 90
   Pimm's mousse 90
pineapple
   Caramel poached pineapple 153
   Pineapple and rum 153
   Pineapple rum gel 153
piping
   piped decorations 29
   piping 31
   piping kisses 32
   Saint Honoré tip 33
pistachio
   Pistachio and yuzu 190
   Pistachio-green chocolate curls 190
   Pistachio mousse 190
plaques, chocolate 73, 82, 107
plaques, matcha chocolate 64
poached apples, vanilla 122
Poached pear balls 135
poached pineapple, Caramel 153
Poached quince 145
Poached rhubarb 70
Poire belle Hélène 135-6

popcorn, caramel 101
poppy
    Lemon, poppy and blackberry 96
    Lemon poppy cake 96
portioning 22
potato chip *see chip*
praline
    Chocolate praline 169
    Hazelnut praline 169
    Praline crémeux 105
    Macadamia praline 49
    Sesame praline 139
    Walnut cornflake crunch 143
    Walnut praline 143
Pudding base 203
pudding, bread and butter 203
pudding, sticky toffee 166
puff pastry 33
Puff pastry layers 132
pumpkin seeds, crystallised 130
purée
    Blackcurrant purée 177
    Butternut purée 129
    fruit purées 12
    kumara purée 205

Q
quenelle 30
quick seeding 25
quince
    Buckwheat and quince 145–6
    Poached quince 145
    Quince compote 145

R
raisin
    Hot cross buns 215
    Raisin jam 215
raspberry
    Ben's Belgian biscuit 200
    Isaphan 56
    Jelly tip 82
    Raspberry, beetroot and chocolate 41
    Raspberry compote 240
    Raspberry jam 200
    Raspberry jelly 82
    Raspberry mousse 53, 56, 67
    Raspberry peanut chocolate discs 89
    Raspberry whipped ganache 200
    Rocky road 67
rhubarb
    Candied rhubarb 43
    Poached rhubarb 70
    Rhubarb and custard 43–4
    Rhubarb compote 70
    Rhubarb elderflower compote 43
    Strawberry and rhubarb 70
Rooky road 67
rum
    Coconut rum mousse 153
    Pineapple and rum 153
    Pineapple rum gel 153
Russian honey cake 228

S
Sabayo cream 197
Sablé Breton base 38
Saint Honoré tip 33
sake
    Mango and sake 102
    Mango sake gel 102
sauce
    Caramel sauce 182
    Chocolate sauce 136
    Sticky toffee sauce 166
seeding 25
sesame
    Sesame and caramel 139
    Sesame mousse 139
    Sesame praline 139
    Sesame tuile 139
Shortcake sponge 241

shortcake, Strawberry 107
slice, Peppermint 181
sliding layers 35
S'mores 114
snickerdoodle base, Butternut 129
soak, Coffee 197
Soft caramel 178
Soft cheesecake 55
Sourdough crumb 172
Speculoos
    Cinnamon cake 216
    Speculoos bûche de Noël 216
    Speculoos chablon 156
    Speculoos crunch 156
    Speculoos spiced sponge 156
    Speculoos topping 205
Spice cake 200, 241
Spiced milk chocolate mousse 225
Spiced mousse 215
splats, chocolate 74
split anglaise 35
sponge (see also cake)
    Chocolate sponge 148
    Choux pastry sponge 43
    Citrus sponge 175
    Dark sugar sponge 153
    Shortcake sponge 241
    Speculoos spiced sponge 156
    Truffle sponge 198
Sprinkle cake 234
squares, chocolate 154
squiggles, chocolate 184
Sticky toffee cake 166
Sticky toffee pudding 166
Sticky toffee sauce 166
storing and serving 35
strawberry
    Pimm's 90
    Strawberry and rhubarb 70
    Strawberry mousse 226, 241
    Strawberry pâte de fruit 107
    Strawberry shortcake 107
substitutions 13
sugar 13
Sweet wine mousse 110
sweetcorn
    Sweetcorn and caramel 101
    Sweetcorn cake 101
    Sweetcorn custard 101
Swiss meringue 241
symphony, the 108
syrup
    Coffee syrup 160
    Mandarin cardamom syrup 175

T
tabling 26
Tarte tatin 231–2
temperatures, tempering 24
tea *see Bergamot, Earl Grey*
tempering
    tempering chocolate 24, 27
    tempering temperatures 24
The symphony 108
Tiramisu 197
toast, A piece of 172
toffee
    Sticky toffee cake 166
    Sticky toffee pudding 166
    Sticky toffee sauce 166
Tonka chocolate 184
topping, honey cream 228
topping, speculoos 205
Tropical egg 212
troubleshooting
    chocolate disasters 35
    collapsing gâteaux 35
    cracking gâteau 34
    it's summer and it's hot and everything is melting! 35
    lumpy or seized caramel 34
    sliding layers 35

split anglaise 35
storing and serving 35
ugly glaze or chablon 35
truffle
    Truffle and white chocolate 198
    Truffle chablon 198
    Truffle sponge 198
    Truffle white chocolate mousse 198
tuile, cocoa 170
tuile, sesame 139

U
ugly glaze or chablon 35

V
vanilla
    Jelly tip 82
    Marble cake 150
    Mille-feuille 132
    Poire belle Hélène 135–6
    S'mores 114
    Vanilla and pear pâte de fruit 135
    Vanilla anglaise 203
    Vanilla bavarois 44
    Vanilla cake 242
    Vanilla crème fraiche 232
    Vanilla marshmallow 114
    Vanilla mascarpone 226, 242
    Vanilla mousse 99, 193, 223
    Vanilla pastry cream 132
    Vanilla poached apples 122
    Vanilla pound cake 70
    Vanilla yoghurt mousse 82
veil, coconut 212
veil, mulled wine 194
vermicelli
    Chestnut vermicelli 177
    Mont Blanc 177
violet, blackcurrant and 46

W
walnut
    Afghan biscuit 143
    Walnut praline 143
whip, mascarpone 81, 121
Whipped caramel 242
Whipped cheesecake 234, 242
Whipped coconut cream 53
Whipped crème fraiche 156, 242
whisking 18
white chocolate
    Caramelised white chocolate mousse 216
    Truffle and white chocolate 198
    Truffle white chocolate mousse 198
    White chocolate mousse 150
White forest 223
wine
    Mulled wine 193
    Mulled wine and pear 193–4
    Mulled wine pâte de fruit 193
    Mulled wine veil 194
    Peach and sweet wine 110
    Sweet wine mousse 110

Y
Yellow chablon 84
yoghurt
    Honey yoghurt mousse 50
    Vanilla yoghurt mousse 82
yuzu
    Blueberry yuzu cheesecake 60
    Pandan, yuzu and coconut 59
    Pandan yuzu crémeux 59
    Pistachio and yuzu 190
    Tropical egg 212
    Yuzu and basil 187–88
    Yuzu basil crémeux 187
    Yuzu basil mousse 188
    Yuzu cake 102, 187, 190
    Yuzu crémeux 190, 242
    Yuzu gel 60
    Yuzu marmalade 187

Please note that recipes labelled as gluten-free, or offering the option of using gluten-free flour, have been tested with a 1:1 gluten-free flour mix. All gluten-free flour mixes are slightly different and may not produce the exact same result as using plain flour. If you have an allergy, or are coeliac, please consult your healthcare practitioner for what is and is not safe for consumption.

Text © Maxine Scheckter, 2025
Photography © Amber-Jayne Bain
The moral rights of the author have been asserted.

Typographical design © David Bateman Ltd, 2025

Published in the UK in 2026 by
Kitchen Press Ltd
1 Windsor Place
Dundee
DD2 1BG
www.kitchenpress.co.uk

First published in New Zealand by David Bateman Ltd.

ISBN: 978-1-7391740-5-7

All rights reserved. No part of this publication may be stored or transmitted in any form or by any means, electronic or mechanical, including recording or storage in any information retrieval systems, without permission in writing from the publisher. No reproduction may be made, whether by photocopying or any other means, unless a licence has been obtained from the publisher or its agent.

A catalogue record for this book is available from the British Library.

Book design: Katrina Duncan & Dan Mercer
Printed in China by Toppan Leefung Printing (Dongguan) Co., Ltd